DIDYMUS THE BLIND AND THE TEXT OF THE GOSPELS

SOCIETY OF BIBLICAL LITERATURE
The New Testament in the Greek Fathers

Edited by
Gordon D. Fee

Number 1
DIDYMUS THE BLIND AND THE
TEXT OF THE GOSPELS

by
Bart D. Ehrman

DIDYMUS THE BLIND AND THE TEXT OF THE GOSPELS

Bart D. Ehrman

Scholars Press
Atlanta, Georgia

DIDYMUS THE BLIND AND THE TEXT OF THE GOSPELS

Bart D. Ehrman

© 1986
The Society of Biblical Literature

Library of Congress Cataloging in Publication Data

Ehrman, Bart D.
 Didymus the Blind and the text of the Gospels.

 (New Testament and the Greek Fathers ; no. 1)
 Bibliography: p.
 1. Bible. N.T. Gospels—Criticism, Textual.
 2. Didymus, of Alexandria, the Theologian, ca.
 313–ca. 398—Knowledge—Alexandrian test of the
 Gospels. I. Title. II. Series.
 BS2551.A26D534   1986   226'.048'0924   86-24845
 ISBN 1-55540-083-3 (alk. paper)
 ISBN 1-55540-084-1 (pbk. : alk. paper)

Printed in the United States of America
on acid-free paper

To Cindy

TABLE OF CONTENTS

Acknowledgments ix

Editor's Preface xi

Introduction 1

Chapter I   Didymus as a Witness to the Text of the
             Gospels: Methdological Problems 4
             Patristic Sources: Their Significance and
                Complexities 4
                The Use of Critical Editions 7
                Source Analysis 7
                Textual Reconstruction 12
             The Special Significance and Peculiar
                Problems of Didymus as a Textual
                Witness 17

Chapter II   Introduction to the Text and Critical
                Apparatus 30
                Presentation of the Text 31
                The Critical Apparatus 34
                Abbreviations used in the Apparatus ... 37

Chapter III Text and Apparatus 38
                Gospel of Matthew 38
                Gospel of Mark 88
                Gospel of Luke 91
                Gospel of John 124
                Indeterminable References and Complex
                  Conflations 172

Chapter IV   The Gospel Text of Didymus: Quantitative
                Analysis 187
                Didymus's Affinities in Matthew 190
                Residual Methodological Concerns 195
                Didymus's Affinities in Mark 202

	Didymus's Affinities in Luke............	204
	Didymus's Affinities in John............	207
	Didymus's Text of the Four Gospels......	218
Chapter V	The Gospel Text of Didymus: Group Profiles.................................	223
	Profile One: Inter-Group Readings.......	228
	Profile Two: Intra-Group Readings.......	234
	Profile Three: Combination Inter- and Intra-Group Readings...............	238
	Profile Four: Didymus's Relationship to Alexandrian Witnesses...............	243
Chapter VI	Conclusions................................	254
	Methods of Textual Analysis and Classification.......................	254
	The Character and History of the Alexandrian Text......................	258
	The Western Text in Alexandria........	258
	The Byzantine Text in Alexandria......	259
	The Caesarean Text in Alexandria......	261
	The Early and Late Alexandrian Texts..............................	262

Appendix One: Didymus in the Apparatus of NA^{26}.......... 268

Appendix Two: Didymus in the Apparatus of UBS^{3}.......... 274

Bibliography... 276

ACKNOWLEDGMENTS

This book grew out of the dissertation I submitted to the faculty of Princeton Theological Seminary in 1985. I would especially like to express my gratitude to the three members of my dissertation committee, each of whom made significant contributions to my labors: Bruce M. Metzger, who spawned in me an interest in the analysis of the Patristic witnesses of the NT text, and whose textual expertise guided me throughout the entire project; Cullen I K Story, whose meticulous attention to detail has always been a source of admiration; and David R. Adams, whose intuitive sense for critical method continues to inspire rigor in his students. Thanks are also due Elizabeth Johnson of New Brunswick Theological Seminary for much generosity and many helpful suggestions, and to my friend Jeffrey Siker who read portions of the MS and gave continual encouragement.

Anyone who reads this study will realize the extent to which I am indebted to the scholarship of Gordon D. Fee. From the very beginning of my work his publications have served as a model of careful research, and I have considered it my great fortune to be able to work with him as the general editor of this project.

I would also like to extend my thanks to Dennis Ford of Scholars Press, who has always been prompt and willing to provide the assistance I have needed.

My deepest appreciation goes to my wife Cindy whose love and patience have been my steady companions throughout the course of my work. It is to her that I have dedicated this book.

EDITOR'S PREFACE

The usefulness of Patristic citations for New Testament textual criticism has long been recognized. Indeed, when a Father's text can be judged as certain (e.g. when he provides commentary on the very words of his text or notes alternative readings), it provides datable **primary** evidence for the New Testament text in a given geographical location.

Unfortunately, however, that usefulness, both for scholar and student alike, has been mitigated by two factors. First, the average scholar or student has very little access to the data, which by and large are the province of the specialist alone--and even the specialist at times has considerable difficulty getting at some of the material, or at other times knowing how to evaluate what he or she does have access to. Second, what access most people do have to the data, namely in the critical editions, is hopelessly inadequate. This is especially true, for example, of the otherwise useful United Bible Societies Greek New Testament, where there are so many inaccuracies that even the correct data are not useful, since one can never know which are correct and which are not.

What has been lacking is an adequate and accessible presentation and evaluation of these data, especially of the Greek Fathers, where to date only that of Clement of Alexandria is available (M. Mees, <u>Die Zitate aus dem Neuen Testament bei Clemens von Alexandrien</u> [Rome, 1970]; who has a full presentation of the data, although the evaluation leaves some things to be desired).

The present volume represents the first in a new series whose aim is to fill up this lacuna. The justification for the series can be found in Dr. Ehrman's Introduction, pp. 1-3. Let me here simply set out the guidelines: (1) The series will present the NT textual data for the Greek Fathers; (2) only data available from critical editions of the Fathers' texts will be included; (3) each volume will include a full presentation of the NT data (or parts thereof) of a given Father or selected works of a given Father; (4) each presentation will also include a minimal evaluation of the Father's citations, as to his citing habits, the reliability of his data, and the degree of certainty with which one may use the data; and finally (5) the author will offer an analysis of the textual data as to the Father's place in the history of the NT text, especially in terms of textual relationships with the other available data. It is hoped that such a presentation will increase our overall confidence in the use of the Father's textual data.

It is a pleasure to introduce the series with Dr. Bart Ehrman's analysis of the text of the four Gospels as it is cited in the commentaries of Didymus the Blind found at Toura in 1941. Dr. Ehrman has not only given us a full presentation and analysis of the data, but has also offered some refinements of method in the task of analysis that help us to move toward greater certainty in that task. This is an auspicious beginning of a series that we trust will prove useful for the ongoing task of NT textual criticism, especially in our ability someday to write the history of the text with even greater clarity.

Perhaps other younger scholars will now be encouraged to look toward this aspect of textual criticism as a possible area for their dissertations, since this series offers them a possiblity of publication.

GORDON D. FEE

Introduction

Recent years have witnessed a renewed interest in the analysis and classification of NT documentary evidence. This renewal had its roots in methodological concerns, as approaches taken to establishing textual consanguinity were systematized and objectified. Two new methods of analysis were devised, one a quantitative method designed to demonstrate on statistical grounds the textual relationships of NT documents, the other a profile method used to classify witnesses according to their patterns of attestation of readings. These developments led to the publication of several analyses of significant textual witnesses, including MSS ℵ and W and the church Fathers Origen, Chrysostom, and Hippolytus, as well as to several important sketches of the NT MS traditions.

The present study seeks, as did most of its predecessors, to utilize and refine methods of textual analysis now common in the field. Far from discussing methodology only in the abstract, however, the study has as its primary objective the application of a refined method of analysis to yet another significant textual witness, Didymus the Blind.

As an ecclesiastical leader in fourth-century Alexandria, Didymus is an important link in the great chain of textual transmission. Alexandria was famous for its classical scholarship and is commonly reputed to have preserved, from earliest times, the purest form of NT text. Furthermore, several of the most important Alexandrian witnesses, including codices ℵ and B, were probably produced during Didymus's lifetime. Thus a study of Didymus's NT quotations can be expected to show whether these other witnesses adequately represent the Alexandrian tradition of the late fourth century. In addition, Didymus's text may cast light on somewhat broader questions concerning the transmission of the NT: it may illuminate, for example, the historical relationship between the so-called "Early" and "Late" Alexandrian texts, and it may show the extent to which other types of text influenced the Alexandrian tradition.

2/ Didymus and the Gospels

The scientific study of Didymus's text of the NT--in this case, of the four Gospels--has become possible only within the past several years. In 1941, in a grotto near Toura, Egypt, Egyptian workers accidentally unearthed nearly 2000 pages of papyrus MSS. Included among these sixth- or seventh-century papyri were fragmentary copies of hitherto unknown expository works of Didymus. Critical editions of these commentaries on Genesis, Job, Psalms, Ecclesiastes, and Zechariah have slowly appeared since 1968. In them Didymus quotes extensively from the NT Gospels. The present study represents the first full-scale textual analysis of these quotations. The analysis focuses on three kinds of issues: (1) Methodological: How can the textual affinities of Didymus's Gospel quotations and allusions best be determined? (2) Textual: What are these affinities? (3) Historical: What does Didymus's Gospel text reveal about the transmission of the NT in Alexandria?

Methodological issues are addressed at the outset of the study. Chapter I considers the problems that are unique to analyses of the Patristic witnesses to the NT text. The chapter pays particular attention to the significance of Didymus as a textual witness and to the peculiar difficulties encountered in the analysis of his Gospel quotations and allusions.

A major portion of the study is devoted to a presentation of Didymus's Gospel text. Chapter II introduces and explains the format of this presentation, which itself is then given in Chapter III. The presentation includes a full listing of every Gospel quotation and allusion found in Didymus's writings, and a critical apparatus which supplies full collations of representative textual witnesses at every point.

These data are subjected to a detailed analysis in Chapters IV and V. Chapter IV uses a quantitative method to demonstrate the proximity of Didymus's text to individual representatives of the major strands of the textual tradition. Chapter V supplements this analysis by examining Didymus's support of readings that characterize each of the textual groups, irrespective of their attestation in any given witness. For this purpose a whole new slate of profiles of group readings is proposed and utilized.

The final chapter summarizes the important methodological refinements made in the course of the study, and demonstrates the significance of the analysis for understanding the history of the text as it was transmitted in Alexandria. Particular attention is paid here to the relationship of the fourth-century Alexandrian text with other known textual groups, and to the historical relationships of the Alexandrian subgroups.

The study concludes with two appendices. The first indicates where the testimony of Didymus can now be cited or corrected in the apparatus of NA^{26}. The second provides similar information with respect to $UBSGNT^3$.

Chapter I

Didymus as a Witness to the Text of the Gospels:
Methodological Problems

Analyses of Patristic witnesses to the NT text encounter a number of serious methodological problems. These problems are of two sorts: those inherent in the Patristic sources generally and those unique to the works of each church Father. For the purposes of the present study, both sets of problems can be considered with reference to the extant writings of Didymus the Blind.[1]

Patristic Sources: Their Significance and Complexities

NT scholars agree that the text of the NT cannot be reconstructed apart from an accurate delineation of the history of its transmission. Patristic evidence figures prominently in this delineation and is, in some respects, more important to it than are the Greek MSS and early versions.[2]

---

[1] See n. 23, p. 17 below, and the discussion of pp. 22-29.

[2] The historical significance of the Patristic evidence was recognized by the earliest pioneers of textual criticism, especially by the eighteenth-century savant Richard Bentley, whose study of Jerome and Origen dictated the scope and method of his critical research. For contemporary assessments of the value of the Patristic sources, see especially Jean Duplacy and Jack Suggs, "Les citations greques et la critique du texte de Nouveau Testament: le passé, le present, et l'avenir," in Le Bible et les pères, eds. André Benoit and Pierre Prigent (Paris: Presses Universitairies de France, 1971) 187-213; Gordon D. Fee, "The Text of John in the Jerusalem Bible: A Critique of the Use of Patristic Citations in New Testament Textual Criticism," JBL 90 (1971) 163-73; Bruce M. Metzger "Patristic Evidence and the Textual Criticism of the New Testament," NTS 18 (1971-72) 379-400; M. J. Suggs, "The Use of Patristic Evidence in the Search for a Primitive New Testament Text," NTS 4 (1957-58) 131-47. The articles by Fee and Metzger are directed, in large measure, against the overly zealous appropriation of Patristic evidence by M.-E. Boismard, whose views and resultant reconstruction of the Greek text of the Gospel of John were taken over by D. Mollat for his translation in the Jerusalem Bible. Boismard developed his position in the following articles: "A propos de Jean v, 39," RB 55 (1948) 5-34; "Critique textuelle et citations patristiques," RB 57 (1950) 388-408; "Lectior brevior, potior," RB 58 (1951) 161-68; "Dans le sein des Père (Jo 1,18)," RB 59 (1952) 23-39; "Problèmes de critique textuelle concernant le

Unlike these other kinds of evidence, Patristic sources can be dated and localized with relative precision. Since the transmission history of the NT cannot be reconstructed without knowing when and where corruption entered the textual tradition, this kind of precision is a <u>sine qua non</u> for the entire critical process.³

Despite this relative advantage, Patristic sources have received far less critical attention than have the Greek and versional evidence. No doubt this scholarly reticence derives, in large measure, from complexities unique to the evidence, complexities stemming both from the loose citation habits of the Fathers and from the faulty transmission of their writings. It is well known that the Fathers did not always make a conscientious effort to cite Biblical texts accurately: with the exception of lengthy citations, quotations were normally drawn from memory without consulting a Biblical manuscript.⁴ The resultant "loose" citations range from paraphrases of Biblical accounts, to adaptations of texts to their syntactical or material context, to complicated conflations of several passages into one. To make matters worse, the Fathers rarely noted the sources of their citations. Thus the "words of the Savior," or the "Holy Apostle," or the "blessed Peter" can be quoted without reference to any of the books of the NT. And frequently a NT quotation is introduced only by a standard quotation formula, such as γέγραπται. Consequently, it often proves difficult not only to ascertain

---

quatrième évangile," <u>RB</u> 60 (1953) 347-71; "Le papyrus Bodmer II," <u>RB</u> 64 (1957) 363-98. Boismard's views lead to the acceptance of the "shorter text" of John at virtually every point, even where the Patristic sources stand alone in their attestation of this text. As will be seen below, the present writer concurs that Boismard's position is untenable. The Patristic sources provide primary evidence for the history of the transmission of the NT text but only secondary evidence for the original text itself.

³See Bruce M. Metzger, <u>The Text of the New Testament: Its Transmission, Corruption, and Restoration</u>, 2nd ed. (New York: Oxford University Press, 1968) 86.

⁴This alone accounts for the ubiquity of "loose" citations in the Patristic sources. See Fee, "The Text of John in the Jerusalem Bible," 167-70; Metzger, <u>Text</u>, 87-88.

the precise wording of a Father's Biblical text, but also to determine the source of a quotation. The latter problem is especially acute, of course, in quotations from the Synoptic Gospels.

The other set of problems unique to Patristic sources concerns the history of their own transmission. The MS traditions of virtually all the church Fathers show that later copyists tended to "correct" quotations of the Bible to the form of text prevalent in their own day. Consequently, Patristic writings that survive only in Medieval MSS or that are available only in uncritical editions, such as Migne's Patrologia Graeca, are of practically no value for establishing the original wording of the NT.[5] Biblical citations in such sources do not necessarily represent the text of the Father, but often only that known to his later copyists.[6]

It has become widely recognized in recent years that these complexities require the critic to follow strict methodological principles when assessing the Patristic evidence.[7] These principles involve three aspects of the analysis: (1) Only critical editions of a Father's works can be used; (2) Only those NT quotations and allusions whose Biblical sources are beyond doubt can be considered; and (3) All of the data--

---

[5] This has been acknowledged at least since the turn of the century. See Frederic C. Kenyon, Handbook to the Textual Criticism of the New Testament (London: Macmillan & Co., 1901) 206. The following is a modern assessment by Gordon Fee: "Over the past eight years I have been collecting the Greek patristic evidence for Luke and John for the International Greek New Testament Project. In all of this material I have found one invariable: a good critical edition of a father's text, or the discovery of early MSS, always moves the father's text of the NT away from the TR and closer to the text of our modern critical editions." (emphasis his) Gordon D. Fee, "Modern Textual Criticism and the Revival of the Textus Receptus," JETS 21 (1978) 26-27.

[6] Among the previous Patristic studies whose findings are compromised by the use of uncritical editions is, significantly, the dissertation of Wilhelm C. Linss, "The Gospel Text of Didymus" (Boston University, 1955). See n. 42, p. below.

[7] In addition to the works cited in n. 2, p. 4, see Gordon D. Fee, "The Text of John in Origen and Cyril of Alexandria: A Contribution to Methodology in the Recovery and Analysis of Patristic Citations," Biblica 52 (1971) 357-94.

i.e. all surviving citations, adaptations, and even allusions--must be analyzed before attempting to delineate the Father's Biblical text.[8] Each of these aspects can now be considered individually.

The Use of Critical Editions

The construction of critical editions of the Fathers' writings obviously lies outside the purview of NT textual criticism. This means that a correct analysis of a Father's text presupposes, in some measure, the validity of previous editorial decisions. The critical editions of Didymus's works were somewhat easier to produce than are those of church Fathers whose writings have survived in numerous but late MSS. Each of Didymus's authentic writings is preserved in only one, relatively early, MS which appears to represent faithfully the original text.[9] Consequently, making critical editions of these works involved primarily three tasks: (1) reconstructing the text wherever lacunae occur, (2) comparing the readings of the original hands of the MSS with those of the correctors (which in some cases numbered six or more),[10] and (3) correcting obvious transcriptional errors. By far the most frequent errors are orthographic, problems of itacism occurring on nearly every page.

The Source Analysis

The first step toward analyzing a Father's NT text involves ascertaining the Biblical source for each citation, adaptation, and allusion.[11] In certain kinds of Patristic

---

[8] The terms "citation," "adaptation," and "allusion" will be carefully differentiated on pp. 13-14 below. At this point it is necessary only to note that the following discussion uses the term "quotation" when speaking of both citations and adaptations, while the term "reference" is used to indicate any of the three kinds of evidence--citation, adaptation, or allusion.

[9] See the works cited in n. 54, p. 25 below.

[10] As in the Zechariah commentary. See Louis Doutreleau, *Didyme l'Aveugle sur Zacharie* (Paris: Les Éditions du Cerf, (1962) 46-50.

[11] Locating all the pertinent references is itself not a difficult matter, involving simply the perfunctory task of

writings, of course, this kind of determination can be made relatively easily--for example in a commentary on the Biblical book in question. Patristic commentaries often supply <u>lemmata</u> before the exposition of each passage. To be sure, these <u>lemmata</u> sometimes represent later additions to a Father's works so that they can be used only as secondary sources for reconstructing his Biblical text. But usually the Father quotes the passage under consideration in the exposition itself, thus providing the critic with ample evidence for a textual reconstruction.[12]

With other genres of Patristic writings, the critic is less fortunate. Patristic sermons on Biblical themes, for example, tend to contain brief, sporadic references to the NT. The situation is similar in commentaries on Biblical books other than those being subjected to textual analysis. Thus one finds that in his OT commentaries, Didymus often quotes half a verse from the NT here, half a verse there, two verses here, three there. Normally he does not mention the Biblical source for these quotations. This obviously complicates the entire text-critical process, since an analysis cannot proceed without first determining the Biblical referents for Didymus's quotations and allusions.[13]

Unfortunately, several previous studies of Patristic witnesses failed to deal adequately with the problem of sources, leading to distorted presentations of evidence. An

---

determining where a Father quotes or alludes to the NT. Naturally the source analysis, as described below, will eliminate some of the data tentatively accepted at the outset of the analysis.

[12] See Fee, "The Text of John in Origen and Cyril," 363-64.

[13] Among the noteworthy studies of Patristic sources that preserve only isolated NT quotations and allusions are the following: Lawrence Eldridge, <u>The Gospel Text of Epiphanius of Salamis</u> (Salt Lake City: University of Utah Press, 1969), Gordon D. Fee, "The Text of John and Mark in the Writings of Chrysostom," <u>NTS</u> 26 (1979-80) 525-47, Alexander Globe, "Serapion of Thmuis as Witness to the Gospel Text Used by Origen in Caesarea," <u>NovT</u> 26 (1984) 97-127, M. Mees, <u>Die Zitate aus dem Neuen Testament bei Clemens von Alexandrien</u> (Rome, 1970), and Carroll Osburn, "The Text of the Pauline Epistles in Hippolytus of Rome," <u>Second Century</u> 2 (1982) 97-124.

outstanding case in point is the landmark study of Chrysostom's text of Mark by J. Geerlings and S. New.[14] As Gordon Fee has recently demonstrated, Geerlings and New drew conclusions about Chrysostom's text of Mark from quotations found in precisely the same form in other Gospels.[15] But obviously a study of Mark's text cannot use as data quotations which might just as well have come from Matthew. This raises the methodological problem of how to determine the Biblical source of a Patristic quotation or allusion.

Sometimes the determination proves to be a relatively simple affair, as when the author names his source. Such a statement can normally, but not always, be trusted.[16] More frequently sources must be determined on the basis of internal considerations, that is, on the ground of verbal correspondence to material found in only one Gospel or another.

Problems of determining sources arise in three kinds of circumstances. The first has to do with Gospel parallels--when verbally identical passages occur in more than one Gospel. The problem can be illustrated from Didymus's writings. In his commentary on Ecclesiastes Didymus states φωνὴν βοῶντος εἶναι ἐν τῇ ἐρήμῳ (EcclT 38:24).[17] This

---

[14] Jacob Geerlings and Silva New, "Chrysostom's Text of the Gospel of Mark," *HTR* 24 (1931) 121-42.

[15] Fee, "The Text of John and Mark in Chrysostom," 538-47.

[16] A striking example of the problem of accepting uncritically an author's declaration of his source can be found in Didymus's commentary on Psalms. In the following passage Didymus points out the different renderings of a dominical saying by Matthew and Luke: τὸν αὐτὸν γὰρ τόπον γράφοντες ὁ μὲν Λουκᾶς λέγει "δώσει ἀγαθὰ τοῖς αἰτοῦσιν αὐτόν," ὁ Μαθαῖος "δώσει πνεῦμα ἅγιον." As the editors of the commentary correctly noticed, the first citation actually derives from Matthew, and the second from Luke! Thus even when the author names his source, the process of internal examination outlined below must be followed.

[17] The following sigla are used for Didymus's commentaries throughout the present study. EcclT=Ecclesiastes commentary of Toura; GenT=Genesis commentary; JobT=Job commentary; PsT=Psalms commentary; ZeT=Zechariah commentary. Thus EcclT 38:24 signifies the Ecclesiastes commentary of Toura, page 38, line 24.

represents an adaptation of the passage found in precisely the same form in all four Gospels: φωνὴ βοῶντος ἐν τῇ ἐρήμῳ (Matt 3:3; Mark 1:3; Luke 3:4; John 1:23). Occasionally the same problem arises when precise verbal parallels are found within the same Gospel, as when Didymus says πᾶσαν νόσον καὶ μαλακίαν θεραπεύοντος (ZeT 139:10), an adaptation of the Matthean θεραπεύων πᾶσαν νόσον καὶ μαλακίαν found in both Matt 4:23 and 9:34 or θεραπεύειν πᾶσαν νόσον κ.τ.λ. found in Matt 10:1. Since the sources of these quotations cannot be determined, they cannot be used in an analysis of Didymus's text. This means that a large number of data must be excluded from the analysis at the outset.

The second kind of problem derives from scribal harmonizations of one Gospel to another in the course of their transmission. Usually each Gospel will contain some unique readings in parallel passages: a different verb tense, the addition or omission of a word or phrase, the use of a synonymn, and the like. If a Father were to quote a passage in one of its distinctive forms, his source would be easily recognized. But since many unique elements of the Gospels were eliminated by well-intentioned scribes who harmonized one passage to another, it is often impossible to determine whether a Father is quoting one of the Gospels in its (originally) unique form or a different Gospel that was later harmonized to it. The nature of the problem can again be illustrated from Didymus's writings. In his commentary on the Psalms, Didymus cites the following saying of Jesus: οὐκ ἔστιν ὁ θεὸς νεκρῶν ἀλλὰ ζώντων (PsT 276:2). The quotation conforms to Matthew's version of the logion. This is significant because it shows Didymus's support for two variants in the tradition: (1) ὁ θεός with UBS[3] B L Δ fam 1 33 against θεός found in א D W and ὁ θεὸς θεός found in TR E (θ) Π Ω (fam 13) 892 1241, and (2) ἔστιν with rell. against ἔστιν δέ found in fam 13 e. But the reasons for considering this citation Matthean evaporate when the MS tradition of Mark is examined more closely. To be sure, Mark's version probably read οὐκ ἔστιν θεός κ.τ.λ. (thus B D L W al.). But the definite article is found in numerous other witnesses, including ℵ A C θ 33. So here it is impossible to determine whether Didymus agrees with B against ℵ in a Matthean citation or with ℵ against B in a Marcan. For this reason, whenever a passage of one Gospel has been harmonized to that of another in a significant strand of the textual tradition, neither passage can be used to establish a Father's textual affinities.

A third problematic situation occurs when a Father, either by accident or design, conflates two or more Biblical passages. Occasionally a conflated reading can be unravelled so as to make the constituent parts and their sources readily discernable. Such is the case, for example, when Didymus says πᾶς...ὃς ἐὰν ὁμολογήσῃ ἐν ἐμοὶ ἔμπροσθεν τῶν ἀνθρώπων ...κἀγὼ ὁμολογήσω αὐτόν (PsT 210:34-45). The first part of the quotation (πᾶς...ἀνθρώπων) must represent a citation of Luke 12:8, the second (κἀγω...αὐτόν) an adaptation of Matt 10:32. In other places, however, conflations are hopelessly complex, making the determination of sources impossible. This is true, for example, in the following quotation from EcclT 358:26-359:2: τίνι ὁμοιώσω τὴν γενεὰν ταύτην;...ὁμοία ἐστὶν παιδίοις ἐν ἀγορᾷ καθημένοις, ἃ προσφωνεῖ ἕτερα πρὸς ἕτερα λέγοντες ηὐλήσαμεν ὑμῖν καὶ οὐκ ὠρχήσασθε, ἐθρηνήσαμεν ὑμῖν καὶ οὐκ ἐκόψασθε...ἦλθεν Ἰωάννης μήτε ἐσθίων μήτε πίνων. Clearly part of this text derives from Matt 11:16-18 and part from Luke 7:31-32. But the two accounts are so intricately interwoven that the source of each phrase cannot be discerned. And part of the text agrees with neither Gospel, deriving from Didymus's own free handling of the materials. Obviously complex conflations of this sort cannot be used when seeking to establish a Father's textual affinities.

A source analysis, then, serves to limit the study of Patristic quotations and allusions to those that are not found in identical form either in the original texts of the Gospels or in their MS traditions, and to those that are not conflated beyond the possibility of disentanglement.

The Textual Reconstruction

The third area of methodological concern has to do with the actual reconstruction of the Father's Biblical text. Here again some genres of literature will be more amenable to the task than others. Biblical commentaries on the passages in question will tend to preserve a relatively high degree of accuracy of citation--if not in the lemmata, at least in the exposition itself.[18] In contrast, quotations in commentaries on other passages will often be allusive and more frequently adapted to the grammatical or material context. The following methodological proposals were developed in view of this latter kind of evidence, given the frequent but sporadic quotations of the NT in Didymus's expository works.

The first step toward reconstructing a Father's Biblical text entails determining the relative value of all the data thus far collected. This determination involves classifying each Biblical quotation and allusion with respect to its verbal correspondence to the NT source. At this point there enters into the critical process the subjective judgment of whether the Patristic author intended to cite the text precisely or willingly altered or paraphrased the text. In theory, one could analyze the manner of citation so as to make this judgment. If, for example, the author introduces the reference by citing his source and using a citation formula (e.g. γέγραπται), one could classify the reference as an intentional citation and, should the passage be sufficiently lengthy, assert that it derives from the author's Biblical MS. In actuality, however, such indicators of authorial intent rarely prove reliable. Citation formulae can just as easily precede paraphrases as citations, and, as previously seen, the notation of sources is sometimes erroneous, making their value in this regard dubious.[19] For these reasons, classification of Biblical references is better made purely on the ground of verbal correspondence to the Biblical text.

In one sense this approach appears problematic, since

---

[18] See the discussion on p. 7-8 above.
[19] See n. 16, p. 9 above.

classifications depend on the proximity of each reference to the Biblical text, while the physiognomy of a Father's text cannot be determined without first establishing the accuracy of his references to it. In practice, however, it is not difficult to distinguish between a faint allusion and a precise citation. The real difficulty comes in distinguishing, say, an intentional citation, which contains one or more small variations from the Father's text, from a slight adaptation of the text made in view of the syntactical or material context. It must be recognized at this stage that all classifications are necessarily provisional and should be viewed as relative points of reference along a continuum ranging from exact citation to distant allusion. No advances in method can overcome the shortcomings of the Patristic data at this point. On occasion it may simply be that what looks like an adaptation of a Biblical text actually derived from the text of the Father's exemplar. On the other hand, since remnants of such an aberrant text would presumably recur elsewhere in the textual tradition, it is relatively safe to assume that these exceptions will be so rare as to make virtually no impact on the analysis.

As already noted, the present study is adopting, with minor modifications, the threefold system of classification advocated by Gordon Fee: citations, adaptations, and allusions.[20] "Citations" consist of accurate quotations of the Biblical passage. Accuracy here is determined solely on the ground of verbal conformity to the Biblical passage, as found in the various strands of the tradition. Thus if the citation varies markedly from the text normally judged to be original, yet conforms with the text as found in a significant element of the tradition, it will still be considered a citation. Naturally, since minor changes may occur, not every citation will be equally precise. Nevertheless, rather than overcrowding the system beyond the point of usefulness--i.e. by labeling citations "very loose," "loose," and "exact"--all

---

[20] See especially "The Text of John in the Jerusalem Bible," 169-70.

14/ Didymus and the Gospels

more or less accurate quotations will be registered as citations.

"Adaptations" are Biblical references which have been significantly modified for one reason or another. Some critics apply this category only to quotations changed in conformity with the grammatical context or in conformity with the point being made in the discussion.[21] But this approach to classification unnecessarily restricts the category to variations whose causes are readily discerned. In point of fact, one would expect that a Father quoting from memory would occasionally adapt a Biblical text to suit his own purposes, whether or not these purposes are transparent. For this reason, it is better to consider any major modification of a Biblical passage an adaptation, so long as the reference maintains a close verbal correspondence to the Biblical text. This broadening of the category does not relieve the critic of the task of finding contextual reasons for adaptations; it does allow the classification to be applied to modifications made for no obvious reason.

Finally, "allusions" consist of Scriptural reminiscences that have only a distant verbal correspondence to the text. References with absolutely no verbal correspondence, of course, cannot help the critic determine the words of the Father's text and so cannot be used in the analysis.

When appropriate classifications have been made, the Patristic references can be analyzed for their witness to the text of the NT. Here too a number of previous studies have fallen short by failing to take into account all of the evidence. Rightly recognizing, for example, that Biblical allusions do not qualify as citations, many earlier critics wrongly discounted the text-critical value of allusions altogether.[22] But even when references to the Biblical text lack

---

[21] Ibid., 170.

[22] This was another shortcoming of Geerlings and New, as shown by G. Fee, "The Text of John and Mark in Chrysostom," 538. Other studies, such as Linss's on Didymus, give citations in full, but only list Scriptural references of allusions. Collations are then made only of the exact quota-

the precision of citations (or of loose adaptations) they can still, on occasion, serve to indicate which of several variants was found in the Father's text. This can be shown by an example drawn from the present study of Didymus. In a clear allusion to Mt. 21:2, 4, Didymus writes ἐπιβεβηκότος ὄνου καὶ πώλου λυθέντων καὶ ἐνεχθέντων ἐκ τῆς κατέναντι κώμης (ZeT 218:6-8). These words must refer to the Matthean passage rather than to either of the parallels in Mark or Luke (note: ὄνου καὶ πώλου!). Significantly, Matthew's use of κατέναντι is attested by most Alexandrian witnesses and several others (UBS^3 ℵ B C D L θ fam 13 33 892) while ἀπέναντι is found in Byzantine witnesses and others (TR E W Δ Π Ω fam 1 1241). Thus, despite the allusive character of Didymus's reference, there can be no doubt that he supports the Alexandrian tradition here.

In other instances the process of establishing the Father's text will be relatively simple, as when he quotes the same passage several times in precisely the same form, or when the minor differences among the citations are not reflected elsewhere in the MS tradition. In such instances it can safely be assumed that the citation which conforms to the common text was also that of the Father; the slightly variant forms represent accidental or intentional modifications.

Two kinds of data have been considered up to this point: (1) allusions and adaptations that give no evidence as to the character of the Father's text of the whole passage, but that do disclose his reading in part of it, and (2) multiple citations that may require the critic to choose one that best represents the Father's text. A third situation occurs when a Father's quotations and allusions are such that his Biblical text can and should be reconstructed. In view here are instances of (1) frequent but partial citations of a passage, and (2) adaptations and allusions which make it possible to discern the original form of the Father's text. Reconstructions can be only tentative, of course, and must be evaluated on the basis of all the relevant data. Both the tentative

---

tions. An alternative method is outlined in Ch. II below.

16/ Didymus and the Gospels

character and the ultimate potential of textual reconstructions can be illustrated, once again, from the data set forth in the following critical apparatus. Didymus preserves two adaptations and one allusion to Matt 5:45--

(a) ἀνατέλλει γὰρ τὸν ἥλιον ὥσπερ ἐπὶ ἀγαθούς (PsT 177:20);

(b) τὸν ἀνατέλλοντα τὸν ἥλιον ἐπὶ ἀγαθοὺς καὶ πονηροὺς καὶ βρέχοντα ἐπὶ δικαίους καὶ ἀδίκους (ZeT 246:11-12);

(c) ἀνατέλλων οὐ μόνον ἐπὶ ἀγαθοὺς τὸν ἥλιον ἀλλὰ καὶ ἐπὶ πονηρούς (PsT 290:21-22).

On the basis of these references, Didymus's text can be reconstructed as follows:
ἀνατέλλει τὸν ἥλιον ἐπὶ ἀγαθοὺς καὶ πονηροὺς καὶ βρέχει ἐπὶ δικαίους καὶ ἀδίκους.

Here it can be seen that Didymus preserves the word order of the Old Latin MS a (ἀγαθοὺς καὶ πονηρούς). This may not be considered significant, given the problem of word order in the versional evidence. But it is worth noting that Didymus also reads καὶ βρέχει...ἀδίκους with the whole tradition against ℵ, which omits it. In a case such as this, the reconstruction must be made conservatively, changing word order or making additions, subtractions, or substitutions only on the basis of hard evidence. As a result, the reconstructed text may preserve some singular readings, as happens twice in the reference just cited (ἀνατέλλει τὸν ἥλιον] ἥλιον ἀνατέλλει; ἥλιον] ἥλιον αὐτοῦ). In view of the character of the evidence, no confidence can be placed in having uncovered some real singular readings by this reconstruction. It could well be that Didymus simply misquoted or adapted the text consistently. But before even this conclusion can be drawn, the data must at least be presented. In this case such a presentation is most adequately achieved through a reconstruction.

Occasionally a reconstruction can be attempted when a solitary adaptation exists, so long as the changes are predominantly syntactical. Here a reconstruction entails little more than the reversion to the passage's original syntax. Thus, for example, Didymus preserves only one, fairly exten-

Methodological Problems /17

sive, adaptation of Matt 22:13:
ὡς καὶ ἐν εὐαγγελίῳ περὶ τοῦ δεθέντος πόσιν καὶ χέρσιν καὶ βληθέντος εἰς τὸ σκότος τὸ ἐξώτερον τὸ ἡτοιμασμένον τῷ διαβόλῳ καὶ τοῖς ἀγγέλοις αὐτοῦ, ἐκεῖ ἔσται ὁ κλαυθμὸς καὶ ὁ βρυγμὸς τῶν ὀδόντων (PsT 247:7-8).
A reconstruction of Didymus's text can be made with a fair degree of confidence.

δήσαντες αὐτοῦ πόδας καὶ χεῖρας βάλετε (αὐτοῦ) εἰς τὸ σκότος τὸ ἐξώτερον, ἐκεῖ ἔσται ὁ κλαυθμὸς καὶ ὁ βρυγμὸς τῶν ὀδόντων

The reconstruction shows that Didymus supports two significant variants of the textual tradition: (1) δήσαντες αὐτοῦ πόδας καὶ χεῖρας with א B L θ f$^{1, 13}$ 892 against both ἄρατε αὐτὸν ποδῶν καὶ χείρων found in D a b e, and δήσαντες αὐτοῦ πόδας καὶ χεῖρας ἄρατε αὐτὸν καί supported by the bulk of later MSS as well as by C 33 and 1241; and (2) βάλετε with D f^{13} 1241 a b e against most other MSS.

The Special Significance and Peculiar Problems of Didymus as a Textual Witness

There can be no doubt about the text-critical significance of the Gospel quotations of Didymus, the blind monk appointed head of the Alexandrian catechetical school by Athanasius.[23] Didymus's life spanned the fourth century (A.D. 313-398). Born and raised in Alexandria, he apparently never left his home city even as an adult. At an early age, perhaps four or five, Didymus became blind, probably the result of a

---

[23] Didymus's life, work, and teachings have been the subject of three monographs in modern times: G. Bardy, Didyme l'Aveugle (Paris: Beauchesne, 1910); J. Leipoldt, Didymus der Blinde von Alexandria (Leipzig: J. C. Hinrichs, 1905); and William J. Gauche, Didymus the Blind: An Educator of the Fourth Century (Washington: Catholic University of America, 1934). Other helpful sketches include Wolfgang A. Bienert, "Allegoria" und "Anagoge" Bei Didymos dem Blinden von Alexandrien (Berlin: Walter de Gruyter, 1972) 1-31; Louis Doutreleau, Sur Zacharie 1-128; Bärbel Kramer, "Didymus von Alexandrien," Theologische Realenzyklopädie, vol. VIII (Berlin: Walter de Gruyter, 1981) 741-46; Johannes Quasten, Patrology, vol. III (Utrecht: Spectrum, 1966) 85-100; and Frances Young, From Nicaea to Chalcedon: A Guide to the Literature and Its Background (Philadelphia: Fortress Press, 1983) 83-91.

childhood disease.[24] Despite this setback, he displayed a great facility for learning, and later in life acquired a reputation for a prodigious memory.[25] His education covered all the major disciplines of the day: mathematics, geometry, astronomy, grammar, rhetoric, dialectic, and philosophy.[26] Best known for his understanding of Scripture, Didymus established himself early in life as a prominent teacher in Alexandria. It was in the midst of the Arian controversy that Athanasius appointed him to be head of the famed cathechetical school,[27] which by this time had lost much of the splendor and reputation it had earlier enjoyed under Clement and Origen.[28] There is no evidence that Didymus publicly lectured to fulfill the duties of his post. More likely he taught from the privacy of his own monk's cell. Nevertheless, his reputation spread far and wide; by life's end he could number among his students such noteworthies as Jerome and Rufinus.[29]

During the course of his career Didymus dictated numerous theological treatises and Biblical commentaries. Most significant for the controversies of his own day were his doctrinal

---

[24]Palladius, Hist. Laus. IV; Jerome Chronicon, VIII; Socrates, Hist. Eccl., IV, 25; Cassiodorus, Historia Tripartia, VIII, 8.

[25]See, e.g., Socrates, Hist. Eccl., IV, 25; Rufinus, Hist. Eccl., II, 7; Jerome, Vir. Ill., 109 and Epist. 50, ad Domnionem.

[26]Rufinus, Hist. Eccl., II, 7; Socrates, Hist. Eccl., IV, 25-26; Theodoret, Hist. Eccl., IV, 26.

[27]The date of his appointment has been widely debated. Proposed dates range from A.D. 335, before Athanasius's first exile (T. de Régnon, Études de Théologie Positive sur la Sainte Trinité, vol. III [Paris, 1898] 19, based on the testimony of Rufinus, Hist. Eccl., II, 7) to A.D. 371 (Carl Andresen, "Didymos 3," in Lexikon der Alten Welt [Zurick: Artemis Verlag, 1965] 732-33). See the discussions of Bardy, Didyme, 6; Bienert, "Allegoria", 5-6; Gauche, Didymus, 78; Leipoldt, Didymus, 6.

[28]See esp. G. Bardy, "Pour l'histoire de l'école d'Alexandria," Vivre et Penser 2 (1942) 80-109; Gauch, Didymus, 36-70.

[29]See Jerome's Epist. 112, ad Augustinius, 4-6; Epist. 84, ad Pammachium et Oceanum; Rufinus, Apology, II, 12; Hist. Eccl., II, 7.

works on the Trinity (De Trinitate)[30] and the Holy Spirit (De Spiritu Sancto).[31] At heart, though, Didymus was a Biblical scholar, having dictated commentaries on much of the Old Testament and most of the New.[32] In addition, some of Didymus's students later published notes taken from his expository lectures on yet other Biblical books.[33]

Didymus is an important witness to the NT text precisely because of his historical context. He studied the NT and quoted its text in Alexandria when the great Alexandrian uncials were being produced.[34] An aura of mystery has always surrounded the Alexandrian text. Was an ecclesiastically-sanctioned recension made there (in the 4th century? or the 2nd?)?[35] When and how extensively did a strain of the Western

---

[30] See the recent critical editions by Jürgen Hönscheid Didymus der Blinde: De trinitate, Buch I (Meisenheim am Glan: Verlage Anton Hain, 1975) and Ingrid Seiler, Didymus der Blinde: De trinitate, Buch II, Kapitel 1-7 (Meisenheim am Glan: Verlag Anton Hain, 1975).

[31] See Louis Doutreleau, "Étude d'une tradition manuscrite: Le 'De Spiritu Sancto' de Didyme," in Kyriakon: Festschrift Johannes Quasten, ed. Patrick Granfield and Josef A. Jungmann, vol. 1 (Münster: Verlag Aschendorff, 1970) 352-89; and idem, "Le De Spiritu Sancto de Didyme et ses éditeurs," RechSR 51 (1963) 383-406. The text can be found in Migne, PG 39, 1031-86.

[32] Doutreleau gives the following as Didymus's commentaries, acknowledging that "cette liste est sans doute incomplète": Genesis, Exodus, Leviticus, Job, Psalms, Proverbs, Ecclesiastes, Song of Songs, Isaiah, Final Vision of Isaiah, Jeremiah, Daniel, Hosea, Zechariah; Matthew, Luke, John, Acts, Romans, 1 and 2 Corinthians, Galatians, Ephesians, Hebrews, Catholic epistles, and Revelation. Sur Zacharie, I, 17-18; 119-26.

[33] This is to be inferred from the character of the Ecclesiastes and Psalms commentaries discovered at Toura, as discussed below, pp. 26-27.

[34] See the discussion of codices ℵ and B in Metzger, Text, 7-8; 42-48.

[35] This view was popularized by Wilhelm Bousset, largely on the basis of his analysis of the Alexandrian fragments commonly designated by the siglum "T": "Die Recension des Hesychius," Textkritische Studien zum Neuen Testament (Leipzig: J. C. Hinrichs, 1894) 74-110. Bousset's position has been discounted by a number of scholars, most recently by Gordon D. Fee, "P75, P66, and Origen: The Myth of Early Textual Recension in Alexandria," in New Dimensions in New

20/ Didymus and the Gospels

text enter the Alexandrian tradition?[36] Were there two streams of transmission there, one early and one late?[37] Or were there two roughly contemporaneous streams?[38] Were elements of a proto-Byzantine text found in Alexandria already by the fourth century?[39] Did the Caesarean text ultimately derive from there?[40] Scholars have addressed many of these issues by analyzing the second- and third-century Alexandrian witnesses, viz. the earliest papyri, Clement, and Origen.[41]

Testament Study, eds. Richard N. Longenecker and Merrill C. Tenney (Grand Rapids: Zondervan, 1974) 19-45.

[36]As early as the third century, Egyptian witnesses such as P29, P38, P45, P48 preserve elements of the Western text. See Metzger, Text, 214. Gordon D. Fee ("Codex Sinaiticus in the Gospel of John: A Contribution to Methodology in Establishing Textual Relationships," NTS 15 [1968-69] 23-44) shows that in John 1:1-8:38 codex Sinaiticus is a leading representative of the Western text.

[37]This view was popularized by Westcott and Hort's differentiation between the "Alexandrian" and "Neutral" texts (The New Testament in the Original Greek, 2 [Cambridge: Macmillan, 1881] 126-32, 164-72). See also the discussion of Carlo Martini, "Is There a Late Alexandrian Text of the Gospels?" NTS 24 (1977-78) 285-96.

[38]This is the position advocated by Martini in the article cited in the preceding note.

[39]See the list of papyrus-supported Byzantine readings in Harry A. Sturz, The Byzantine Text-Type and New Testament Textual Criticism, 3rd ed. (La Mirada, Cal: Biola College Bookstore, 1980) 107-222, and the conclusions drawn there. See also C. C. Tarelli, "The Chester Beatty Papyrus and the Western and Byzantine Texts," JTS 41 (1940) 253-60, and Gunther Zuntz, The Text of the Epistles: A Disquisition Upon the Corpus Paulinum (London: Oxford University, 1953) 55.

[40]The origin of the Caesarean text has sometimes been traced back to the text Origen brought to Caesarea when he moved from Alexandria. Thus Robert P. Blake, Kirsopp Lake, and Silva New, "The Caesarean Text of Mark," HTR 21 (1928) 207-404. See Bruce M. Metzger, "Caesarean Text of the Gospels," in Chapters in the History of New Testament Textual Criticism (Leiden: E. J. Brill, 1963) 47, 62-67.

[41]In addition to the works cited in nn. 35, 36, 39, and 40 above, see especially P. M. Barnard, The Biblical Text of Clement of Alexandria (Cambridge: University Press, 1899); Gordon D. Fee, "Origen's Text of the New Testament and the Text of Egypt," NTS 28 (1982) 348-64; M. Mees, Die Zitate; Calvin Porter, "Papyrus Bodmer XV (P75) and the Text of Codex Vaticanus," JBL 81 (1962) 363-76; Reuben J. Swanson, "The Gospel Text of Clement of Alexandria" (Ph.D. dissertation, Yale University, 1956).

Methodological Problems /21

Now another link in the chain can be forged by studying the writings of Didymus, a fourth-century Alexandrian church Father.

It should be noted that two previous scholars have analyzed Didymus's text. The first was Wilhelm Linss, whose doctoral dissertation is rendered virtually useless by its methodological inadequacies and by the publication of newer discoveries since its completion in 1955.[42] More recently Carlo Martini probed the issues raised by Didymus's text as preserved in the Toura commentaries, but did not provide a thoroughgoing presentation and analysis of the data.[43] Both of these former studies will be considered at appropriate junctures in the analyses of Chapters IV and V below.

In addition to the complexities inherent in all Patristic sources, as already discussed, the citations of any particular Father will pose unique difficulties for a text-critical analysis. For Didymus, additional complexities arise from the circumstance of his blindness and from the problems of determining the authenticity of various writings attributed to him.

Didymus's blindness poses obvious problems for the analysis of his NT text. Whereas other church Fathers frequently chose to quote Scripture from memory, Didymus always did so out of necessity; whereas others could check their citations against Biblical MSS whenever they wished, Didymus never could; whereas others learned Scripture by reading available MSS, Didymus did not. Didymus went blind before he could read, so that his vast knowledge of Scripture came by memorizing what was read to him. Since different ones of his early teachers presumably used different Biblical MSS, each with its

---

[42] With the exception of Zoepfl's edition of the *Expositio in septum canonicorum epistolarum* (see n. 47 below), Linss had access only to Migne's uncritical edition of Didymus's writings. Just as importantly, the authorship of most of these works has since come under attack, as will be discussed below. Furthermore, Linss sought to establish Didymus's textual affinities largely by tabulating agreements in variation from the TR. Thus Linss's study provides incomplete data drawn from an uncritical edition of writings that may well not be authentic.
[43] Martini, "Is There a Late Alexandrian Text?"

own textual peculiarities, Didymus would have learned an "eclectic" text at the very beginning of his life. Furthermore, as an author, Didymus could not have written any of his treatises himself, but would have had to dictate them to various amanuenses. It is not impossible that different amanuenses recorded Didymus's Scriptural citations, not as he gave them, but in the form of text they themselves had learned. It seems reasonable to assume that this would have led only to minor modifications of the text. But if such modifications did occur, then even before Didymus's works were released to the public, his citations of Scripture differed from the text as he had it memorized. Taking all these problems into account, it looks as though the task of establishing Didymus's Gospel text is very great indeed, perhaps insurmountable.

On closer examination, however, these problems appear no greater than those that obtain in the analysis of any other Patristic writer. Yes, Didymus would have learned Scripture by memorizing passages from various MSS. But, presumably, so too would have most Christians in his day. Furthermore, however "mixed" the resultant memorized text would have been, it would have been a text with its various constituent parts coming from fourth-century Alexandrian exemplars. It must be borne in mind that an analysis of a Father's text is concerned primarily with the date and location of the data, not simply with their source. Yes, Didymus would have been forced to quote from memory. But so too did most of the Fathers. And on this score Didymus could perhaps be said to have an advantage, given his reputation for a superior memory. Yes, Didymus would have used different amanuenses who could conceivably have changed his quotations of Scripture before they even came to the page. But this in no way affects the analysis of Didymus's text, since, again, changes of this sort would necessarily represent readings found in fourth-century Alexandria. Thus the problems deriving from the circumstance of Didymus's blindness should have little bearing on an analysis of his NT quotations and allusions.

Somewhat more complicated is the issue of the authenti-

Methodological Problems /23

city of the various works attributed to Didymus. Clearly if Didymus's text is to be analyzed, only his writings can be studied. But since the publication of the commentaries discovered at Toura, Egypt in 1941 (see below) the authorship of virtually all of the theological and expositional works previously attributed to him has come into dispute. The history of the attribution of various writings to Didymus is interesting but involved. Here only a brief sketch will be provided so as to show the rationale for restricting the present investigation to the Toura commentaries.[44]

By the early eighteenth century, three works were commonly ascribed to Didymus: Jerome's Latin translation of a treatise on the Holy Spirit, De Spiritu Sancto;[45] a little tractate directed against the Manichaeans, Contra Manichaios;[46] and a commentary on the seven Catholic epistles, Expositio Septem Canonicarum Epistolarum.[47] Then in 1758 J. Mingarelli discovered a three-volume work on the Trinity. Some eleven years later, in the preface to his edition of the work, Mingarelli argued for Didymian authorship on three grounds: (1) the early church historian Socrates (ca. A.D. 440) knew of a three-volume work on the Trinity by Didymus; (2) the author of the work makes several references to his former treatise on the Holy Spirit, presumably De Spiritu

---

[44] The following survey of research is particularly indebted to the discussion of Bienert, "Allegoria", 8-31. See also Quasten, Patrology, III, 86-93.

[45] See note 31, above.

[46] Preserved in Latin translation with only fragments of the Greek text extant. See Migne, PG, 39, 1085-1110.

[47] Cassiodorus states that Didymus's commentary on the Catholic epistles was translated into Latin by Epiphanius (De Institutione Divinarum Litteratarum, 8, in Migne PL, 70, 1120). But already by the early eighteenth century some scholars questioned whether the extant document is this translation, or whether instead it represents a commentary originally written in Latin (and hence not Didymus's). See especially Dom R. Ceillier, Histoire générale des Auteurs Sacrés et Écclesiastiques, 2nd ed. vol V (Paris, 1860) 739-41. The text of the commentary can be found in Migne, PG 39, 1749-1818, or in the critical edition prepared by F. Zoepfl, Didymi Alex. in epistolas canonicas brevis enarratio (Münster: Aschendorffsche Verlagsbuchhandlung, 1914).

24/ Didymus and the Gospels

Sancto; and (3) a number of formal and material parallels can be found between these two works.[48] Mingarelli's position was widely accepted among scholars for nearly 200 years.

In the late 19th and 20th centuries other works were attributed to Didymus, largely on the basis of formal and material parallels to De Trinitate. Thus Pseudo-Basil's Adversus Eunomium IV-V,[49] Pseudo-Gregory's Adversus Arium et Sabellium,[50] Pseudo-Hieronymus's On the Vision of the Seraphim,[51] the Pseudo-Athanasian Dialogues,[52] and Contra Montanus,[53] were all assigned to Didymus at one time or another. Even before the Toura finds, none of these attributions was universally accepted. But with the discovery and publication of Didymus's Old Testament commentaries, a cloud of doubt was cast over the authorship of De Trinitate, and consequently over all other writings attributed to Didymus on the basis of similarities to it.

In August of 1941, a crew of Egyptian workers, digging out a grotto for use as a munitions depot in Toura, Egypt (twelve kilometers south of Cairo), unearthed eight ancient papyrus codices, totaling some 2000 pages. When the codices

---
[48] Mingarelli's preface to De Trinitate was reprinted in Migne PG 39, 139-216.

[49] First attributed to Didymus by F. X. Funk, "Die zwei letzen Bücher der Schrift Basilius' des Gr. gegen Eunomius," Kirchengeschictliche Abhandlungen und Untersuchungen, II (Paderborn: F. Schöningh, 1899) 291-329. For the course of the subsequent debate, see Bienert, "Allegoria", 10-12. The strongest case against Didymian authorship was made by Chr. Bizer, "Studien zu den pseudoathanasian Dialogen, Der Orthodoxos und Aëtios" (Dissertation, Bonn, 1966) 213ff.

[50] K. Holl, "Über die Gregor von Nyssa zugeschriebene Schrift 'Adversus Arium et Sabellium,'" ZKG 25 (1904) 380-98. Holl's arguments were rejected by several subsequent scholars. See especially Bardy, Didyme, 17ff.

[51] W. Dietsche, Didymus von Alexandrien als Verfasser der Schrift über die Seraphvision (Freiburg: Blumer, 1941). For a contrary view, see B. Altaner, "Wer ist der Verfasser des Tractatus in Isaiam VI, 1-7" ThRev 42 (1943) 147-51.

[52] See especially A. Günthor, Die 7 pseudoathanasianischen Dialoge, ein Werk Didymus' des Blinden von Alexandrien (Rome: Herder, 1941) 23ff.

[53] Ibid., contra Bizer, Studien.

finally reached the hands of papyrologists, it was realized that a discovery of the first order had been made.[54] Along with copies of several works of Origen were sixth or seventh-century fragmentary copies of commentaries on Genesis, Job, Psalms, Ecclesiastes, and Zechariah. The attribution of the Genesis, Job, and Zechariah commentaries to Didymus came almost immediately.[55] Within several years the other two works were likewise assigned to him.[56] These attributions, which today are accepted by virtually all scholars, were based on the following considerations. The Genesis and Job commentaries contain numerous linguisic and material parallels to the expositions preserved in Didymus's name in the Medieval catanae.[57] The extent and character of these parallels leave little room for doubt as to the authorship of the commentaries. The commentary on Zechariah was attributed to Didymus largely on the basis of Jerome's testimony. In the preface to his own commentary on Zechariah, Jerome stated that Didymus had previously written a five-volume commentary on that book

---

[54] The first notice of the discovery was made by O. Guerand "Note préliminaire sur les papyrus d'Origène découverts à Toura," RHR 131 (1946) 85-108. Shortly thereafter a number of brief appraisals of the find were published: B. Altaner, "Ein grosser, aufstehen erregender patrologischer Papyrusfund," ThQ 127 (1947) 332-33; O. Cullmann, "Die neuesten Papyrusfunde von Origenestexten und gnostischer Schriften," ThZ 5 (1949) 153-57; J. de Ghellinck, "Récentes découvertes de littérature chrétienne antique," NRTh 71 (1949) 83-86; E. Klostermann, "Der Papyrusfund von Tura," ThLZ 73 (1948) 47-50; H.-Ch. Puech, "Les nouveaux écrits d'Origène et de Didyme découverts à Toura," RHPhR 31 (1951) 293-329. The best discussion of the find prior to the publication of any of the texts was by Louis Doutreleau, "Que savons-nous aujourd'hui des Papyrus de Toura," RechSR 43 (1955) 161-93. Doutreleau updated this discussion twelve years later with the assistance of Ludwig Koenen, "Nouvelle inventaire des papyrus de Toura," RechSR 55 (1967) 547-64.

[55] Guerand, "Note préliminaire," 90.

[56] Doutreleau, "Que savons-nous," 167-68.

[57] Doutreleau and Koenen, "Nouvelle inventaire," 551, 561; Bienert "Allegoria", 23-24. As A. Heinrichs has shown, some of the Job catenae preserved under the name of Nicetas (eleventh century) actually derive from Didymus, and these also find parallels in the Toura commentary. Didymos Der Blinde: Hiob Kommentar, I, 14-15.

at his request.[58] The Toura commentary comprises five books and shows numerous similarities to Jerome's work. In the opinion of L. Doutreleau, the parallels demonstrate not only that Didymus authored this commentary, but that Jerome made extensive use of it in producing his own.[59]

The authorship of the Psalms commentary proved somewhat more difficult to establish, since very few verbal parallels exist between this exposition and the catenae fragments of the Psalms that bear Didymus's name.[60] Nevertheless, extensive material similarities do occur between the two expositions[61] and the vocabulary and style of this commentary conform closely to what is found in the three already attributed to Didymus. These considerations have led a number of scholars to conclude that while the catenae fragments and the Toura commentary both derive from Didymus,[62] they represent different expositions, or, possibly, different stages of the same exposition, the text of the catenae perhaps representing a later redaction of Didymus's work.[63] The Ecclesiastes commentary was obviously written by the author of the Psalms commentary, as is shown by the remarkable similarities in vocabulary and style of exposition. Furthermore, it likewise conforms in outlook, theology, and style to the three other Toura commentaries.[64] It should be noted that of these five commentaries, those on Genesis, Job, and Zechariah appear to represent actual literary productions, dictated and revised by

---

[58] See Migne, PL, 25, 1486.

[59] Doutreleau, Sur Zacharie, 129-37.

[60] See the detailed comparisons and discussion by Adolphe Gesché, La Christologie du 'Commentaire sur les Psaumes' découvert à Toura (Gembloux: J. Duculot, 1962) 327-51.

[61] See the discussion of Aloys Kehl, ed. Der Psalmenkommentar von Tura, Quaternio IX (Köln: Westdeutschen Verlag, 1964) and, especially, that of Gesché, La Christologie, 322-417.

[62] So Bienert, "Allegoria", 27. See the discussion of possible alternatives to this view in Gesché, La Christologie, 347-50.

[63] Bienert, "Allegoria", 27-28.

[64] Ibid., 28.

Didymus with the intention of publication, while those on Psalms and Ecclesiastes appear to have been produced by Didymus's students from lecture notes taken while sitting at their master's feet.[65] Interestingly, in these latter two works the textual exposition is periodically interrupted by a student's question which, along with the teacher's answer, has been dutifully recorded.

In a landmark article written some sixteen years after the discovery of the Toura commentaries, L. Doutreleau reopened the question of the authorship of De Trinitate.[66] With the authorship of the Toura commentary on Zechariah so firmly established by the testimony of Jerome, Doutrelaeu asked how this new evidence affected the earlier conclusions of Mingarelli. Doutreleau argued that the two works could not have come from the same author, largely because of their irreconcilable expositions of Zech. 3:8-4:10. The differences extend to the style, diction, and especially the content of the expositions. A glaring inconsistency, for example, comes in the interpretation of the "mountain" of Zech 4:7: in the Toura commentary it signifies the Redeemer, while in De Trinitate it is said to represent the Devil.[67]

While Doutreleau's arguments were not persuasive to all scholars,[68] they did clear the way for a reexamination of the

---

[65] See especially the discussions of Gerhard Binder and Leo Liesenborghs, Didymos der Blinde: Kommentar zum Ecclesiastes 1:1 (Bonn: Rudolf Habelt Verlag, 1979) x-xiii, and Aloys Kehl, Der Psalmenkommentar, 39-43.

[66] "Le 'De Trinitate' est-il l'oeuvre de Didyme l'Aveugle?" RechSR 45 (1957) 514-57.

[67] See De Trinitate II, 14 (in Migne PG 39, 701A-708A) and ZeT 54:9-75.

[68] Especially unconvinced was Ludwig Koenen ("Ein theologischer Papyrus des Kölner Sammlung: Kommentar Didymos' des Blinden zu Zach 9,11 u. 16," Archiv für Papyrusforschung, 17 [1960] 60-105), who dates De Trinitate ca. A.D. 395--that is, some eight years after the Zechariah commentary. Koenen argued that the two works were not only written at different times, but also in radically different contexts (De Trinitate was written during an Origenist controversy) and for different purposes (only De Trinitate was written for publication). These factors, Koenen maintained, could easily account for any exegetical discrepencies. See the discussions of Bienert,

28/ Didymus and the Gospels

evidence originally set forth by Mingarelli. In 1963 L. Beranger showed that when the author of De Trinitate mentioned his prior work on the Holy Spirit, he did not refer to another treatise, but to his discussion earlier in the same document.[69] Furthermore, it is now generally recognized that the parallels between the De Spiritu Sancto and the De Trinitate derive from a mutual dependence on the same sources, rather than from a common author.[70] More recently W. Bienert has argued that Mingarelli overlooked one major tension between De Spiritu Sancto and De Trinitate that renders the view of mutual authorship doubtful: whereas Didymus explicitly states in De Spiritu Sancto that no pagan could understand the things of the Spirit without the witness of the Scriptures, the author of De Trinitate uses numerous pagan authors as corollary witnesses to the truth of his doctrine.[71]

It is not the purpose of this brief overview to determine whether Didymus wrote the various works sometimes attributed to him. A perusal of the Patrologies and secondary literature shows that no consensus has emerged.[72] This situation is not in the least surprising, given the uncertainty of the authorship of De Trinitate. But now the question naturally arises: which writings should be studied when analyzing Didymus's Gospel citations? Surely there is no methodologically sound alternative to using only those works that are universally

---

"Allegoria", 16-20 and Hönscheid, De Trinitate, 5-7.

[69] "Sur deux enigmes du 'De Trinitate' de Didyme l'Aveugle," RechSR 51 (1963) 255-67.

[70] Thus the use of Isa 6, John 12:40-41, and Acts 28:25-27 to establish the Deity of the Father, Son, and Holy Spirit in both works had been appealed to by L. Chavoutier ("Querelle origèniste et controverses trinitaires à propos de Tractatus contra Origenem de Visione Isaiae," VC 14 [1960] 9-14) as proof that Didymus wrote De Trinitate. But this view was discounted by M. Tetz ("Zur Theologie des Markell von Ancyra I," ZKG 75 [1964] 217-70) who showed that this concatenation of passages was first made by Marcellus of Ancyra.

[71] Bienert, "Allegoria", 19.

[72] See, for example, Altaner, Patrology, 324-25, Bienert, "Allegoria", 8-31, Quasten, Patrology, 86-92, and Young, From Nicaea to Chalcedon, 85.

assigned to Didymus and that are found in critically reliable editions. Of what value would this kind of analysis be if it were later discovered that some of the evidence did not derive from a fourth-century Alexandrian but a fifth-century Caesarean? Or how could reliable results be obtained by consulting editions which had not removed scribal corruptions of this fourth-century text? Thus, despite the natural urge to extend the data base as far as possible, the present study will not take into account the works whose authenticity has not been decided with reasonable certainty. Essentially, this leaves the critic with Contra Manichaios, De Spiritu Sancto, the catenae fragments, and the Toura commentaries. Of these, De Spiritu Sancto exists only in Latin translation, which, coupled with the complexities of Patristic evidence generally, virtually nullifies its text-critical value. The Contra Manichaios is extant only in a late sixteenth-century MS, and no critical edition exists. Furthermore, the catenae, with their incredibly complex history of transmission, are at best of secondary usefulness for textual criticism.[73] This leaves the critic with the editions of the Toura commentaries as the only reliable sources for recovering the Gospel text of Didymus.

---

[73]Even the critical edition of the Psalm catanae by Ekkehard Mühlenberg (Psalmenkommentare aus der Katenenüberlieferung, 3 vols. [Berlin: Walter de Gruyter, 1975-78]) is of little use for the present study, in view of the problems of the catenae generally: the medieval scribes normally would have used late MSS of Didymus's writings in compiling the catenae, so that even if the attribution of various comments to him are correct--of which there can be little assurance--his NT citations will have suffered during the course of transmission. As to the problems concerning the relationship of the Psalm catenae and the Toura commentary generally, see above pp. 26-27.

Chapter II

Introduction to the Text and Critical Apparatus

One methodological issue not yet considered involves the presentation of textual data once they have been collected from a Patristic source. When a Father's quotations of the Bible are frequent but sporadic, as is the case with Didymus's OT commentaries, what is the most effective way to set forth his Biblical text?

A common approach to this task involves listing all textual variants found among representative witnesses in passages quoted by a Father. The value of this system lies in its manageability: it allows the reader to see textual alignments at every point of variation while conserving space by not citing the author's text in full. Yet this advantage also proves to be the system's greatest flaw, since a listing of variants can indicate points of disagreement among witnesses but not corresponding points of agreement. This drawback can be readily illustrated. Were Didymus known to cite a verse of twenty words in which variation among representative textual witnesses occurs only in one verb tense or in the substitution of a synonym, a notation of the variant and its supporting documents would not inform a reader either of the length of Didymus's citation or of his extensive agreement with all the witnesses. As a result, still other MSS could not be compared with Didymus's text _per se_, but only with his text at one unit of variation. The situation would be even worse for the portions of text in which _no_ variation is found among the witnesses consulted. Here a reader would not know even that Didymus quotes the passage.

This inadequate manner of citing textual variation can, in cases of textual reconstruction, actually prove to be deceptive. As already observed, a reconstruction must be based on every available citation, adaptation, and allusion. Each reconstruction is more or less tentative, of course, depending on the extent and reliability of the evidence. But when variants from a reconstructed text are presented apart

Introduction to Text and Apparatus /31

from a full listing of the relevant data, a reader is misled into thinking that the Father's text is unambiguous when in fact it is not.

In view of such problems, Gordon Fee has issued an urgent plea for critics to present <u>all</u> the relevant data when setting forth the text of a church Father.[1] This kind of presentation involves listing all of a Father's Biblical citations, adaptations, and allusions, and providing a critical apparatus which shows every variant found among the representative textual witnesses. Only when such a procedure is adopted can other critics collate additional witnesses against the Father's text, evaluate the adequacy of the occasional reconstructions, and detect errors in the analysis. This, therefore, is the mode of presentation used in the following chapter. The purpose of the chapter is twofold: (1) to give in its entirety the Gospel text of Didymus as preserved in the Toura commentaries, and (2) to provide a critical apparatus of representative witnesses for every portion of this text.

The Presentation of the Text

All of Didymus's Gospel references are listed and classified with respect to their verbal correspondence to the Biblical passage. Citations, indicated by [C], consist of more or less verbally exact quotations; adaptations [Ad] comprise greater or lesser modifications of a passage, usually, but not exclusively, in view of the syntactical or material context; allusions [All] represent distant echoes of a Biblical text which nonetheless contain conceptual and verbal affinities with the passage. Normally the first hand of Didymus's Toura commentaries is cited, except in cases of editorial corrections of itacism and nonsense readings. Restored lacunae are placed in square brackets [].

As suggested earlier, the problems arising from Gospel parallels occasionally make it impossible to determine the

---

[1]"The Text of John in Origen and Cyril of Alexandria: A Contribution to Methodology in the Recovery and Analysis of Patristic Citations," <u>Bib</u> 52 (1971) 358-64.

parallels occasionally make it impossible to determine the source of Didymus's quotations and allusions. In a similar vein, Didymus not infrequently creates a complex conflation of passages in which the individual components cannot be reliably discerned. Whenever the source of a quotation or allusion cannot be ascertained with confidence, the relevant texts are listed separately in the appendix at the end of Chapter III. In rare instances a complex conflation preserves a variant which must have been derived from the MS tradition of only one of the Gospels. In such cases the reference is given both in the appendix and in the appropriate critical apparatus.

The Gospel references are given in their canonical sequence, with a critical apparatus provided immediately beneath those passages for which Didymus's text can be considered secure. Citations of a passage are listed first, followed by adaptations and allusions.

It would obviously be of little help to cite all variants from Didymus's adaptations and allusions, since these do not represent his Gospel text *per se*, but only give clues as to what that text may have looked like. Some means was needed, therefore, to indicate which of the looser references were determined valuable for establishing Didymus's textual consanguinity. The procedure that was used in making this determination is as follows. For each of Didymus's Gospel references, including even distant allusions, all the representative documents were collated against one another. Whenever genetically significant variation was found, Didymus's reference was consulted to ascertain whether it supports one of the variant readings. When it does, a critical apparatus that indicates the variants and their supporting documents is provided, just as is done for all the citations. Adaptations and allusions thus found to support one variant over another are marked with an asterisk (*). Hence [Ad]* and [All]* indicate adaptations and allusions which support a reading for some or all of the units of variation listed in the critical apparatus. Other differences between Didymus and the representative witnesses are not listed. Consequently, adaptations and allusions not marked with an asterisk have been judged to be of no help for establishing Didymus's textual alignments. In every instance this is either because no variation was found among the textual witnesses consulted, or because Didymus's reference does not provide clear evidence of his text at this point. In either case Didymus's reference is deemed of no text-critical significance.

Didymus sometimes refers to a text in a way that **seems** to support a variant of the tradition, yet the quotation departs so radically from the original wording of the text that its witness to the variant in question is vitiated. Such adaptations are not marked with an asterisk, but a critical apparatus is provided to show that the vagaries of Didymus's reference disallow his apparent attestation of the reading in question.

Occasionally Didymus cites the same passage in several slightly different forms. Rather than making a reconstruction that reproduces one of the citations verbatim, the citation taken to be as representative of Didymus's text is marked with a double asterisk ([C]**). When none of the references appears to be representative, a reconstruction of Didymus's text has been attempted. Such reconstructions are based only on the portions of text preserved in the extant references, emendations being restricted to the fairly logical reversion of syntactical adaptations--the shift of genitive absolutes back into finite clauses, the change of verb tenses, etc. As a result, the reconstructions will sometimes be incomplete, with lacunae occurring in the middle of the text. These lacunae will not be taken into account in the collations. In the layout of the text, reconstructions will be given after the list of quotations and allusions.

Didymus sometimes makes a solitary loose reference to a passage, thus disallowing a reconstruction. When such references show his support for a variant reading, but in a slightly modified form, they are marked with an asterisk, and the critical apparatus cites Didymus's support in parentheses.

The Critical Apparatus

The critical apparatus lists all variants uncovered in the collations of the representative documents. Only those variants previously adjudged to be genetically immaterial are not included: nu-movable, οὕτω/οὕτως, nonsense readings, itacism, and other minor spelling differences, including, normally, the spelling of proper names.[2] Furthermore, Didymus sometimes cites a passage which is preserved in shorter and longer forms in the tradition. When the additions or omissions occur at the end of such a passage, and Didymus seems to cite the shorter form, his witness normally cannot be used. Instead of preserving the shorter text, he may simply have quoted a portion of the passage germane to his discussion.[3] Only when it seems natural to assume that Didymus would have included the longer text had he known it can his testimony be given in support of the shorter text.

With the exception of such unusable readings, all variants are given in the apparatus in the order of their occurrence in the text. Those supported by two or more witnesses are cited first, followed by a list of all singular variants, including those singular to Didymus. Any witness which clearly supports a variant reading, but in a slightly modified form, is cited in parentheses. The abbreviation "vid" (= *videtur*) is used with MSS that are partially fragmentary at the point of variation, but that nonetheless appear to attest the reading in question. In the first unit of variation of each text, all supporting documents are cited in full. In subsequent variants, the support for one reading is normally designated by the abbreviation "rell" (= *reliqui*). The apparatus designates the witnesses which are lacunose for each passage with the abbreviation "Lac." Witnesses partially

---

[2] One notable exception, occasioned by textual alignments which suggest a genetic significance, is the spelling of βεεζεβούλ in Matt 12:24 and Luke 11:15.

[3] See B. M. Metzger's trenchant criticisms of Boismard's proposed reconstruction of the text of John. "Patristic Evidence and the Textual Criticism of the New Testament," NTS 18 (1971-72) 387-95.

lacunose are placed in parentheses.

For each unit of variation, Didymus's reading is given first. Occasionally Didymus's witness will be split--i.e. he sometimes supports one variant, sometimes another. When, as a consequence, his text cannot be determined with certainty, his support is listed for both variant readings and is tabulated as agreeing with each set of witnesses against the other.

The Old Latin evidence is always difficult to interpret. In some kinds of variation, such as the presence or absence of the article, its testimony is mute. In others, such as word order, its testimony may be helpful, but is often ambiguous. In still other instances, such as the inclusion or exclusion of words or phrases, its testimony is unequivocal. Only when the Old Latin support of a variant is judged to be relatively certain will it be included in the critical apparatus. When the textual tradition splits three or more ways the Old Latin is sometimes found to support either of two variants, but not a third (as when two of the variants differ only in the presence or absence of the article). In such cases the Old Latin MSS are cited in parentheses for each of the two possible variants against the third.

The following witnesses were chosen as representative of the major text-types in each of the Gospels.[4] Commonly accepted designations for these groupings (Early Alexandrian, etc.) will be used here as a matter of convenience. As can be seen, in addition to the representative MSS, the texts of UBS[3] and TR are also cited.

---

[4] See the discussion in Metzger, <u>The Text of the New Testament: Its Transmission, Corruption, and Restoration</u>, 2nd ed. (New York: Oxford Press, 1968) 36-66, 213-18.

Matthew
    Early Alexandrian: UBS^3 ℵ B
    Late Alexandrian: C L 33 892 1241
    Western: D a b e k
    Caesarean: Θ fam 1 fam 13
    Byzantine: TR A E W Δ Π Ω

Mark
    Early Alexandrian: UBS^3 ℵ B
    Late Alexandrian: C L Δ Ψ 33 579 892 1241
    Western: D W (1:1-5:30) a b e k
    Caesarean: Θ fam 1 fam 13
    Byzantine: TR A E Π Ω

Luke
    Early Alexandrian: UBS^3 P^{75} ℵ B
    Late Alexandrian: C L W (1:1-8:12) Ψ 33 579 892 1241
    Western: D a b e
    Caesarean: Θ fam 1 fam 13
    Byzantine: TR A W (8:13-24:53) Δ Π Ω

John
    Early Alexandrian: UBS^3 P^{66} P^{75} ℵ (8:39-21:25) B
    Late Alexandrian: C L W Ψ 33 579 892 1241
    Western: ℵ (1:1-8:38) D a b e
    Caesarean: Θ fam 1 fam 13
    Byzantine: TR A Δ Π Ω

Abbreviations

[Ad]   Adaptation

[Ad]* Adaptation that supports variation given in the critical apparatus

[All] Allusion

[All]* Allusion that supports variation given in the critical apparatus

[C]   Citation

[C]** Citation taken to be representative of Didymus's text (and used as a base for collation)

[ ]   Lacuna in the MS

Lac.   Lacunose Witness

( )   Witness supports the reading, but in a slightly modified form; or, a partially lacunose witness

vid.   *videtur*. Witness appears to support the reading

rell. *reliqui*. All other witnesses support the reading

TR   Textus Receptus

UBS^3 United Bible Societies' Greek New Testament, 3rd edition

Chapter III

Text and Apparatus

Matt. 1:1

βιβλ[ος γε]νεσεως Ιησου Χριστου (GenT 145:19) [C]

βιβλος γενεσεως [Ιησο]υ Χριστου υιου Δαυιδ υιου Αβρααμ
(ZeT 103:25) [C]
───────────────────
βιβλος γενεσεως Ιησου Χριστου TR UBS³ ℵ B E L W (Δ) Π Ω
fam 1. 13 33 892 1241 a] liber generalis (=βιβλος κοινος?)
k

Lac.: A C D Θ b e

Matt. 1:6

Δαυιδ δε εγεννησεν τον Σολομων (Ecc1T 5:8-9) [C]
───────────────────
δε UBS³ ℵ B fam 1. 13 k] δε ο βασιλευς TR C E L W Δ
Π Ω 33 892 1241 a^{vid}

Lac.: A D Θ (a) b e

Matt. 1:16

Ιακωβ δε εγεννησεν [τον Ιωσ]ηφ τον ανδρα Μαριας, εξ ης
εγεννηθη ο Χριστος (PsT 153:5-6) [C]
───────────────────
τον ανδρα Μαριας εξ ης εγεννηθη TR UBS³ ℵ B C E L W
(Δ) Π Ω fam 1 33 892 1241] ω μνητευθεισα παρθενος
Μαριαμ εγεννησεν θ fam 13 a (b) (k)

τον$^{(2)}$ rell] omit Δ

ο Χριστος] ο λεγομενος Χριστος fam 1; Ιησους Χριστος k;
Ιησους ο λεγομενος χριστος rell

Lac.: A D e

Matt. 1:17

απο μεν του Αβρααμ εως του Δαυιδ τω οντι γενεαι δεκατεσσαρες
εισιν (PsT 304:4) [Ad]
───────────────────
μεν του Αβρααμ εως του] Αβρααμ εως TR UBS³ ℵ B C E L
W Δ Θ Π Ω fam 1. 13 33 892 1241

τω οντι] omit rell

38

Matt. 1:17 (cont.)

εισιν b] omit rell

Lac.: A D e

Matt. 1:21

οτι αυτος σωσε[ι] τον λαον απο των αμαρτιων αυτου
(ZeT. 219:25) [Ad]

Matt. 1:21-23

δια τουτο ετεκεν η Μαρια, οπως πληρωθη ιδου [εν γ]αστρι
εξει (EcclT 218:12-13) [All]

Matt. 1:23

ινα κ[λη]θη ονομα αυτω μεθ' ημων ο θεος. τουτο γαρ
αποσημαινει μ[εθ]ερμηνευομενον το Εμμανουηλ (ZeT
102:13-14) [All]
τις γαρ ουτω σωζων και σωτηρ του κοσμου η ο μεθ' ημων
θεος Εμμανουηλ (ZeT 219:18-19) [All]

Matt. 2:1-2

αινιττεται η κλησις των απο ανατολης μαγων ελθοντων απο
ανατολων επι τα Ιεροσολυμα προσκυνησαι τω τεχθεντι
εκει βασιλει, ποδηγουμενοι υπο αστερος φανεντος
αυτοις (ZeT 202:4-7) [All]

Matt. 2:11

δηλουν ον προσηνεγκαν οι μαγοι τω εκ της Μαριας τεχθεντι
παιδιω μετα χρυσου και σμυρνης λιβανον (ZeT 267:18)
[All]

Matt. 3:12

ου το πτυον εν [τη χει]ρι αυτ[ο]υ και διακ[α]θαριει τ[ην
αλ]ωνα αυτου και συναξει τον [σιτον] εις αποθηκην, το
δε αχυρον κ[α]τακαυσει πυρι ασβεστω (JobT 157:2-6) [C]

40/ Didymus and the Gospels

Matt. 3:12 (cont.)

σιτον E L fam 13 892 a b] σιτον αυτου TR UBS³ ℵ B C
W Δ Π Ω fam 1 33 1241

αποθηκην rell] αποθηκην αυτου B E L W 892 b

τον rell] τον μεν fam 13

Lac.: A D θ e k

Matt. 4:1-2

εν τω ερημω εστη αντικειμενος εκ δεξιων νηστευοντι
τεσσερακοντα ημερας και νυκτας ισας (ZeT 44:22)
[All]

Matt. 4:4

ου...επ' αρτω μονω ζησεται ανθρωπος, αλλ' επι π[αντι]
ρηματι εκπορευομενω δια στοματος θεου (GenT 71:16-18)
[C]

ανθρωπος TR E Π Ω fam 13 1241] ο ανρθωπος UBS³ ℵ B C
D L W Δ θ fam 1. 33 892

επι rell] εν C D fam 13

εκπορευομενω δια στοματος rell] omit D a b

αλλ'...θεου rell] omit in toto k

Lac.: A e

Matt. 4:9

ταυτα παντα δωσω σοι...εαν πεσων προσκυνησης μοι (ZeT
45:2) [C]

παντα δωσω σοι] σοι παντα δωσω UBS³ ℵ B C W fam 1
33; παντα σοι δωσω rell

Lac.: A e

Text and Apparatus /41

Matt. 4:19

δευτε...οπισω μου, [και ποιησω υμας α]λεεις ανθρωπων
(Ecc1T 286:20-21)   [C]

δευτε οπισω μου, και ποιησω υμας αλεεις ανθρωπων
(GenT 61:15-16)   [C]

υμας TR UBS³ א B C E L W Δ Π Ω fam 1.13 892 1241]
υμας γενεσθαι D 33 a b k

Lac.: A θ e

Matt. 5:3

ο γαρ πτωχος τω πνευματι εχει την βασιλειαν του θεου
(JobT 5:24)   [Ad]*

μη γαρ ο πτωχος τω πνευματι ουκ εχει τας αλλας αρετας
(PsT 186:25)   [All]*

μακαριοι ο[ι πτ]ωχ[οι τω πν]ευματι (PsT 202:24) [C]

τω πνευματι TR UBS³ א B C E W Δ Π Ω fam 1.13 33 892
1241] πνευματι D

Lac.: A L θ e

Matt. 5:4

μακαριοι...οι πενθουντες ν[υν], οτι αυτοι παρακληθησονται
(Ecc1T 198:6)   [C]

νυν 33 892] omit TR UBS³ א B C D E W Δ θ Π Ω fam 1.13
1241 a b k

Lac.: A L e

Matt. 5:5

μακαριοι...οι πραεις, οτι αυτοι κληρονομησουσι την γην
(GenT 104:20-21)   [C]

μακαριοι οι πραεις οτι αυτοι κληρονομησουσι την γην
(GenT 218:10-11)   [C]

μακαριοι οι πραει[ς οτι] αυτοι κλ[η]ρονομησουσι την γην
(JobT 70:32-71:1)   [C]

42/ Didymus and the Gospels

Matt. 5:5 (cont.)

    την TR UBS³ ℵ B C D E W Δ Θ Π Ω fam 1.13 33 892]
          omit 1241

    Lac.: A L e

Matt. 5:6

μακαριοι οι πεινωντες και διψωντες την δικαιοσυνην, οτι
αυτοι χορτασθησονται (PsT 50:16-17) [C]

    Text: TR UBS³ ℵ B C D E W Δ Θ Π Ω fam 1.13 33 892 1241
          a b k

    Lac.: A L e

Matt. 5:7

μακαριοι οι ελεημονες οτι αυτοι ελεηθη[σονται] (PsT 179:22)
[C]

    Text: TR UBS³ ℵ B C D E W Δ Θ Π Ω fam 1.13 33 892 1241
          (a) (b) (k)

    Lac.: A L e

Matt. 5:8

ως προς το καθαρα καρδια τον θεον [ο]ραν ματαια εισιν
(EcclT 11:5) [All]

...καθαραν εχει καρδιαν, ουτω και αυτον τον θεον οραν
δυναται (PsT 83:17-18) [All]

...η καθαρα καρδια ητις και τον θεον βλεπει (PsT 84:25)
[All]

...καθαρου ο εχων ορα θεον (PsT 93:2) [All]

μακ[αρ]ιοι οι καθαροι τη καρδια (EcclT 44:18) [C]

μακαριοι οι καθαροι τη κα[ρδ]ια οτι αυτοι τον θεον οψονται
(GenT 248:18) [C]

μακαριοι οι καθαροι τ[η] καρδια (JobT 213:12) [C]

μακαριοι οι καθαροι τη καρδια (PsT 53:19) [C]

μακαριοι...οι καθαροι τη καρδια οτι αυτοι τον θεον οψονται
(PsT 209:20) [C]

Matt. 5:8 (cont.)

μακαριοι...οι καθαροι τη καρδια, οτι αυτοι τον θεον οψονται
(PsT 240:16) [C]

μακαριοι οι καθαροι τη καρδια, οτι αυτοι τον θεον οψονται
(ZeT 192:12) [C]

θεον TR UBS³ ℵ B C D E W Δ Θ Π Ω fam 1.13 33 892
1241 a b] Dominum (=κυριον) k

Lac.: A L e

Matt. 5:9

λεγει προς ετεροις τους ειρηνοποιους μακαριους ειναι
οτι υιοι θεου εισιν (PsT 227:18) [All]*

μακαριοι οι ειρηνοποιοι, οτι υιοι θεου κληθησονται
(JobT 306:33-34) [C]

οτι ℵ C D fam 13 a b] οτι αυτοι TR UBS³ B E W Δ Θ Π Ω
fam 1 33 892 1241 k

Lac.: A L e

Matt. 5:11-12

χαιρετε και αγαλλιατε οταν ονειδιζωσιν υμας (PsT 277:22-23)
[Ad]

οτε ουν οι αποστολοι χαιρουσιν και αγαλλιωνται ονειδιζομενοι
υπερ Χριστου (PsT 318:10) [All]

Matt. 5:13

υμεις εστε το αλας της γης (EcclT 305:12-13) [C]

αλας TR UBS³ B C E Δ Θ Π Ω fam 1.13 33 892 1241]
αλα   ℵ D W

Lac.: A L e

Matt. 5:14

υμεις εστε το φως του κοσμου (GenT 38:22) [C]

υμεις εστε το φως του κοσμ[ου] (PsT 193:6) [C]

44/ Didymus and the Gospels

Matt. 5:14 (cont.)

υμεις εστε το φως του κοσμου   (ZeT 305:17) [C]

υμεις εστε [το] φως το[υ κ]οσμου (ZeT 376:1) [C]

    Text: TR UBS³ ℵ B C D E W(Δ)ΘΠΩ fam 1. 13 33 892 1241
    a b k

    Lac.: A L e

Matt. 5:16

...την σωτηρα...ου λαμπει τα εργα εμπροσθεν των ανθρωπων
οια φως (PsT 24:1-3) [All]*

θελει το φως αυτου λαμπειν ε[μ]προσθεν των ανθρωπων ιν'
ιδοντες εκεινοι δοξασωσιν τον θεον (PsT 189:28-29) [All]

λαμψατω...το φως υμων ενπροσθεν των ανθρωπων, οπως ιδωσιν
υμων τα καλα εργα και δοξασωσιν τον πατερα τον εν τοις
ουρανοις (PsT 231:24-25) [C]

    εργα TR UBS³ ℵ D E L W Δ Θ Π Ω fam 1. 13 33 892 1241
    a b k] omit B

    πατερα] πατερα υμων rell

    Lac.: A C e

Matt. 5:17

ο εληλυθως Σωτηρ πληρωσαι τον νομον και τους προφητας
(ZeT 40:11) [All]

ο εληλυθως πηληρωσαι τον νομον και τους προφητας
(ZeT 372:19) [All]

Matt. 5:19

ος αν ποιηση και διδαξη τους ανθρωπους ουτος μεγας
κληθησεται εν τη βασιλεια των ουρανων (ZeT 183:26) [Ad]*

    ουτος TR UBS³ B E L Δ Θ Π Ω fam 1. 13 33 892 1241] sic
    (= ουτως) a (k); sic hic (= ουτως ουτος) b

    ος αν...των ουρανων] omit in toto ℵ D W

    Lac.: A C e

Matt. 5:20

εαν μη περισσευει υμων η δικαιοσυνη πλεον τ[ων] γραμματεων
και φαρισσαιων   (EcclT 43:6-7)   [C]

εαν μη περισσευση υμων η δικαιοσυνη πλεον των γραμματεων
και φαρισσαιω[ν]   (PsT 287:9)   [C]**

υμων η δικαιοσυνη   UBS³ ℵ B E L W Δ Θ Π Ω fam 13 892
1241] η δικαιοσυνη υμων   TR fam 1 33 a b (k)

πλε(ι)ον   rell]   πληωνα   L

εαν μη...φαρισσαιων   rell]   omit in toto   D

Lac.: A C e

Matt. 5:25

ισθι ευνοων τω αντιδικω σου εως οτου ει μετ' αυτου εν τη
οδω   (PsT 212:20)   [C]

μετ' αυτου εν τη οδω   UBS³ ℵ B D L W fam 1. 13 33 892
a b] εν τη οδω μετ' αυτου   TR E Δ Θ Π Ω 1241 k

οτου   rell]   ου   fam 13 1241;   του   L

σου]   σου ταχυ   rell

εως   rell]   omit   D

Lac.: A C e

Matt. 5:28

ειδεν τις γυναικα προς επιθυμιαν   (PsT 263:10)   [All]

Matt. 5:34

ο ετοιμας ων προς το δεξασθαι τους του θεου νομους ουκ
ομνυει ολως   (PsT 69:5)   [All]

εγω δε λεγω υμιν μη ομοσαι ολως   (ZeT 185:27)   [C]

Text: TR UBS³ ℵ B D E (L) W Δ Θ Π Ω fam 1. 13 33 892
1241 a b k

Lac.: A C e

46/ Didymus and the Gospels

Matt. 5:41

εαν τις σε ενγαρευσει μιλ[ιον] εν, υπαγε μετ' αυτ[ου δυο]
(EcclT 123:26)   [C]

εαν (א Δ 33 892)] omit TR UBS³ B D E L W θ Π Ω fam 1.13
1241 a b k

σε rell] omit L Δ

τις] οστις rell

ενγαρευσει (or αγγ-, or -ση) rell] αγγαρευει D

Lac.: A C e

Matt. 5:42

τον θελοντα απο σου δανισασθαι μη αποστραφης   (JobT 139:2-3)
[C]

τον θελοντα TR UBS³ א B E L W Δ θ Π Ω fam 1.13 33 892
1241] τω θελοντι D, (volenti) a b, (ab eo qui
voluerit) k

απο σου rell] omit D (k)

Lac.: A C e

Matt. 5:45

ανατελλει γαρ τον ηλιον ωσπερ επι αγαθο[υ]ς   (PsT 177:20)
[Ad]*

ανατελλων ου μονον επι αγαθους τον ηλιον αλλα και επι
πονηρους (PsT 290:21-22) [All]*

τον ανατελλοντα τον ηλιον επι αγαθους [και πονηρου]ς και
βρεχοντα επι δικαιους και αδικους   (ZeT 246:11-12) [Ad]*

Reconstruction: ανατελλει τον ηλιον επι αγαθους και πονηρους
και βρεχει επι δικαιους και αδικους

αγαθους και πονηρους a] πονηρους και αγαθους   TR UBS³ א
B D E L W Δ θ Π Ω fam 1.13 33 892 1241 b k

ανατελλει τον ηλιον] τον ηλιον ανατελλει rell

ηλιον] ηλιον αυτου rell

και βρεχει...αδικους rell] omit א

Lac.: A C e

Text and Apparatus /47

Matt. 5:48

οταν τις γενηται τελειος ως ο πατηρ ο ουρανιος   (PsT 68:19)
   [Ad]*

κατα το δεκτικον του γενεσθαι τελειος ως ο πατηρ ο εν
   τοις ουρανοις τελειος εστιν   (PsT 130:29-30)   [Ad]*

γινεσθε...τ[ελειοι ως] ο πατηρ υμων ο ουρανιος τελειος
   εστιν   (GenT 180:4-5)   [C]
   ─────────────

   ως   UBS³ ℵ B E L fam 1. 13 33]   ωσπερ   TR D W Δ Θ Π Ω
      892;   ως και   1241

   ουρανιος   UBS³ ℵ B E L W fam 1. 13 33 892 1241 a]
      εν τοις ουρανοις   b k rell

   Γινεσθε] εσεσθε ουν υμεις   rell

   Lac.:   A C e

Matt. 6:1

ουτω και οι ελεημοσυνην παρεχοντες προς το θεαθηναι τοις
   ανθρωποις απεχουσιν εαυτων τον μισθον, ουδεν απο θεου
   εχοντες   (GenT 125:4-6)   [All]*

ουχ ουτως οι ελεημοσυνην ποιουντες προς το θεαθηναι υπ'
   ανθρωπων ενεργουσιν   (GenT 212:16-17)   [All]*
   ─────────────

   ελεημοσυνη   TR E L₂ W Δ Θ Π Ω fam 13 33 892 1241 k]
      δικαιοσυνη   UBS³ ℵ B D fam 1 a b

   θεαθηναι   rell] μη θεαθηναι   Δ

   Lac.:   A C e

Matt. 6:2

βουλεται δε τον ελεον μη μετα σ[αλ]πιγω[ν γινεσθ]αι
   (GenT 180:2-3)   [All]

συ δε [οταν] ποιης ελεημοσυνην, μη σ[αλπι]σης ωσπερ οι
   υποκριται π[οιο]υσιν   (JobT 37:18-20)   [Ad]

συ...ποιων ελεημοσυνην, μη σαλπισης εμπροσθεν σου
   (ZeT 238:8-9)   [Ad]

48/ Didymus and the Gospels

Matt. 6:5

αλλως δε περι [των γ]ωνιων εστι φαναι ως εφευσμενων,
εν αις οι υποκριται ε[στη]κοτες προσευχονται
(ZeT 386:17)   [All]

Matt. 6:14

εαν αφητε τοις ανθρωποις τα παραπτωματα αυτων, αφησει
και υμιν ο πατηρ ο ουρανιος τα παραπτωματα υμων (ZeT 126:14) [C

και υμιν   TR UBS³ ℵ B E L W Δ Θ Π Ω fam 1.13 33
892 1241] υμιν και   D b k; υμιν   a

ουρανιος   rell] εν τοις ουρανοις   Θ a b k

τα παραπτωματα υμων   L fam 13] omit   rell

εαν   D L] εαν γαρ   rell

πατηρ] πατηρ ημων   E; πατηρ υμων   rell

Lac.: A C e

Matt. 6:19

μη θησαυριζετε υμιν θησαυρου[ς επι τη]ς γης   (PsT 276:25-26)
[C]

θησαυριζετε   TR UBS³ ℵ B E L W Δ Θ Π Ω fam 1.13 33
892 1241 a b k] θησαυρισετε   D

υμιν   rell] εν υμιν   Δ

Lac.: A C e

Matt. 6:20-21

α δει σκοπειν τους τα ανω βλεποντας τους θησαυριζοντας
εν ουρανοις   (EcclT 6:23)   [All]

Matt. 6:20-21 (cont.)

θησαυρισαντες εν ουρανοις εκει την καρδιαν εχουσιν
(EcclT 35:18-19) [All]

οπου ο θησαυρος, εκει και η καρδια σου εσται
(PsT 53:18-19) [Ad]*

θησαυριζετε θησαυρους εν ουρανω. επει γαρ οπου ο
θησαυρος εκει και ο νους εστιν καρδια ονο[μα]ζομενος...
(PsT 276:25-26) [Ad]*

πως γαρ...εν ουρανω σκοιη την καρδιαν, μη θησαυρισας εν
ουρανω   (ZeT 22:1-2)   [All]

εν ουρανω θησα[υ]ρισαντες εκει [την] καρδιαν σχωμεν
(ZeT 407:10)   [All]

καρδια σου UBS³ ℵ B a b k] καρδια υμων   TR E L W Δ
Θ Π Ω fam 1. 13 33 892 1241

και   rell] omit   B

Lac.: A C D e

Matt. 6:24

ουδεις [δυν]αται δ[υσι κυριοι]ς δουλευειν· η γαρ τον ενα
μισησει και τ[ον ετερ]ον αγ[απησει] η ενος ανθεξεται
και του ετερου κατα[φρονησει]. ου δ[υνασθ]ε θεω
δουλευειν και μαμωνα   (GenT 175: 14-17)   [C]

ουδεις δυναται δυσιν δυριοις δουλευειν (PsT 84:4) [C]

ουδεις   TR UBS³ ℵ B E W Θ Π Ω fam 1. 13 33 892 a b k]
ουδεις οικετης   L Δ 1241

γαρ   rell] omit   b

θεω   rell] Domino (= κυριω)   k

Lac.: A C D e

Matt. 6:33

ζητειτε πρωτον την βασιλεια[ν] και την δικαιοσυνην, και
ταυτα παντα προστεθησεται υμιν   (EcclT 84:16-17)   [Ad]

50/ Didymus and the Gospels

Matt. 6:33 (cont.)

ζ[η]τειτε...πρωτον την δικαιοσυνη [και τ]ην βασιλειαν του
θεου, και παντ[α τ]αυτα προστεθησεται υμιν (EcclT 193:
22-24) [Ad]

Matt. 6:34

μη με[ριμ]ν[η]σητε [π]ερι της αυριον (JobT 395:14-15)
[Ad]

μη a b] μη ουν TR UBS³ ℵ B E L W Δ Θ Π Ω fam 1.13
33 892 1241 k

περι της] εις την rell

Lac.: A C D e

Matt. 7:6

ου βαλλω[ν τα αγι]α τοις κυσιν ουδε τους μαργαριτας
εμπροσθεν των χ[οιρων] (GenT 72:13-14) [Ad]*

το αγιον κυσιν μη διδοναι μηδε τας μαργαριτας χοιροις
παραβαλλειν (ZeT 276:27) [Ad]*

ουτως ουδε χοιροις παραβαλλειν προσηκει τους θειους
μαργαριτας (ZeT 277:19) [All]

μη δωτε το αγιον τοις κυσιν, μηδε βαλητε τους μαργαριτας
ενπροσθεν των χοιρων, μηποτε στραφεντες ρηξωσιν υμα[ς]
και καταπατησωσιν (EcclT 352:4-5) [C]

μη βαλητε τα αγια τοις κυσιν μηδε τους μαργαριτας υμων
εμπροσθεν των χοιρων...μηποτε καταπατησουσιν αυτους
και στραφεντες ρηξωσιν υμας (GenT 111:2-4) [C]

μη βαλητε τα αγια τοις κυσιν (GenT 196:7-8) [C]

Reconstruction: μη δωτε το αγιον τοις κυσιν μηδε βαλητε
τους μαργαριτας υμων εμπροσθεν των χοιρων, μηποτε
[καταπατησωσιν/καταπατησουσιν] αυτους και στραφεντες
ρηξωσιν υμας

καταπατησωσιν Did^pt TR ℵ E Δ Π Ω fam 1 892 1241 a b k]
καταπατησουσιν Did^pt UBS³ B C L W Θ fam 13 33

ρηξωσιν rell] ρηξουσιν 33 1241

βαλητε rell] βαλλετε L

Text and Apparatus /51

Matt. 7:6 (cont.)

αυτους rell] αυτοις Δ

αυτους] αυτους εν τοις ποσιν αυτων rell

Lac.: A D e

Matt. 7:9-10

τις...εξ υμων, ον αιτηση ο υιος αυτου αρτον, μη λιθον
επιδωσει αυτω; η ιχθυν [αιτη]ση, μη οφιν επιδωσει
[αυτ]ω; (EcclT 314:4-5) [C]

τις B L 1241 b] τις εστιν TR UBS³ ℵ C E W Δ Θ Π Ω
     fam 1.13 (33) 892 (a) k

αιτηση (or -σει)⁽¹⁾ UBS³ ℵ B (C) Θ a b] (ε)αν
αιτηση (or -σει) rell

η 892 a b k] και TR E L W Δ Θ; η και rell

αιτηση (or -σει)⁽²⁾ UBS³ ℵ B C Δ fam 1 33 892 1241]
(ε)αν αιτηση (or -σει) rell

υμων] υμων ανθρωπος rell

ον rell] ο fam 13

αιτηση (or -σει)⁽¹⁾ rell] αιτησεις C

μη rell] omit k

Lac.: A D e

Matt. 7:11

...κ[αι αγ]αθα, α διδωσιν ο πατηρ τοις αιτουσιν αυτον
(EcclT 78:15) [All]

ει διδοται παρα θεου αυτω αγαθα, διδωσιν δε αγαθ[α] το[ι]ς
αιτουσιν αυτον (EcclT 293:14-15) [Ad]

κυριος αγαθα δωσει τοις αιτουσιν αυτον (PsT 61:1) [Ad]

...τα αγαθα εκεινα, α διδωσιν ο θεος τοις αιτουσιν αυτον...
(PsT 245:6) [All]

δωσει...αγαθα τοις αιτουσιν αυτον (PsT 101:9) [C]

δωσει αγαθα τοις αιτουσιν αυτον (PsT 109:15) [C]

52/ Didymus and the Gospels

Matt. 7:11 (cont.)

Text: TR UBS³ א B C E (L) (W) Δ (Θ) Π Ω fam 1. 13 33
892 1241 a b k

Lac.: A D e

Matt. 7:13

...ποιει της πλατειας οδου, ητις επι την απωλειαν αγει
(GenT 166:2) [All]*

η αγωγη η κατα τον περιγειον τοπον και η κατα κακιαν
λεγεται πλατεια ειναι και ευρυχωρος (PsT 141:27-28)
[All]*

καθως εν τω ευαγγελιω πολλοι ειναι λεγονται οι την
ευρυχωρον οδον οδευοντες, τελος εχουσαν απωλειαν
(ZeT 211:13-15) [All]

πλατεια [π]υλη και ευ[ρυ]χωρος οδος υπαρχουσα τοις φαυλοις
και [φιλη]δονοις, ως πολλους περιπιπτειν τη α[πω]λεια
(ZeT 271:12-14) [All]*

...της πλατειας και ευρυχωρου απαγουση[ς] ει[ς] τ[ην
α]πωλειαν (ZeT 387:23) [All]*

πλατεια...και ευρυχωρος η οδος η απαγουσα εις την απωλειαν,
και πολλοι εισιν οι εισερχομενοι εις αυτην (GenT 102:
20-21) [C]

πλατεια Did^pt א a b k] πλατεια η πυλη Did^pt TR UBS³
B C E L W Δ Θ Π Ω fam 1.13 33 892 1241

εισερχομενοι rell] εισπορευομενοι fam 1 1241;
ερχομενοι L fam 13

εισιν rell] omit א

εις αυτην] δι' αυτης rell

Lac.: A D e

Matt. 7:14

και η οδος, εν η τυγχανομεν, στενη εστιν (PsT 142:2) [All]

ονπερ γαρ τροπον τοις δικαιοις στενη εσ[τι]ν η πυλη και
τεθλιμμενη η οδος τοις εν τω ορθως πο[λι]τευεσθαι
ζητουσιν την ζωην αιωνιον (ZeT 271:10-12) [All]*

Text and Apparatus /53

Matt. 7:14 (cont.)

τι στενη η πυλη και τεθλιμμενη η οδος η απαγουσα εις την
ζωην   (GenT 102:18-19)   [C]

τι   UBS³ C E L W Δ (θ) Π Ω fam 1.13 33 892 1241 a b k]
οτι   TR ℵ B

η πυλη   rell] πυλη   L θ 1241; omit   a k

Lac.: A D e

Matt. 7:15

εξωθεν μεν προ[βα]του δορα[ν] περιβαλλομενοι, εσωθεν δε
οντες λυκοι αρπαγες (GenT 125:19-21)   [All]

απο της [αυ]τ[ης] κακιας και υποκριται συνισ[τ]ανται
εσωθεν οντες λυκοι αρπαγες, εξωθεν δε προβατα φαινομενοι
(JobT 254:2-5)   [All]

ουτω και οι ψευδοπροφηται δοραν προβατου περιβεβλημε[ν]οι
εσωθεν ησαν λυκοι αρπαγες (JobT 401:19-22)   [All]

οιον οι ψευδοπροφηται λυκοι αρπαγες κατα την γνωμην οντες
επιφερονται δοραν προβατου, ινα προβατα νομισθωσιν
(PsT 232:1-2)   [All]

ο λυκος οτε δοραν περικειμενος προβατου προσεισιν τη
Χριστου ποιμνη   (PsT 274:20)   [All]

Matt. 7:21

δουλος δε εστιν ο δουλευων θεω, ο και διαθεσει και εργω
ομολογων την δεσποτειαν, ο ποιων το θελημα του εν τοις
ουρανοις πατρος   (PsT 85:15)   [All]*

ο τοινυν ουτω κυριον Ιησουν καλων τω το θελημα του πατρος
αυτου ποιειν του ουρανιου   (PsT 281:31)   [All]*

ου π[ας] ο λεγων με κυριε, κυριε εισελευσεται εις την
βασιλειαν των ουρανων, αλλ' ο π[ο]ιων το θελημα του
πατρος μου του εν τοις ουρανοις   (EcclT 208:7-8)   [C]

ου πας...ο λεγων με κυριε, κυριε, εισελευσεται εις την
βασιλειαν των ουρανον, αλλ' ο ποιων το θελη[μα τ]ου
πατρος μου του εν τοις ουρανοις   (PsT 229:6)   [C]

ου πας ο λεγων με κυριε κυριε, εισελευσεται, αλλ' ο ποιων
το θελημα του πατρος μου   (PsT 231:3)   [C]

Matt. 7:21 (cont.)

    τοις UBS³ ℵ B C Θ Ω fam 1 33 892] omit TR E L W Δ Π fam 13 1241

    με] μοι a b k rell

    το θελημα rell] τα θεληματα ℵ

    Lac.: A D e

Matt. 7:22

    πολλοι ερουσιν μοι εν εκεινη τη ημερα· Κυριε, Κυριε (PsT 281:29) [C]

    τη TR UBS³ ℵ B C E L W Θ Π Ω fam 1. 13 33 892 1241] omit Δ

    Lac.: A D e

Matt. 7:23

    αποχωρειτε εργαται ανομιας· ουδεποτε υμας εγνων (GenT 194:17-18) [Ad]*

    αποχωρειτε απ' εμου, εργαται ανομ[ια]ς· ουδεποτε υμας εγνων (JobT 383:6-8) [Ad]*

    ουδεποτε υμας εγνων (PsT 281:29-30) [Ad]*

    αποχωρειτε απ' εμου, εργαται ανομιας· ουδεποτε υμας εγνων (ZeT 177:19) [Ad]*

    αποχωρειτε TR UBS³ ℵ B C E (L) W Δ Π Ω fam 1 33 892 1241] αναχωρειτε Θ fam 13

    εμου a k rell] εμου παντες L Θ fam 13 b

    εργαται ανομιας a] οι εργαζομενοι την ανομιαν rell

    υμας εγνων k] εγνων υμας rell

    ουδεποτε rell] non (= ου) a b

    υμας rell] αυτους E

    Lac.: A D e

Matt. 7:24

ο τους Ιησου λογους ακουων και ποιων αυτους οικιαν
οικοδομει επι την πετραν   (EcclT 310:23-24)   [All]

ο οικοδομων την εαυτου οικιαν επι την πετραν
(EcclT 311:3-4)   [All]

οταν γαρ λεγη τον τους Ιησου λογους ακηκοοτα και μεταβαλοντα
εις εργα οικοδομειν την εαυτου οικιαν επι την πετραν
(EcclT 342:5-6)   [All]

ος αν ακουση το[υς λο]γους μου και ποιηση, ομοιο[ς ε]στιν
ανδρι φρονιμω, οστις ω[κοδ]ομησεν την οικιαν αυτου επι
την πετραν   (JobT 147:15-19)   [Ad]*

οικοδομησα[ς βεβ]αιον ο φρονιμος επι την [πετρα]ν
εθεμελιωσεν   (JobT 148:24-26)   [All]

κατα τον ακουοντα τους λογους Ιησου και οικοδομουντα την
εαυτου οικι[α]ν ο εστιν του βιου ουκ επι πετραν
αισθητην, αλλ' επι τον Χριστον   (JobT 312:18-22)   [All]

ο γαρ τους Ιησου ακουσας και εις εργα μεταβαλων αυτους
οικοδομει οικιαν επι την πετραν   (PsT 145:1-146:1)   [All]

οι...εις πραξεις μεταβαλ[ο]ντες τας εντολας του
κρατουντος αυτων και παιδευσαν[το]ς ωκοδομησαν
τον βιον αυτων οια οικον επι την πετραν τον Χριστον
(ZeT 107:9)   [All]

...ομοιωθησεται ανδρι φρονιμω   (ZeT 183:22)   [C]

    ομοιωθησεται   UBS³ ℵ B θ fam 13 33 892 1241 a b]
    ομοιωσω αυτον   TR C E L W Δ Π Ω k; ομοιωθησεται αυτον
    fam 1

    την οικιαν αυτου   TR E L Δ Π Ω fam 13 a b k] αυτου την
    οικιαν   rell

    Lac.:   A D e

Matt. 7:25

οι ανεμοι μετα βροχης και ραγδαιων ποταμων μνημονευονται
επερχομενοι επι τω προσκρουσαι και σφοδρως πνευσαι τας
οικιας των ακουσαντων τους Ιησου λογους   (ZeT 31:7-9)
[All]

και κατεβη η βροχη, επνευσαν οι ανεμοι, ηλθον οι ποταμοι,
και ουκ εσεισθη η οικι[α]   (JobT 147:19-22)   [Ad]

56/ Didymus and the Gospels

Matt. 7:26

ο Ιησου τους λογους ακουων και μη ποιων παραβαλλεται ανδρι μω[ρω] (EcclT 290:9) [Ad]*

ανδρι μωρω ομοιουμ[ε]νου, ος ωκοδομησεν την οικ[ιαν] αυτου επι την αμμον (JobT 148:5-8) [Ad]*

του φαυλου επι την αμμον οικοδομουντος (PsT 146:1-2) [All]

κατασπωντες την οικοδομην του ακουσαντες τους θειους λογους και μη ποιησαντς επειπερ επι την αμμον την κρηπιδα αυτης κατεβαλετο (ZeT 31:12-14) [All]

ο ακουων...μη ποιων TR UBS³ ℵ B C E L W Δ Π Ω fam 1 33 892 1241 a b k] οστις ακουει...μη ποιει θ fam 13

την οικιαν αυτου TR C E L Δ Π Ω fam 13 33 a b k] αυτου την οικιαν rell

Lac.: A D e

Matt. 8:11

πολλοι απο ανατολων και δυσμων ηλιου ηξουσιν και ανακλιθησοντα[ι] εν τη βασιλεια των ουρανων μετα Αβρααμ και Ισαακ και Ιακωβ (ZeT 161:11-12) [C]

ηλιου] omit TR UBS³ ℵ B C E L W Δ θ Π Ω fam 1. 13 33 892 1241 a b k

εν τη βασιλεια των ουρανων] post Ιακωβ rell

Lac.: A D e

Matt. 8:12

οι υιοι της βασιλειας εκβληθησεσθε εις το σκοτος το εξωτερον (PsT 260:29-30) [Ad]*

οι υιοι της βασιλειας εξελευσονται εις το σκοτος το εξωτερον (PsT 55:6) [C]

βασιλειας TR UBS³ ℵ B C E L W θ Π Ω fam 1. 13 33 892 1241 a k] βασιλειας αυτης Δ b

εξελευσονται Did^{pt} ℵ, (exient) k, (ibunt) a b] εκβληθησονται (-σεσθε Did^{pt}) TR UBS³ B C E L W Δ θ Π Ω fam 1. 13 33 892; εμβληθησονται 1241

Text and Apparatus /57

Matt. 8:12 (cont.)

οι] οι δε   rell

Lac.: A D e

Matt. 9:33

εκβαντος του δαιμονιου ελαλησεν ο κωφος   (PsT 268:2)   [Ad]*

εκβληθεντος...του δαιμονιου ελαλησεν ο κωφος   (PsT 267:33) [C]

κωφος   TR UBS³ א B C D E L W Δ Θ Π Ω fam 1. 13 33 892 a b]
Moses (Μωσης)   k

Lac.: A 1241 e

Matt. 10:9

χαλκον εις [τ]ας ζ[ω]νας   (JobT 138:29)   [C]

Text: TR UBS³ א B C D E L W Δ Θ Π Ω fam 1. 13 33 892
  a b k

Lac.: A 1241 e

Matt. 10:10

αξιος ο εργατης της τροφης αυτου   (ZeT 317:9)   [C]

της τροφης   TR UBS³ א B C D E L W Δ Θ Ω fam 1. 13 33 k]
του μισθου   Π 892 a b

αυτου   UBS³ א B C L fam 1. 13 892] αυτου εστιν   rell

αξιος] αξιος γαρ   rell

Lac.: A 1241 e

Matt. 10:16

γινεσθε φρονωιμοι ως οι οφεις και ακεραιοι ως αι περιστεραι
(GenT 93:3)   [C]

γινεσθε   k] γινεσθε ουν   TR UBS³ א B C D E L W Δ Θ Π Ω
fam 1. 13 33 892 a b

ως οι (2x)   rell]   ωσει   L

Matt. 10:16 (cont.)

    οι οφεις   rell] ο οφις   ℵ

    ακεραιοι   rell] απλουστατοι   D

    Lac.:   A 1241 e

Matt. 10:28

    μη φοβεισθε τους αποκτεννοντας το σωμα   (PsT 47:7)   [Ad]*

    μη φοβεισθε απο των αποκτεννοντων το σωμα, την δε ψυχην μη δυναμενων αποκτειναι· φοβηθητε δε τον δυναμενον και ψυχην και σωμα απολεσαι εν γεενν[η]   (GenT 56:5-8) [C]**

    μη φοβεισθε απο των α[πο]κτεννοντων το σωμα   (JobT 86: 29-31)   [C]

    μη φοβ[εισθε α]πο των αποκτεννοντ[ων το] σωμα, την δε ψυ[χ]ην μη δυναμενων αποκτε[ιν]αι   (JobT 347: 12-15)   [C]

    μη φοβεισθε απο των αποκτεννοντων το σωμα την δε ψυχην μη δυναμενων αποκτειναι   (PsT 52:27-53:1)   [C]

    μη φοβεισθε απο των αποκτεννοντων το σωμα, την δε ψυχην μη δυν[αμενων αποκτ]ειναι   (PsT 194:31-32)   [C]

    φοβηθητε ουν τον δυναμενον ψυχην και σωμα απολεσαι εν γεεννη   (PsT 209:16-17)   [C]

        φοβεισθε   UBS³   ℵ C E L Δ Π fam 13] φοβηθητε   TR B D W Θ Ω fam 1   33   892

        φοβηθητε   TR D E L Δ Θ^{vid} Π Ω fam 1. 13 33] φοβεισθε rell

        δε$^{(2)}$] μαλλον   L fam 1;   δε μαλλον   a b k rell

        και$^{(1)}$ rell] omit   Θ fam 13   a b

        ψυχην$^{(2)}$ rell]   την ψυχην   E W Δ Θ fam 13

        σωμα$^{(2)}$ rell]   το σωμα   ℵ E W Δ Θ fam 13

        εν γεεννη   rell]   εις γεενναν   D, (in gehennam) a b

        αποκτειναι   rell]   σφαξαι   D

        Lac.:   A 1241 e

Text and Apparatus /59

Matt. 10:29

ουχι δυο στρουθ[ι]α α[σσα]ριου πωλειται; και ου[χ] εν
[αυτ]ων εμπεσειται εις [π]αγι[δα αν]ευ του πατρος
του εν τ[οι]ς ο[υρανοι]ς   (JobT 317:10-13)   [Ad]*

   πωλειται   TR UBS³ ℵ B C E L W Δ Θ Π Ω fam 1. 13 33
   892] πωλουνται   D, (veneunt) a, (veniunt) b k

   ανευ του πατρος   rell] sine voluntate patris (=ανευ
   της βουλης του πατρος?)   a b

   του εν τοις ουρανοις   892 b] omit   rell

   ασσαριου   rell] του ασσαριου   D

   Lac.: A 1241 e

Matt. 10:32-33

πα[ς ος α]ν ομολογηση εν εμοι εμπροσθεν των ανθρωπων,
ομ[ολογ]ησω καγ[ω] εν αυτω, και πας ος αν αρνησηται...
αρνησομαι καγω αυτον   (GenT 176:10-12)   [Ad]*

   καγω αυτον   UBS³ ℵ B D W Δ Θ fam 1   33 a b k] αυτον
   καγω   TR C E L Π Ω fam 13   892

   Lac.: A 1241 e

Matt. 10:34

ουκ ηλθον βαλειν ειρηνην, αλλα μαχαιραν   (GenT 98:26-27) [C]

μη νομισητε...οτι ηλθον ειρηνην βαλειν επι της γης,
αλλα μαχαιραν   (ZeT 319:25)   [C]

Reconstruction: μη νομισητε οτι ηλθον ειρηνην βαλειν
επι της γης, ουκ ηλθον βαλειν ειρηνην, αλλα μαχαιραν.

   ειρηνην βαλειν   ℵ (k)] βαλειν ειρηνην   TR UBS³ B C D
   E L W Δ Θ Π Ω fam 1. 13 33 892 a b

   βαλειν ειρηνην   rell] ειρηνην βαλειν   a b k

   της γης] την γην   rell

   επι της γης   rell] omit   fam 13

   Lac.: A 1241 e

60/ Didymus and the Gospels

Matt. 10:37

ο φιλων πατερα η μητερα υπερ εμε ουκ εστιν μου αξιος
(PsT 112:8-9) [C]

πατερα...μητερα TR UBS³ ℵ B C D E L W Δ Θ Π Ω fam 1. 13 33 892 a b] μητερα...πατερα k

Lac.: A 1241 e

Matt. 10:40

ο εμε δεχομενος δεχεται τον αποστειλαντα με (ZeT 371:29-372:1) [C]

ο   TR UBS³ B C E L W Δ Θ Π Ω fam 1. 13 33 892]
ο δε ℵ

Lac.: A D 1241 e

Matt. 11:12

βιασται την βασιλειαν αρπαζουσιν (GenT 166:7) [All]

βιασται γαρ αρπαζο[υσι] την βασιλειαν (JobT 136:23-24) [All]

Matt. 11:18

ελθοντος γαρ του Ιωαννου μηδε εσθιοντος μηδε πινοντος
(Ecc1T 73:10-11) [Ad]*

γαρ   TR UBS³ ℵ B C D E W Δ Π Ω fam 1 33 892 a b k]
γαρ προς υμας (L) Θ fam 13

Lac.: A 1241 e

Matt. 11:20

ηρξατο ο Ιησους ονειδιζειν τας πολει[ς εν αις ε]γενοντο
αι πλεισται δυναμεις αυτου οτι ου μ[ετενοησαν]
(GenT 181:1-2) [C]**

τοτε Ιησους ηρξατο ονειδιζειν τας πολεις εν αις εγενοντο
αι πλεισται δυναμεις αυτου, οτι ου μετενοησαν
(GenT 232: 15-17) [C]

ο Ιησους C L W Θ Π fam 1.13 892] omit TR UBS³ ℵ B D E
Δ Ω 33 a b k

Text and Apparatus /61

Matt. 11:20 (cont.)

εγενοντο   rell] γεγονεισαν   D, (factae fuerant) k

αυτου   rell] omit   D

Lac.:   A 1241 e

Matt. 11:21

ουαι σοι Χοραζιν, ουαι σοι Βηθσαϊδαν, οτι ει εν Τυρω
και Σιδονι εγενοντο αι δυναμεις αι γενομεναι εν σοι,
παλαι αν εν σακκω και σποδω μετενοησαν   (GenT 232:
15-20)   [C]

ουαι σοι Χοραζιν, ουαι σοι Βηθσαϊδα, οτι ει εν Τυρω
και Σιδονι εγενοντο αι δυναμεις, παλαι αν εν σακκω
και σποδω μετενοησαν   (ZeT 202:29)   [C]**

Χοραζιν ουαι σοι   TR UBS³ ℵ B C E L W Δ Θ Π Ω fam 1.13
33 892] Χοραζιν και   D a b k

εγενοντο   rell] εγενηθησαν   33 892; εγεγονεισαν   D

σποδω   rell] σποδω καθημενοι (or -μεναι)   ℵ C Δ fam 1
33 892

ει   rell] omit   L

σοι] υμιν   rell

Lac.:   A 1241 e

Matt. 11:28

δευτε προς εμε παντες οι κοπιασαντες και πεφορτισμενοι...
εγω γαρ αναπαυσω υμας   (EcclT 317:4-6)   [Ad]*

δευτε...προς εμε, αναπαυσω γαρ υμας   (PsT 262:21-22)   [Ad]

[παντα]ς ερχομενους εγω υμας αναπαυσω   (ZeT 406:3)   [All]

δευτε προς εμε παντες οι κεκοπωμενοι   (PsT 257:124-25)   [C]

δευτε προς με, παντες οι κοπιωντες και πεφορτισμενοι,
και εγω αναπαυσω υμας   (ZeT 133:10)   [C]

δευτε προς εμε παντες οι κοπιωντες και πεφορτισμενοι
(ZeT 260:21)   [C]

δευτε προς [εμε κ]αγω αναπαυσω υμας   (ZeT 260:29)   [C]

Matt. 11:28 (cont.)

πεφορτισμενοι   TR UBS³ ℵ B C E L W Δ Θ Π Ω fam 1.13 33
892] πεφορτισμενοι εστε   D, (onerati estis)   a b k

Lac.: A 1241 e

Matt. 11:29

ο μαθων παρα Ιησου οτι πραυς εστιν και ταπεινος τη
καρδια   (PsT 265:21-22) [Ad]

μαθετωσαν υπο Ιησου οτι πραυς εστιν και ταπεινος τη
καρδια, ινα ευρωσιν αναπαυσιν   (ZeT 12:6-8) [Ad]

...παρα Ιησου οτι πραυς και ταπεινος τη καρδια εστιν
(ZeT 96:14-15) [Ad]

ε[υρη]σετε...αναπαυσιν ταις ψυχαις υμων   (EcclT 319:12-13)
[C]

μαθετε απ' εμου οτι πραυς ειμι και ταπεινος τη καρδια
(GenT 71:1-2) [C]

αρατε τον ζυγον μου εφ' υμας και μαθετε απ' εμου οτι πραυς
ειμι κ[α]ι τα[πε]ινος τη καρδια και ευρησετε αναπαυσιν
ταις ψυχαις υμ[ω]ν   (GenT 189:1-4) [C]**

μαθετε απ' εμου οτι πραυς ειμι και ταπεινος τη καρδια
(GenT 212:22-23) [C]

μαθετε απ' εμου, οτι πραυς ειμι και ταπεινος τη καρδια
(PsT 81:12-13) [C]

μαθετε απ' εμου, οτι πραυς ειμι   (PsT 81:15-16) [C]

μαθετε απ' εμου, οτι πραυς ειμι και ταπεινος τη καρδια
(PsT 202:25) [C]

μαθετε...απ' εμου, οτι πραυς ειμι και ταπεινος τη καρδια
(PsT 246:13-14) [C]

ειμι και ταπεινος τη καρδια, και ευρησετε αναπαυ[σιν...]
(PsT 257:24-25) [C]

και αρατε τον ζυγον και μαθετε απ' εμου οτι πραυς ειμι
(ZeT 133:11-12) [C]

μαθετε απ' εμου οτι πραυς ειμι και ταπεινος τη καρδια
και ευρησετε αναπαυσιν ταις ψυχαις υμων   (ZeT 185:8-9)
[C]

Matt. 11:29 (cont.)

μαθετε απ' εμου οτι πραυς ειμι και ταπεινος τη καρδια,
και ευρησετε αναπαυσιν ταις ψυχαις υμων (ZeT 201:
16-17) [C]

αρατε το ζυγον μου εφ' υμας, και μαθετε απ' εμου οτι
πραυς ειμι και ταπεινος τη καρδια (ZeT 220:19-21) [C]

και ευρησετε αναπαυσιν ταις ψυχαις υμων· και αρατε τον
ζυγον μου εφ' υμας, και μαθ[ετε απ'] εμου οτι πραυς
ειμι και ταπεινος τη καρδια (ZeT 260:22-24) [C]

μαθετε απ' εμου οτι πραυς ειμι και ταπεινος τη καρδια,
και εηρησετε αναπαυσιν ταις ψυχαις υμων (ZeT 306:3-5)
[C]

μαθετε απ' εμου οτι πραυς και ταπεινος ειμι τη καρδια
(ZeT 335:16) [C]

ευρησετε [αναπ]αυσιν τ[αις ψ]υχαις υμων (ZeT 406:6) [C]

   απ' εμου TR UBS³ B C D E L W Δ Θ Π Ω fam 1. 13 33 892
     a b k] omit ℵ

   Lac.: A 1241 e

Matt. 11:30

ο γαρ ζυγος μου χρηστος εστιν και το φορτιον μου ελαφρον
(PsT 262:22-23) [C]

ο γαρ ζυγος μου χρηστος και το φορτιον μου ελαφρον εστιν
(ZeT 220:19-20) [C]**

ο ζυγος μου χρηστος (ZeT 221:16) [C]

[ο γαρ ζυγ]ος μου χρηστος και το φορτιον ελαφρον εστιν
(ZeT 260:24-25) [C]

   χρηστος TR UBS³ ℵ B C D W Δ Θ Π Ω fam 1 33 892 a b k]
   χριστος E L fam 13

   Lac.: A 1241 e

Matt. 12:24

[ο]υτος ουκ εκβαλλει τα δαιμον[ια] ει μη εν τω βεεζεβουλ
(PsT 294:9) [C]

64/ Didymus and the Gospels

Matt. 12:24 (cont.)

τω TR UBS³ ℵ B C E L W Δ Θ Π Ω fam 1.13 892 1241]
omit E 33

βεεζεβουλ ℵ B] βελζεβουλ L b k; βεελζεβουλ a rell

εκβαλλει rell] εβαλλει Δ

Lac.: A (1241) e

Matt. 12:33

ποιησατε το δενδρον καλον και τους καρπους αυτου καλους,
η ποιησατε το δενδρον σαπρον και τους καρπους αυτου
σαπρους (JobT 369:17-20) [C]

το⁽²⁾ TR UBS³ ℵ B C E L W Δ Π Ω fam 1.13 33 892]
τον D θ

τους καρπους αυτου καλους...τους καρπους αυτου
σαπρους a] τον καρπον αυτου καλον...τον καρπον
αυτου σαπρον b k rell

Lac.: A 1241 e

Matt. 12:35

ει δε παλι[ν λεγεται, οτι δει] τα κακα φυλαττειν,
εκβαλλειν δε τα αγαθα (EcclT 78:18-19) [All]*

τα⁽²⁾TR ℵ C L Δ Ω fam 1 33] omit UBS³ B D E W Θ Π
fam 13 892

Lac.: A 1241 e

Matt. 12:36

περι παντος αργου ρηματος δ[ωσειν] ανθρωπους λογον εν
ημερα κρισεως (GenT 174:13-14) [All]

Matt. 12:37

εκ των εαυτου τις λογων δικαιουται και εκ των λογων
καταδικαζεται (GenT 88:27-89:1) [Ad]*

εκ των λογων εαυτου δικαιουται τις, και εκ [των λο]γων
αυτου καταδικαζεται (PsT 255:10) [Ad]**

Matt. 12:37 (cont.)

εκ των λογων τις εαυτου δικαιουται και εκ των λογων αυτου
κατακρινεται (PsT 272:22-23) [Ad]*

———

εαυτου τις δικαιουται...αυτου καταδικαζεται (or -κρινεται)
(a) (b)] σου δικαιωθηση...σου κατακικασθηση (or
-κριθηση) TR UBS³ ℵ B C D E L W Δ Θ Π Ω fam 1. 13
33 892 k

και rell] η D a

καταδικασθηση (-ζεται Did^pt) rell] κατακριθηση
(-νεται Did^pt) L Ω 33

εκ των λογων σου rell] omit a

λογων⁽²⁾ rell] λογον εργων θ

Lac.: A 1241 e

Matt. 12:40

οτε ο σωτηρ ημελλεν εις τον καταχθονιον τοπον απιεναι
εν τη καρδια της γης (EcclT 92:9) [All]

ωσπερ γαρ Ιωνας εμενεν [εν τη κ]οιλια του κητους ουτως...
εν τη καρ[δια τ]ης γης τρεις ημερας και τρεις νυκτας
(GenT 189:19-21) [Ad]

Matt. 12:43

οταν το ακαθαρτον...[π]νευμα εξελθη απο του ανθρωπου,
διερχεται δι' ανυδρων τοπων ζητουν αναπαυσιν και
ουχ ευρισκει (JobT 398:21-26) [C]

———

οταν L] οταν δε TR UBS³ ℵ B C D E W Δ Θ Π Ω fam 1. 13
33 892 a b k

Lac.: A 1241 e

Matt. 13:11

αγνην εχει καρδιαν...ο τα μυστηρια της βασιλειας εν
ψυχη λαβων (PsT 75:9) [All]*

υμιν δεδοται γνωναι τα μυστηρια της βασιλειας των
ουρανων (ZeT 147:27) [C]

υμ[ιν δεδο]ται γνωναι τα μυστηρια της βασιλειας των
ουρα[νων] (ZeT 162:28) [C]

———

Matt. 13:11 (cont.)

τα μυστηρια TR UBS³ ℵ B C D E L W Δ Θ Π Ω fam 1.13
33 892 1241 b e] mysterium (a), sacramentum (k)
(= τον μυστηριον) a k

των ουρανων rell] omit a b e k

Lac.: A

Matt. 13:17

πολλοι προφηται και δικαιοι επεθυμησαν ιδειν α βλεπετε
και ουκ ειδον (PsT 247:4-5) [C]

και ουκ ειδον TR UBS³ ℵ B C E L W Δ Θ Π Ω fam 1.13
33 892 1241 b] και ουκ ηδυνηθησαν ιδειν D; et
non audierunt (= και ουκ ηκουσαν) a k; omit e

και δικαιοι rell] omit B

Lac.: A

Matt. 13:23

ο μεν γαρ εκατον, ο δε εξηκοντα, ο δε τριακοντα εκαρποφορησαν
(EcclT 146:1) [Ad]

ινα καρποφορηση εκατον, εξηκοντ[α, τρια]κοντα (JobT 152:13) [Ad

εκαρποφορησεν η εις εκατον και εξηκοντα και τριακοντα (PsT
67:28) [All]

Matt. 13:24

ομοιωθη κατα ευ[αγ]γελ[ικ]ον ουτος ο ανθρωπος τη βασι[λει]α
τω[ν] ουρανων εν τω αγρω τη εαυτ[ου] καρδια σπειρων
(JobT 152:9-13) [Ad]

Matt. 13:28

εχθρος ανθρωπος τουτο εποιησεν (GenT 164:23-24) [C]

Text: TR UBS³ ℵ B C D E L W Δ Θ Π Ω fam 1.13 33
892 1241 a b e k

Lac.: A

Text and Apparatus /67

Matt. 13:38

το καλον σπε[ρμ]α υιοι της βασιλειας εισιν   (JobT 156:2-3) [Ad]

σπερμα   k] σπερμα ουτοι   TR UBS³ ℵ B C D E L W Δ Θ Π Ω fam 1. 13 33 892 1241 a b e

το] το δε   rell

υιοι] οι υιοι   rell

υιοι της βασιλειας εισιν] εισιν υιοι της βασιλειας   rell

Lac.: A

Matt. 13:43

οι εκλαμψαντες ως ο ηλιος εν τη βασιλεια του πατρος εαυτων   (EcclT 195:11) [Ad]*

εκλαμπων ως ο ηλιος εν τη βασιλεια του πατρος (JobT 178:24-26) [Ad]*

εκλαμψουσιν...οι δικ[αιοι][ω]ς ο ηλιος εν τη βασιλεια του πατρος αυτων   (EcclT 46:8-9) [C]**

εκλαμψωσιν...οι δικαιοι ως οι ηλιος   (EcclT 163:4-5) [C]

εκλαμψωσιν ως ο ηλιος εν τη βασιλεια του πατρος αυτων (EcclT 194:18-19) [C]

εκλαμψουσιν οι δικαιοι ως ο ηλιος εν τη βασιλεια τ[ου] πατρος εαυτων   (GenT 39:9-10) [C]

οι δικαιοι εκλαμψουσιν ως η ηλιος εν τη βασιλεια πατρος εαυτων   (ZeT 375:21) [C]

εκλαμψουσιν οι δικαιοι   Did^pt 1241] οι δικαιοι εκλαμψουσιν   Did^pt TR UBS³ ℵ B C (D) E L W Δ Θ Π Ω fam 1. (13) 33 892 a b e k

εκλαμψουσιν   rell] λαμψουσιν   D fam 13, (fulgebunt) a b e k

του πατρος αυτων   rell] των ουρανων   θ fam 13

αυτων   rell] mei (μου)   e

Lac.: A

Matt. 13:45

τους ουτω τιμαλφεστατ[ου]ς καλους μαργαριτας ους ο της βασιλειας εμπο[ρο]ς ζητει   (ZeT 278:6-7) [All]*

68/ Didymus and the Gospels

Matt. 13:45 (cont.)
καλους μαργαριτας TR UBS³ א B C D E L W Δ Θ Π Ω fam 1.13 33 892 1241 e k] bonam margaritam (=καλον μαργαριτην) a b
Lac.: A

Matt. 13:47
η γαρ πλοκη της θειας παιδευσεως και της ευαγγελικης διδασκαλιας σαγηνη εστιν βληθεισα εις την θαλασσαν και απο παντος γενους συναγει (EcclT 228:7-8) [All]*

γενους TR UBS³ א B C D E L W Δ Θ Π Ω fam 1.13 33 892 1241 k] genere piscium (=γενους ιχθυων) a b e

συναγει] συναγουση θ; συναγουσιν L; συναπαγουση Δ; συναγαγουση rell
Lac.: A

Matt. 13:52
ο κατα αλλην παραβολην του ευαγγελιου προφερων εκ του θησαυρου νεα κ[α]ι [παλαι]α (EcclT 65:18) [All]

ο...προφερων] οστις προφερει fam 1, proferit (a) b (e) k; οστις εκβαλλει TR UBS³ א B C D E L W Δ Θ Π Ω fam 13 33 892 1241
Lac.: A

Matt. 14:21
του γαρ σωτηρος [τους] πεντε αρτους κλασαντος, εξ [ων] εκορεσεν πεντακισχιλιους ανδρας ο ευαγγλιστης απομνη-[μον]ευει λεγων, χωρις γυναικων και παιδιων (JobT 31: 25-29) [All]*

γυναικων και παιδιων TR UBS³ א B C E L W Δ Π Ω fam 13 33 892 1241] παιδιων και γυναικων D (Θ) (fam 1) a b e

παιδιων rell] παιδων θ fam 1
Lac.: A k

Text and Apparatus /69

Matt. 15:6

ακυροντες την εντολην του θεου δια την επιβλαβη
παραδοσιν αυτων   (ZeT 309:5)   [All]*

την εντολην TR E L W (Δ) Π Ω fam 1 33 1241] τον λογον
UBS³ B D θ 892 a b e; τον νομον   ℵ C fam 13

Lac.: A k

Matt. 15:8

ο λαος ουτος τοις χειλεσιν με τιμα, η δε καρδια αυτων
πορρω απεχει απ' εμου   (ZeT 309:2-3)   [C]

ο λαος ουτος UBS³ ℵ B D L θ fam 13 33 892 a b e]
εγγιζει μοι ο λαος ουτος τω στοματι αυτων και   TR
C E W (Δ) Π (Ω) 1241; ο λαος ουτος εγγιζει μοι
fam 1

τοις χειλεσιν με τιμα   rell] omit W Ω

απεχει   rell] εστιν   D a b e

με τιμα   rell] αυτων τιμωσι με   1241

αυτων   rell] αυτου   θ

Lac.: A k

Matt. 15:9

ματην δε σεβονται με διδασκοντες ενταλματα και διδασκαλιας
ανθρωπων   (ZeT 309:3-5)   [Ad]*

ενταλματα και διδασκαλιας] διδασκαλιας ενταλματα   TR
UBS³ ℵ B C D E L W Δ θ Π Ω fam 1. 13 33 892 1241;
doctrinas et mandata (praecepta e) (=διδασκαλιας
και ενταλματα) a b e

με   rell] omit   Δ

Lac.: A k

Matt. 15:13

υπ' εκεινην γινομενος την φυτ[ει]αν, ην [ο] πατηρ ουκ
εφυτευσεν, ητις και εκριζωθησεται   (JobT 223:33-224:1)
[Ad]

70/ Didymus and the Gospels

Matt. 15:13 (cont.)

εκκο[πτον] πασαν φυτειαν ην ουκ εφυτευσεν ο ουρανιος
πατηρ   (ZeT 80:14)   [Ad]

Matt. 15:14

τυφλος τυφλον εαν οδηγη, αμφοτε[ροι εις] βοθρον πεσουντ[αι]
(EcclT 301:9-10)   [C]

    εαν οδηγη   TR UBS³ ℵ B C (D) E L W Δ Π Ω fam 1 33
    892 (1241) a e] οδηγων σφαλησεται και   θ fam 13

    εις rell] εις τον   θ fam 13

    βοθρον   D fam 1] βοθυνον   rell

    εις βοθρον (or βοθυνον) (εμ)πεσουνται   TR UBS³ ℵ B C E W
    Δ Π Ω 33 892 a e] (εμ)πεσουνται εις βοθρον (or
    βοθυνον) rell

    πεσουνται rell] εμπεσουνται   D W

    τυφλος] τυφλος γαρ   1241; τυφλος δε   rell

    Lac.:   A b k

Matt. 15:19

εσωθεν εκ της καρ[διας εξερχονται διαλ]ογισμοι πονηροι
(EcclT 280:20-21) [Ad]*

εκ γαρ της καρδιας εξερχοντ[αι] διαλογισμοι πονηροι
(JobT 217:32-33)   [C]

    γαρ   TR UBS³ B C D E L Δ θ Π Ω fam 1. 13 33 892 1241 a e]
    omit ℵ W (homeoeteleuton)

    εξερχονται rell] εξερχεται   W

    Lac.:   A b k

Matt. 16:16

συ ει ο χριστος ο υιος του θεου του ζωντος   (GenT 114:
14-15)   [C]

    του ζωντος   TR UBS³ ℵ B C E L W Δ θ Π Ω fam 1. 13 33
    892 1241 a b e] του σωζοντος   D

    Lac.: A k

Matt. 16:17

σαρξ και αιμα ουκ απεκαλυψεν αυ[τω] τον υιον, αλλ' ο
γεννησας αυτον ουρ[α]ν[ιος] πατηρ   (EcclT 331:13)
[Ad]

Matt. 16:18

και ως Πετρος δια το στερρον της πιστεως ης εσχεν πετρας
καλουμενης παρωνομασθη Πετρος   (EcclT 355:24-25) [All]

συ ει Πετρος και επι ταυτη τη πετρα οικοδομη[σω] μου την
εκκλησιαν, και πυλαι αδου ου κατισχυσουσιν αυ[της]
(GenT 114:15-17) [C]**

...ουδε πυλαι αδου κατισχυουσιν αυτης   (GenT 195:6) [C]

συ ει Πετρος, και επι ταυτη τη πετρα οι[κο]δομησω μου
την εκκλησιαν   (JobT 148:1-3) [C]

συ ει Πετρος, και επι ταυτη τη πετρα οικοδομησω μου την
εκκλησιαν (JobT 312:23-25) [C]

συ ει Πετρος, και επι ταυτη τη πετρα οικοδομησω μου την
εκκλησιαν, και πυλαι αδου ου μη κατισχυσουσιν αυτης
(ZeT 107:17-18) [C]

  μου την εκκλησιαν TR UBS³ ℵ B C E L W Δ Θ Π Ω fam 1.
  13 33 892 1241] την εκκλησιαν μου D a b e

  ταυτη τη πετρα rell] τη πετρα ταυτη E ; ταυτη πετρα θ;
  ταυτην την πετραν D; ταυτην τη πετρα Δ

  κατισχυσουσιν rell] κατισχυουσιν Δ

  Lac.: A k

Matt. 16:19

οι υπο Ιησου λαβοντες τας κλεις της βασιλειας των ουρανων
(ZeT 187:4-5) [All]*

  κλεις ₃TR C D E Δ Π Ω fam 1. 13 33 892 1241] κλειδας
  UBS³ ℵ B L W θ

  Lac.: A k

Matt. 16:27

...αποδιδοντος τε εκαστω κατα την πραξιν... (ZeT 78:18)
[All]*

72/ Didymus and the Gospels

Matt. 16:27 (cont.)

την πραξιν TR UBS³ B C D E L W Δ Θ Π Ω fam 13 33
892 1241 e] τα εργα ℵ fam 1 a b

Lac.: A k

Matt. 18:3

ο στραφεις κατα την υφηγησιν Ιησου και γενομενος ως τα παιδια, εκεινος εν ακακια γεγονεν (PsT 91:5-6) [All]

Matt. 18:6

ος εαν σκαν[δ]αλιση εν[α τω]ν μικρων τουτων των πιστευοντων εις εμε, συμφερει αυτω, ει μυλος ονικο[ς κρ]εμασθειη περι τον τραχηλον και καταποντισθειη εν τω πελαγει της θαλασ[ση]ς (EcclT 306:3-6) [Ad]*

ορατε μη σκανδαλισητε ενα των μικρων τουτων των πιστευοντων εις εμε (PsT 194:26-27) [Ad]*

περι τον τραχηλον UBS³ ℵ B L 33 892] εις τον τραχηλον E W Δ Θ Π Ω fam 1.13 1241, (in collum) e; επι τον τραχηλον TR D; in collo (=εν τω τραχηλω) a b

μυλος ονικος rell] λιθος μυλικος L

Lac.: A C k

Matt. 18:7

ουαι τω ανθρωπω δι' ου το σκανδαλον ερχεται (EcclT 113:3) [c]

ανθρωπω UBS³ ℵ D L fam 1 892] ανθρωπω εκεινω TR B E (W) Δ Θ Π Ω fam 13 33 1241 a b (e)

το σκανδαλον rell] τα σκανδαλα fam 13; omit Θ

Lac.: A C k

Matt. 18:10

και οι εν τη εκκλη[σ]ια μικροι εχουσιν αγγελους βλεποντας δια π[αντος] το προσωπον του πατρος (EcclT 344:22-23) [All]

Matt. 18:10 (cont.)

ως αγγελοι δια παντος βλεποντες το προσωπον του εν
ουρανοις πατρος   (GenT 89:15-16)   [Ad]*

οι γαρ αγγελοι αυτων δια παντος βλεπουσιν το προσωπον
του πατρος ημων του εν τοις ουρανοις   (GenT 194:26)
[Ad]*

οι αγγελοι των εν τη εκκλησια το προσωπον δια παντος
βλεπουσιν του εν τοις ουρανοις πατρος   (ZeT 194:13)
[Ad]*

αυτων   fam 1   e] αυτων εν ουρανοις   TR UBS^3 א D E L W
Δ Θ Π Ω fam 13   (892) 1241 a b; εν τω ουρανω   B
(33)

τοις   Did^{pt} D 33 892] omit Did^{pt} TR UBS^3 א B E L W
Δ Θ Π Ω fam 1. 13 1241

Lac.:   A C k

Matt. 18:20

οτι οτε συμφωνοι εισιν οι δυ[ο] εχουσι[ν το]ν σωτηρα
μεσον α[υτων]   (EcclT 127:6)   [All]

[ου γαρ εισιν δυο] η τρεις συνηγμενοι, εγω εκει ειμ[ι]
(EcclT 127:6-7)   [Ad]*

ου γαρ εισιν...εκει   TR UBS^3 א B E L W Δ Θ Π Ω fam 1.
13 33 892 1241 a b e] ουκ εισιν γαρ...παρ' οις ουκ
D

η   rell] omit א

εκει   rell] omit e

Lac.:   A C k

Matt. 18:21

ποσαχις αμαρτανει; λεγει εως επτα;   (PsT 107:21)   [Ad]

Matt. 18:22

ου λεγω σοι εως επτα μονον, αλλα και εβδομηκοντακις
επτα (PsT 107:21-22) [Ad]*

επτα$^{(2)}$ TR UBS^3 ℵ B E L W Δ Θ Π Ω fam 1. 13 33 892
1241] επτακις D, (septies) a b e

Lac.: A C k

Matt. 18:35

ουτω και υμιν ο πατηρ ποιησει αν μη αφητε εκαστος απο
της καρδιας υμων τοις οφειλουσιν υμιν (ZeT 126:23-24)
[Ad]

Matt. 19:12

δια την τοιαυτην στειρ[ωσ]ιν [κ]αι ο ευνου[χισ]θεις ου
δια την βασιλειαν των [ουρα]νων... (ZeT 398:16)
[All]

Matt. 19:28

καθισεσθε και υμεις εν τη παλινγενεσια επι θρονους
δωδεκα (PsT 225:14) [Ad]*

ουτοι δ'εισιν οι εν τη παλιγγενεσια τη κατα την
αναστασιν των νεκρων καθημενοι προ προσωπου του
σωτηρος, κριτου και βασιλεως οντος, κρινοντες τας
δωδεκα φυλας του Ισραηλ (ZeT 56:8-10) [All]*

καθησεσθε και υμεις επι δωδεκα θρονους κρινοντες τας
δωδεκα φυλας του Ισραηλ (JobT 327:12-15) [C]

Reconstruction: εν τη παλινγενεσια...καθησεσθε και
υμεις επι δωδεκα θρονους κρινοντες τας δωδεκα φυλας
του Ισραηλ

υμεις TR UBS^3 B C E W Δ Θ Π Ω fam 13 33 1241 a b e]
αυτοι ℵ D L fam 1 892

καθησεσθε (or καθισεσθε) rell] καθεσθησεσθε fam 1

δωδεκα$^{(1)}$ rell] δεκαδυο D

τας rell] omit D

Lac.: A k

Matt. 20:32

τι θελετε ινα ποιησω υμιν (GenT 54:9-10) [C]

ινα L 892] omit TR UBS³ ℵ B C D E W Δ Θ Π fam 1.13
33 1241 a b e

Lac.: A Ω k

Matt. 21:2

τ[ην] εκκειμενην προφητειαν πεπληρωσθαι φασιν οι ευαγγελ-
ισται υπο του Ιησου επιβεβηκοτος ονου και πωλου
λυθεντων και ενεχθεντων εκ της κατεναντι κωμης
(ZeT 218:6-8) [All]*

κατεναντι UBS³ ℵ B C D L Θ fam 13 33 892] απεναντι TR
E W (Δ) Π Ω fam 1 1241

Lac.: A k

Matt. 21:10

ως δε ηλθεν Ιησους εις Ι[εροσο]λυμα, εσεισθη πασα η
πολις (GenT 180:25-26) [Ad]

Matt. 21:19

ου μηκετι εκ σου καρπος γενηται εις τον αιωνα
(GenT 85:27-86:1) [C]

ου B L] omit TR UBS³ ℵ C D E W Δ Θ Π Ω fam 1.13
33 892 1241

γενηται rell] γενοιτο ℵ Θ

Lac.: A k

Matt. 21:31

αι πορναι και οι τελωναι προαγουσιν υμας εν τη βασιλεια
(PsT 55:2-3) [C]

αι πορναι και οι τελωναι a b e] οι τελωναι και αι
πορναι TR UBS³ ℵ B C D E L W Δ Θ Π Ω fam 1.13 33
892 1241

εν τη βασιλεια (in regno) a b e] εις την βασιλειαν
rell

76/ Didymus and the Gospels

Matt. 21:31 (cont.)

προαγουσιν rell] προαγωσιν Δ

Lac.: A k

Matt. 22:13

ως και εν ευαγγελιω περι του δεθεντος ποσιν και χερσιν και βληθεντος εις το σκοτος το εξωτερ[ον το] ητοιμασμενον τω διαβολω και τοις αγγελοις αυτου, εκει εσται ο κλαυθμος και ο βρυγμος των οδοντων (PsT 247:7-8) [Ad]*

Reconstruction: δησαντες αυτου ποδας και χειρας βαλετε (αυτου?) εις το σκοτος το εξωτερον, εκει εσται ο κλαυθμος και ο βρυγμος των οδοντων

δησαντες αυτου ποδας και χειρας UBS³ ℵ B L θ fam 1.13 892] αρατε αυτον ποδων και χειρων D a b e; δησαντες αυτου ποδας και χειρας αρατε αυτον και TR C E W Δ Π Ω 33 (1241)

βαλετε D fam 13 1241 a b e] εκβαλετε rell

ποδας και χειρας rell] χειρας και ποδας 1241

Lac.: A k

Matt. 22:19

επιδειξατε μοι το νομισμα (ZeT 309:10) [C]

μοι TR UBS³ ℵ B C D E L W Δ Θ Π Ω fam 1.13 33 892 1241 a e] omit b

νομισμα rell] denarium (=δηναριον) e

Lac.: A k

Matt. 22:44

λεγει κυριος τω κυριω μου (PsT 7:23) [C]

κυριος UBS³ ℵ B D] ο κυριος TR E L W Δ Θ Π Ω fam 1.13 33 892 1241

λεγει] ειπεν rell

Lac.: A C k

Matt. 22:45

ει εν πνευματι αγιω κυριον αυτον ειπεν, πως υιος αυτου
εστιν   (PsT 7:23-24)   [Ad]*

    ει εν πνευματι (+αγιω Did.) D Δ Θ Π fam 13 a b] ει
    TR UBS³ ℵ B E L W Ω fam 1 33 892 1241 e

    Lac.: A C k

Matt. 23:2

επι της καθεδρας Μωσεως εκαθισαν οι γραμματεις
(JobT 327:15-17)   [C]

    καθεδρας Μωσεως   D Θ fam 13 a b e] Μωσεως καθεδρας
    TR UBS³ ℵ B E L W Δ Π Ω fam 1 33 892 1241

    Lac.: A C k

Matt. 23:14

κλειετε την βασιλειαν των ουρανων, αυτοι ουκ εισερχεσθε
ουδε τους εισερχομενους αφιετε εισελθειν   (JobT 322:
28-31)   [Ad]

Matt. 23:25

τα αυτα οντα τοις ταφοις κατα αλληγοριαν τοις εξωθεν
κεκονιαμενοις, εσωθεν γεμουσιν πασης ακρασιας
(ZeT 88:22-24)   [All]*

    ακρασιας   TR UBS³ ℵ B D L Δ Θ Π fam 1.13 33 892 1241
    a e] αδικιας   C E Ω; ακρασιας αδικιας   W

    Lac.: A b k

Matt. 23:27

τα αυτα οντα τοις ταφοις κατα αλληγοριαν τοις εξωθεν
κεκονιαμενοις   (ZeT 88:22-23)   [All]

τι παρομοιαζετε ταφοις κεκονι[αμ]ενοις· εσωθεν γεμουσιν
οστεων νεκρων και πασης ακαθ[αρ]σιας   (GenT 125:21-23)
[C]

    παρομοιαζετε   TR UBS³ ℵ C D E L W Δ Θ Π Ω fam 13 33
    892 1241] ομοιαζετε   B   fam 1

78/ Didymus and the Gospels

Matt. 23:27 (cont.)

τι] οτι   rell

εσωθεν] εσωθεν δε   rell

γεμουσιν   rell] γεμει   D

Lac.:   A (b)

Matt. 23:30

ει ημεν εν ταις ημεραις των πατερων ημων, ουκ αν ημεθα κοινωνοι αυτων εν τω αιματι των προφητων   (ZeT 82: 20-22)   [C]

ημεν   TR W Π Ω fam 1 33] ημεθα   UBS³ ℵ B C D E L Δ θ fam 13 892 1241

ημεθα   rell] ημεν   TR W Π Ω fam 1. 13   33

κοινωνοι αυτων   rell] αυτων κοινωνοι   UBS³ B D fam 1. 13; κοινωνοι   θ; (κοιν. α. post προφητων)   1241

ουκ αν...προφητων   a b rell] omit in toto   e

Lac.:   A k

Matt. 23:31

ωστε μαρτυρειτε οτι υιοι εστε των αποκτεινάντων τους προφητας   (ZeT 82:22-23)   [C]

μαρτυρειτε] μαρτυρειτε εαυτοις   TR UBS³ ℵ B C D E L W Δ θ Π Ω (fam 1. 13) 33 892 1241 a b e

αποκτεναντων] φονευσαντων   rell

Lac.:   A k

Matt. 23:32

πληρωσατε ουν και υμεις το μετρον των πατερων υμων   (ZeT 82:23-24)   [C]

πληρωσατε   TR UBS³ ℵ C E L W Δ θ Π Ω fam 1. 13   33 892 1241 a b] πληρωσετε   B e; επληρωσατε   D

ουν] omit   rell

Text and Apparatus /79

Matt. 23:32 (cont.)

και υμεις] ante πληρωσατε   rell

Lac.: A k

Matt. 23:33

οφεις γεννηματα εχιδνων   (GenT 96:19-20)   [C]

οφεις   TR UBS³ ℵ B C D E L W Δ Θ Π Ω fam 1. 13 33 892
1241 a e] omit   b

Lac.: A k

Matt. 23:35

ο γαρ πατηρ του βαπτιστου Ιωαννου Ζαχαριας και βαραχιας
ο τουτου γονευς προσηγορευοντο   (!)   (ZeT 2:5-6)   [All]*

υιου βαραχιου   TR UBS³ B C D E L W Δ Θ Π Ω fam 1. 13
33 892 1241 a b e]   omit   ℵ

Lac.: A k

Matt. 23:37

ποσακις ηθελησα επισυναγαγειν τα τεκνα σου, ον τροπον
ορνις επισυναγει τα νοσσια υπο τας πτερυγας και ουκ
ηθελησατε   (GenT 171:25-172:1)   [C]

ορνις επισυναγει   UBS³ ℵ B D L Θ fam 1. 13 33 892
a b e] επισυναγει ορνις   TR C E W Δ Π Ω 1241

νοσσια   B] νοσσια(ε)αυτης   rell

πτερυγας   rell] πτερυγας αυτης   Δ a b e

Lac.: A k

Matt. 24:3

τι το σημειον της παρουσιας και συντελειας του αιωνος
τουτου   (EcclT 87:4)   [C]

ποτε ταυτα εσται, και τι το σημε[ιο]ν της σης παρουσιας
και συντελειας του αιωνος   (GenT 73:20-22)   [C]**

80/ Didymus and the Gospels

Matt. 24:3 (cont.)

συντελειας UBS³ ℵ B C L θ Ω fam 1 33 892] της
συντελειας TR D E W Δ Π fam 13 1241

ποτε rell] τοτε C

σης παρουσιας rell] παρουσιας σου D

και⁽²⁾ a b rell] omit e

του αιωνος rell] omit e

Lac.: A k

Matt. 24:5

πολλοι ελευσονται εν τω ονοματι μου λεγοντες· Εγω ειμι
ο χριστος (GenT 221:5-6) [C]

πολλοι] πολλοι γαρ TR UBS³ ℵ B C D E L W Δ θ Π Ω
fam 1. 13 33 892 1241 a b e

εν] επι rell

λεγοντες rell] λεγοντες οτι C

Lac.: A k

Matt. 24:12

οτε πληθυνει, ψυχομενης [τ]ης των πολλων αγαπης, συντελεια
εσται (GenT 44:16-17) [All]

δια το πληθυνθηναι την ανομιαν ψυγησεται η αγαπη των
πολλων (GenT 193:3-4) [C]

πληθυνθηναι TR UBS³ ℵ B E L W Δ θ Π Ω fam 1. 13 33
892 1241] πληθυναι D

Lac.: A C k

Matt. 24:14

δει κηρυχθηναι το ευαγγελιον τουτο της βασιλειας εν
ολω τω κοσμω εις μαρτυριον πασιν τοις εθνεσιν
(Ecc1T 357:21-22) [Ad]*

πασιν TR UBS³ ℵ B D E L Δ θ Π Ω fam 1. 13 33 892
1241 a b e] omit W

Lac.: A C k

Text and Apparatus /81

Matt. 24:22

ει μη εκολοβωθησαν αι ημεραι εκειναι, ουκ αν εσωθη πασα
σαρξ   (ZeT 73:1-2)   [C]

Text: TR UBS³ ℵ B D E L W Δ Θ Π Ω fam 1. 13 33 892
1241 a b e

Lac.: A C k

Matt. 24:29

ευθεως μετα την θλιψιν των ημερων εκεινων ο ηλιος
σκοτισθησεται, και η σεληνη ου δωσει φως αυτης
(PsT 14:24-26)   [C]

ευθεως a] ευθεως δε TR UBS³ ℵ B D E L W Δ Θ Π Ω
fam 1. 13 33 892 1241 b e

φως] το φεγγος   rell

Lac.: A C k

Matt. 24:30

φ[υλαι οψοντ]αι τον υιον το[υ ανθρωπου] ερχομενον επι
των νεφελων του [ουρα]νου μετα δυν[αμεω]ς και δοξης
πολλης   (ZeT 375:2-4)   [C]

και δοξης πολλης TR UBS³ ℵ B E L W Δ Θ Π Ω fam 1. 13
33 892 1241] πολλης και δοξης D a b e

φυλαι] πασαι αι φυλαι της γης, και   rell

Lac.: A C k

Matt. 24:36

περι της ωρας και της ημερας εκεινης ουδεις οιδεν, ουτε
οι αγγελοι ουτε ο υιος, ει μη ο πατηρ μονος   (ZeT 377:
17-18)   [Ad]*

της ωρας και] και (της) ωρας post εκεινος TR UBS³ ℵ B
D E W Δ Θ Π Ω fam 1. 13 (33) 1241 a (b) e; omit L 892

της ωρας TR Θ fam 1 33] ωρας   rell

και rell] η 33, (vel) b

Matt. 24:36

    ουτε (or ουδε) ο υιος UBS³ ℵ B D θ fam 13 a b]
    neque filius hominis (= ουτε ο υιος του ανθρωπου)
    e; omit rell

    πατηρ rell] πατηρ μου TR E W Ω 1241

    Lac.: A C k

Matt. 24:40

    [δυ]ο ειν[αι εν] τω [αγ]ρω, ενα παρλαμβανομ[ε]νον και
    [ε]να [α]φ[ι]ε[μενον] (EcclT 346:15-16) [Ad]*

    Reconstruction: δυο εσονται εν τω αγρω, ο εις παραλαμ-
    βανεται και ο εις αφιεται

    δυο εσονται TR UBS³ D E L W Δ θ Π Ω fam 1.13 33 1241
    a b e] εσονται δυο ℵ B 892

    Lac.: A C k

Matt. 25:1

    τοτε ομοιωθησεται η βασιλεια των ουρανων δεκα παρθενοις
    (ZeT 197:14) [C]

    ομοιωθησεται TR UBS³ ℵ B C D E L Δ θ Π Ω fam 1.13 33
    892 1241 a b] ωμοιωθη W

    Lac.: A e k

Matt. 25:3-4, 10

    αι δε μη λαβουσαι ελαιον εν τοις αγγειοις...απηλθαν
    αγορασαι και ουκετι ευρον τους πωλουντας (EcclT 349:
    20-21) [All]

Matt. 25:6

    μεσον νυκτος κραυγη γεγονεν· ηλθεν ο νυμφ[ι]ος, εξελθατε
    εις υπαντησιν (EcclT 349:18-19) [Ad]*

    εξερχεσθε (Did.) TR UBS³ ℵ A B C (D) E L W Δ
    Π Ω fam 13 33 892 1241] εγειρεσθε θ fam 1 (b)

    γεγονεν rell] εγενετο B

    Lac.: a e k

Matt. 25:15

δε[δω]κεν εκαστω των δουλων αυτου τα [θη]τικα αυτου
αγρυρια εκαστω κατα [τ]ην ιδιαν δυναμιν, τω μεν
πεντε, τω δε δυο, τω δε εν   (Ecc1T 164:18-20)   [All]*

εκαστω [κ]ατα την ιδιαν δυναμιν...και τω μεν δεδωκεν
πεντε, τω δε δυο, τω δε εν   (PsT 251:15-17)   [Ad]*

ιδιαν δυναμιν TR UBS³ ℵ A B C E L W Δ Θ Π Ω fam 1. 13
33 892 1241] δυναμιν αυτου D

εν rel1] ενα D

Lac.: a e k

Matt. 25:16

ο τα πεντε λαβων ταλαντα ειργασατο εν αυτοις και
εδιπλασιασεν αυτοις   (PsT 251:17)   [Ad]*

εν TR UBS³ ℵ A B C D E L W Δ Π Ω fam 13 33 892
1241] επ' θ fam 1

Lac.: e k

Matt. 25:18

ο το εν λαβων και εις την γην αυτο κατακρυψας ουδε
ειργασατο εν αυτω ουδε απεδωκεν τοκους, αυτο εις την
γην κατεκρυψεν   (PsT 251:18-19)   [All]

Matt. 25:25

ιδε εχεις τοκον (PsT 251:21) [Ad]

φοβηθεις εκρυψα σου το αργυριον εις την γην, και ουδενι
αυ[το εδω]κα (PsT 251:22-23) [Ad]

Matt. 25:31

οταν καθιση επι θρονου δοξης αυτου (ZeT 178:1) [Ad]

Matt. 25:32

παντα τα εθνη παρασταθησεται επιπροσθεν του βασιλεως του
ερχομενου σωτηρος, ωστε αφορισαι αυτον τας εριφους
απο των προβατων (Ecc1T 321:25-322:2) [All]

Matt. 25:33

και τα μεν προβατα εκ δεξιων στηση, τα δε εριφια εξ
ευωνυμων   (EcclT 322:2-3)   [Ad]*

   μεν   TR UBS³ ℵ A B E L W Δ Θ Π Ω fam 1.13 33 892 1241]
   omit   D a b

   δεξιων   ℵ A] δεξιων αυτου   rell

   ευωνυμων   rell] ευωνυμων αυτου   ℵ

   Lac.:   C e k

Matt. 25:41

ακουει τα εριφια·   υπαγετε εις το πυρ το αιωνιον
(EcclT 322:4-5)   [Ad]

[το] ητοιμασμενον τω διαβολω και τοις αγγελοις αυτου
(PsT 247:7-8)   [C]

εις το πυρ το ητοιμασμενο[ν τω] διαβολω και τοις αγγελοις
αυτου   (ZeT 83:14-15)   [C]

πορευεσθε οι κεκατηραμενοι, εις το πυρ το αιωνιον, το
ητοιμασμενον τω διαβολω και τοις αγγελοις αυτου
(ZeT 178:6-8)   [C]**

   οι   TR UBS³ A D E W Δ Θ Π Ω fam 1.13 892] omit   ℵ B
   L 33 1241

   το ητοιμασμενον   rell] ο ητοιμασεν ο πατηρ μου   D fam 1
   a b

   πορευεσθε] υπαγετε απ' εμου ℵ ; πορευεσθε απ' εμου
   rell

   κεκατηραμενοι] κατηραμενοι   rell

   Lac.:   C e k

Matt.26:15

τι θελετε μοι δουναι, καγω παραδωσω υμιν αυτον
(PsT 93:15-16)   [Ad]*

τι μοι θελετε δουναι, καγω παραδιδωμι υμιν αυτον
(PsT 293:21)   [Ad]*

τι μοι θελετε δουναι, καγω υμιν αυτον παραδωσω
(PsT 294:4)   [Ad]*

Matt. 26:15 (cont.)

παραδωσω   TR UBS³ ℵ A B D E L Δ Θ Π Ω fam 1. 13 33
892 1241 a b] παραδω   W

Lac.:   C e k

Matt. 26:31

παταξω τον ποιμενα και διασκορπισθησεται τα προβατα
(ZeT 354:16)   [C]

———

διασκορπισθησεται   TR D E W Δ Θ Π Ω fam 1] διασκορπισ-
θησονται   UBS³ ℵ A B C L fam 13 33 892 1241 a b

Lac.:   e k

Matt. 26:52

παντες οι λαβοντες μαχαιραν μαχαιρη απολουνται
(PsT 85:25-26)   [C]

παντες οι λαβοντες μαχαιραν μαχαιρη απολουνται
(PsT 247:28)   [C]

———

παντες a] παντες γαρ   TR UBS³ ℵ A B C D E L W Δ Θ Π Ω
fam 1. 13 33 892 1241 b

μαχαιρη] εν μαχαιρη   UBS³ ℵ A B C E L Θ 33; εν μαχαιρα
rell

απολουνται   rell] αποθανουνται   W Δ Ω fam 13 1241

λαβοντες   rell] λαμβανοντες   fam 1

Lac.:   e k

Matt. 26:53

η δοκεις οτι ουκ εδυναμην παρακαλεσαι τον πατερα μου και
εδωκεν αν μοι πλειους δωδεκα λεγιωνων αγγελων
(GenT 225:18-20)   [Ad]*

———

δοκεις οτι ου δυναμαι (Did.)   TR UBS³   ℵ B
(C) D E L W Δ Θ Π Ω fam (1). 13 33 892 (1241)] ου
δοκεις οτι δυναμαι   a b

δοκεις   rell] δοκει σοι   C^vid fam 1 1241

εδυναμην...μοι] δυναμαι...μοι αρτι   UBS³ (ℵ) B L 33
892; δυναμαι αρτι...μοι   rell

86/ Didymus and the Gospels

Matt. 26:53 (cont.)

μοι rell] μοι ωδε ℵ θ fam 1

πλειους rell] πλειω UBS³ ℵ B D

δωδεκα UBS³ ℵ B D L θ b] η δωδεκα rell

λεγιωνων αγγελων ℵ A C L θ fam 13 33] λεγιωνων αγγελους Δ Π; λεγεωνας αγγελων rell

δωδεκα] XII milia (=δωδεκα χιλαδες) b

Lac.: e k

Matt. 26:55

καθ' ημεραν διδασκω εν τη συναγωγη και νυν ως επι ληστην ηλθατε (PsT 294:5) [Ad]

Matt. 27:3, 5

ειδως...οτι κατεκριθ[η α]πελθων απηγ[ξατο] (PsT 293:30) [All]

Matt. 27:25

εφ' ημας το αιμα αυτου και επι τα τεκ[να η]μων (ZeT 161:25) [Ad]

Matt. 27:40

ει υιος ει του θεου, καταβηθι απο του σταυρου (ZeT 341:8) [C]

ει του θεου TR UBS³ ℵ A D E L W Δ θ Π Ω fam 1. 13 33 892 1241] θεου ει B a b

θεου rell] θεου και UBS³ ℵ A D a b

Lac.: C e k

Matt. 27:52-53

πολλους, λεγει, εθεωρησαν εν τη αγια πολει (PsT 186:28) [All]

Text and Apparatus /87

Matt. 28:19

οπερ οι μακαριοι αποστολοι πεποιηκασι αποσταλεντες
μ[αθ]ητευσαι παντα τα εθνη (JobT 402:38-403:2) [All]

πορευθεντες μαθητευσατε παντα τα εθνη (ZeT 263:17) [C]

πορευθεντες TR UBS³ ℵ A B E W Δ Θ Π Ω fam 1. 13 33
892 1241 a b] πορευεσθε D e

μαθητευσατε   ℵ A E Ω fam 13] νυν μαθητευσατε D a b;
ουν μαθητευσατε rell

Lac.: C L k

Matt. 28:20

ιδου εγω εσομαι μεθ' υμων (Eccl 239:26) [Ad]

εως συντελειας του αιωνος τουτου (EcclT 87:3) [Ad]*

ιδου εγω μεθ' υμων πασας τας ημερας εως της συντελειας
του αιωνος τουτου (EcclT 239:17-18) [Ad]*

εως συντελειας του αιωνος τουτου (PsT 12:7) [Ad]*

τουτου] omit TR UBS³ ℵ A B D E W Δ Θ Π Ω fam 1. 13
33 892 1241 a b e

Lac.: C L k

Mark 1:15

μετανοιετε και πιστευετε εν τω ευαγγελιω (PsT 157:30)
[C]

Text: TR UBS³ ℵ A B D E L W Δ Θ Π Ω fam 1.13 33 579 892 1241 a b

Lac.: C Ψ e k

Mark 3:17

ταυτης της βροντης ηκουσαν οι αμφι τον Ιακοβ και Ιωαννην· εχρηματισαν γαρ υιοι βροντης (EcclT 355:23) [All]*

και Ιακωβον τον του Ζεβεδαιου και Ιωαννην τον αδελφον του Ιακωβον και επεθηκεν αυτοις ονοματα (Ιακοβ... βροντης Did) TR UBS³ ℵ A (B) C (D) E L Δ Θ Π Ω fam 1.13 33 579 892 1241 a b] κοινως δε αυτους εκαλεσεν W e

Lac.: Ψ k

Mark 4:10

λοιπον ερω[τω]σι[ν] περι των παραβολων (EcclT 10:3)
[All]*

τας παραβολας (Did) UBS³ ℵ B C L Δ 892] την παραβολην TR A E Π Ω fam 1 33 579 1241; τις η παραβολη αυτη D W Θ fam 13 a b

Lac.: Ψ e k

Mark 4:11

οταν λεγη τας παραβολας τοις εξω. οτ[ε ουκ] εκκλησιαζει, τοτε κατ' ιδιαν τοις ιδιοις λαλει και λεγει το μυστηριον τουτο εμοι και τοις ε[μ]ου (EcclT 5:26-27) [All]*

ου λεγεις τους μα[θ]ητας Ιησου εν τοις οχλοις τοις εξω παρειναι οτε αι παραβολας ελεγοντο (EcclT 10:1) [All]*

λαλει τας παραβολας τοις πολλοις τοις εξω (EcclT 7:23) [All]*

το μυστηριον TR UBS³ ℵ A B C D E L W Δ Θ Π Ω fam 13 33 579 892 a b] τα μυστηρια fam 1 1241

εξω rell] εξωθεν B

Lac.: Ψ e k

Mark 4:28

πρωτον γαρ χορτωδες εσται το φυομενον ως και ο Σωτηρ
φησιν...ειτεν σταχυν   (GenT 104:2-3)   [All]*

ειτεν (or ειτα) σταχυν TR UBS³ A B C D E L W Δ Θ Π Ω
fam 1. 13 33 579 892 1241 a b e] omit ℵ

σταχυν rell] σταχυας D; σταχυει W

Lac.: Ψ k

Mark 4:34

ε[πι]λυει τας παραβολας ενδον τοις μαθηταις εισωτερικω
λογω   (EcclT 7:24)   [All]

Mark 7:6

ο λαος ουτ[ος τοι]ς χειλ[εσιν με] τιμα, τη δε καρδια
πορρω απεστιν α[π εμου]   (GenT 176:18-19)   [C]

ο λαος ουτος B D b] ουτος ο λαος TR UBS³ ℵ A E L
W Δ Θ Π Ω fam 1. 13 33 579 892 1241; ο λαος a

τιμα rell] αγαπα D W a b

απεστιν L Θ 892] est (= εστιν) a b; αφεστηκεν D;
εχει W; απεστη Δ; απεχει rell

τη δε καρδια] η δε καρδια αυτων rell

Lac.: C Ψ e k

Mark 9:49

πας πυρι αλισθησεται   (ZeT 207:6)   [C]

πας πυρι αλισθησεται   (ZeT 358:25)   [C]

πας (a)] πας γαρ TR UBS³ ℵ A B C (D) E L W Δ Θ Π Ψ Ω
fam 1. 13 579 892 1241 (b) (k)

πας (γαρ) (εν) πυρι rell] πασα γαρ θυσια αλι D a b k

πυρι rell] εν πυρι ℵ C

αλισθησεται rell] αλισγηθησεται W; αναλωθησεται Θ

Lac.: 33 e

Mark 11:2

γραφεται περι του απο της κατεναντι κωμης λυθεντος πωλου, ινα προς τον Ιησουν ελθη, εξημερωθησομενου επιβαντος αυτω του Σωτηρος· ειρηται γαρ οτι ουπω τοτε εκαθισεν επ' αυτον ανθρωπων τις (ZeT 221:21-24) [All]*

ουπω UBS³ ℵ B C L W Δ Π Ψ fam 13 892 (adhuc b)] πωποτε A 1241 (b); omit TR D E Θ Ω fam 1 579 a k

εκαθισεν rell] κεκαθικεν TR A D E Π Ω fam 1. 13; επικεκαθεικεν W

Lac.: 33 e

Mark 14:33

ηρξατο γουν Ιησους θαμβεισθαι και αδημονειν (PsT 282:3) [Ad]*

ηρξατο θαμβεισθαι και αδημονειν (PsT 43:20) [C]

ηρξατο θαμβεισθαι και αδημονειν (PsT 222:10) [C]

ηρξατο...θαμβεισθαι και αδημονειν (PsT 293:7) [C]

θαμβεισθαι] εκθαμβεισθαι TR UBS³ ℵ A B C D E L W Δ Θ Π Ψ Ω fam 13 579 892; λυπεισθαι fam 1; αθυμεισθαι 1241

ηρξατο a b k rell] ηρξαντο L

αδημονειν rell] ακηδεμονειν D

Lac.: 33 e

Luke 1:2

οι απ' αρχης αυτοπται και υπηρεται του λογου   (ZeT 329:23)
[C]

οι   TR UBS³ ℵ A B C D L W Δ Θ Π Ψ Ω fam 1 33 579 892 1241] omit fam 13

υπηρεται] υπηρεται γενομεναι   b e rell

Lac.: P^{75} a

Luke 1:15

ουτως ηλθον μετα του θεον σε εχειν ως ο Ιωαννης. το ετι πλησθησεται ου λεγεται γαρ το ετι περι του μηδ' ολως εσχηκοτος   (PsT 31:22)   [All]

και πνευματος αγιου πλησθησεται ετι εκ κοιλιας μητρος αυτου   (PsT 30:9)   [C]

εκ κοιλιας   TR UBS³ ℵ A B C D L Δ Θ Π Ψ Ω fam 1.13 33 579 892 1241 a b] εν κοιλια W e

ετι rell] omit b

Lac.: P^{75}

Luke 1:17

προεληλυθοτος ενωπιον Κυριου εν πνευματι και δυναμει Ηλιου   (ZeT 68:1-2)   [Ad]*

προελευσεται   (Did) TR UBS³ ℵ A D W Δ Θ Π Ψ fam 1.13 33 579 892 1241 a b e] προσελευσεται B C L

κυριου Δ] αυτου   rell

Lac.: P^{75} Ω

Luke 1:28

χαιρε κεχαριτωμενη, ο κυριος μετα σου   (GenT 161:24)
[C]

χαιρε κεχαριτωμενη   TR UBS³ ℵ A B C D L W Δ Θ Π Ψ fam 1.13 33 579 892 1241 a e] omit b

Lac.: P^{75} Ω

Luke 1:32-33

ελαβεν τον θρονον Δαυιδ του πατρος αυτου· ιν' εις τους
αιωνας βασιλευη, της βασιλειας αυτου ουκ εχουσης
τελος   (ZeT 109:4-6)   [Ad]

Luke 1:34

και ποθεν μοι τουτο, επει ανδρα ου γινωσκω   (ZeT 179:22)
[Ad]*

πως εσται μοι τουτο, επει ανδρα ου γιγνωσκω   (GenT 118:1-2)
[C]

μοι θ fam 1. 13 33 892 1241] omit   TR UBS^3 ℵ A B C D
L W Δ Π Ψ Ω 579 a e

γινωσκω   rell] μετεχω   579

πως...γιγνωσκω   rell] omit in toto b

Lac.: p^{75}

Luke 1:35

δυναμις ην υψιστου, ουτος εστιν, επεσκιασεν την Μαριαν
(PsT 5:14)   [Ad]

η Μαρια συνειληφεν του πνευματος του αγιου επελθοντος
επ' αυτην και της δυναμεως του υψιστου επισκιασης
αυτην   (PsT 29:21-22)   [Ad]

πνευματος αγιου επελθοντος εν τη Μαρια, και της του
υψιστου δυναμ[ε]ως επισκιασασης αυτη   (PsT 285:9-10)
[Ad]

αλλ' εκ πνευματος αγιου επελθοντος τη παρθενω τη πειραν
ανδρος ουκ εχουση και η η του υψιστου δυναμις επεσκιασεν
ως αγιον χραματισαι το γεννηθεν ανευ γαμου   (ZeT 41:2-5)
[All]

επελθοντος του αγιου πνευματος επι την αγιωτατην παρθενου
Μαριαμ, της του υψιστου δυναμεως επισκιασασης αυτην
(ZeT 166:20)   [Ad]

πνευμα αγιον επελευσεται επι σε και δυναμις υψιστου
επισκασει σοι   (JobT 215:29-31)   [C]

π[νε]υμα αγιον επελευσεται επι σε, και η δυναμις υψιστου
επισκιασει σοι, διο το γεννωμενον εν σοι αγιον
κληθησεται υιος θεου   (JobT 274:18-22)   [C]

Luke 1:35 (cont.)

πνευμα κυριου επελευσεται επι σε...και δυναμις υψιστου
(PsT 18:20-22) [C]

πνευμα αγιον επελευσεται επι σε, και δυναμις υψιστου
επισκιασει σοι (ZeT 68:4-5) [C]

διο e] διο και TR UBS³ ℵ (A) B C D L (W) Δ Θ Π Ψ Ω
fam 1. 13 33 579 892 1241 a b

διο rell] διοτι A W

εν σοι] εκ σου C Θ fam 1 33 a^vid e; omit rell

Lac.: p^{75}

Luke 1:38

ιδου η δουλη κυριου· γενοιτο μοι κατα το ρημα σου
(EcclT 236:20) [C]

ιδου...η δο[υλη] κυριου· γεν[οιτο μο]ι κατα το ρημα σου
(PsT 295:29) [C]

Text: TR UBS³ ℵ A B C D L W Δ Θ Π Ψ Ω fam 1. 13 33
579 892 1241 a b

Omit in toto: e

Lac.: p^{75}

Luke 1:44

και Ιωαννης εν γαστρι της μητρος σκιρτων και αγαλλιωμενος
(JobT 57:25-27) [All]

Luke 1:53

ειρηται γουν επι τω τοκετω της Μαριας ως ενεπλησθησαν
αγαθων οι προτερον λιμωττοντ[ες] (ZeT 258:10) [All]

πεινωντας ενεπλησεν αγαθων και [π]λουσιους εξαπεστειλεν
κενους (PsT 196:18-19) [C]

πλουσιας] πλουτουντας TR UBS³ ℵ A B C D L W Δ Θ Π Ψ Ω
fam 1. 13 33 579 892 1241

Lac.: p^{75}

Luke 1:68

ευλογητος κυριος ο θεος Ισραηλ, ος επεσκεψατο και εποιησεν λυτρωσιν (ZeT 220:14-15) [C]

κυριος TR UBS³ ℵ A B C D L Δ Θ Π Ψ Ω fam 1.13 33 579 892 1241 e] omit W a b

ος (qui) e] οτι rell

θεος] θεος του rell

επεσκεψατο και rell] omit e

Lac.: p^{75}

Luke 1:69

ηγειρεν κερας σωτηριας ημιν εξ οικου Δαυιδ (ZeT 105:29) [C]
ηγειρεν κερας σωτηριας ημιν εν οικω Δαυιδ (ZeT 220:15-16) [C]**

εν UBS³ ℵ B C D L W fam 1.13 33 579 892 1241] εν τω TR A Δ Θ Π Ψ Ω

Lac.: p^{75}

Luke 1:78-79

ανατολη εξ υψους επεφανεν τοις εν σκοτει και σκια θανατου (PsT 323:22) [Ad]*

ανατολη εξ υψους επιλαμψαι τοις εκ σκοτει και σκια θανατου καθημενοις (ZeT 57:17) [Ad]*

επεφανεν τοις εν σκοτει και σκια θανατου καθημενοις (ZeT 105:20) [Ad]*

επιφαναι (Did) TR UBS³ ℵ A B C L W Δ Θ Π Ψ Ω fam 1.13 33 579 892 1241 a b e] επιφαναι φως D

Lac.: p^{75}

Luke 2:11

ετεχθη υμιν σημερον σωτηρ...ος εστιν χριστος κυριος, εν πολει Δαυιδ (ZeT 22:3-4) [C]

Text and Apparatus /95

Luke 2:11 (cont.)

σημερον σωτηρ TR UBS³ ℵ A B D L W Δ Θ Π Ψ Ω fam 1.13
33 579 892 a b e] σωτηρ σημερον 1241

χριστος κυριος rell] κυριος χριστος W; Christus Iesus
Dominus (=χριστος Ιησους κυριος) e

Lac.: P⁷⁵ C

Luke 2:14

δοξα εν υψιστοις θεω και επι γης ειρηνη (PsT 20:8) [C]

Text: TR UBS³ ℵ A B D L W Δ Θ Π Ψ Ω fam 1.13 33 579 892
1241 a b e

Lac.: P⁷⁵ C

Luke 2:34

ιδου ουτος κειται εις πτωσιν και αν[αστα]σιν [πολ]λων
(ZeT 392:1-2) [C]

και TR UBS³ ℵ A B Γ W Δ Θ Π Ψ Ω fam 1.13 33 579
892 1241 a b e] και εις D

Lac.: P⁷⁵ C

Luke 2:35

και σου αυτης την ψυχην διελευσεται ρομφαια (PsT 41:26-27)
[C]

σου B L W Ψ 579 b] σου δε TR UBS³ ℵ A D Δ Θ Π Ω
fam 1.13 33 892 1241 a e

Lac.: P⁷⁵ C

Luke 2:36

Αννα η προφητις, ζησασα μετα ανδρος ετη επτα απο της
παρθενιας αυτης (ZeT 154:21-22) [C]

μετα ανδρος ετη επτα UBS³ ℵ B L W Δ Θ Ψ fam 13 33
579 892 1241 a (e)] ετη μετα ανδρος επτα TR Ω
fam 1 (b); ετη επτα μετα ανδρος A D Π

ανδρος rell] viro suo (=ανδρος αυτης) b e

Luke 2:36 (cont.)

ζησασα rell] χηρευσασα ℵ
Lac.: p⁷⁵ C

Luke 2:37

διαμεινασα επι πολυ χηρα εως ετων ογδοηκοντα τεσσαρων
(ZeT 154:23-24) [C]

εως UBS³ ℵ A B L Ψ 33 579] ως TR W Δ Θ Π Ω fam 1. 13
892 1241; omit D a b e

ογδοηκοντα rell] εβδομηκοντα ℵ
Lac.: p⁷⁵ C

Luke 3:8

ποιησατε γαρ καρπους αξιους της μετανοιας (ZeT 79:23)
[C]

καρπους αξιους TR UBS³ ℵ A C L Δ Θ Π Ψ Ω fam 1. 13
33 579 892 1241 a b] καρπον αξιον D W e; αξιους
καρπους Β

γαρ] ουν rell

γαρ (ουν) rell] ergo vobis (=ουν σεαυτοις) e
Lac.: p⁷⁵

Luke 4:5

και δειξας πασας τας βασιλειας της οικουμενης και τας
δοξας αυτων (ZeT 45:1-2) [All]*

της οικουμενης TR UBS³ ℵ A B L Δ Θ Π Ψ Ω fam 1. 13
33 579 892] του κοσμου D 1241; της γης W
Lac.: p⁷⁵ C

Luke 4:9

βαλε σεαυτον εντευθεν κατω (ZeT 44:25) [C]

κατω TR UBS³ ℵ A B D L W Δ Θ Π Ψ Ω fam 1. 13 33 579
892 1241 b e] omit a
Lac.: p⁷⁵ C

Text and Apparatus /97

Luke 4:13

απεστη ο διαβολος απ' αυτου...αχρι καιρου   (PsT 43:27)
[C]

απεστη αχρι καιρου   (PsT 44:14)   [Ad]*

απεστη ο διαβολος] ο διαβολος απεστη   TR UBS^3 ℵ A
B D L W Δ Θ Π Ψ Ω fam 1.13 33 579 892 1241 a b e

καιρου rell] χρονου D

Lac.: p^{75} C

Luke 4:17

και επεδοθη αυτω το βιβλιον του προφητου Ισαιου
(PsT 336:20)   [C]

το 579] omit   TR UBS^3 ℵ A B L W Δ Θ Π Ψ Ω fam 1.13
33 892 1241

βιβλιον του προφητου Ισαιου   a b rell] βιβλιον Ισαιου
του προφητου   TR A Δ Π Ω fam 1 1241 e; ο προφητης
Ησαιας D

Lac.: p^{75} C

Luke 4:18

του εληλυθοτος   κηρυξαι αιχμαλωτοις αφεσιν   (ZeT 11:25-26)
[Ad]

πνευμα κυριου επ' εμε, ου εινεκεν εχρισεν με, ευαγγελισασθαι
πτωχοις, κηρυξαι αιχμαλωτοις αφεσιν   (ZeT 38:2-4)   [C]

πνευμα κυριου επ' εμε, ου εινεκεν εχρισεν με, ευαγγελ[ισασ]θαι
πτωχοις απεστ[α]λκεν με, κηρυξαι αιχ[μα]λωτοις αφεσιν
και τυφλοις αναβλεψιν   (ZeT 393:11-13)   [C]

με$^{(2)}$ UBS^3 ℵ B (D) L W fam 13 33 579 892 a b e] με
ισασθαι τους συντετριμμενους την καρδιαν   TR A Δ
Θ Π Ψ Ω fam 1 (1241)

ευαγγελισασθαι rell] ευαγγελιζεσθαι   TR

απεσταλκεν με rell] απεσταλμαι   D

Lac.: p^{75} C

98/ Didymus and the Gospels

Luke 4:22

και παντες εθαυ[μαζον επ]ι το[ις λο]γοις της
χαρ[ιτο]ς τοις εκπορευομενοις εκ του στομ[ατ]ος
αυτου (PsT 336:20-21) [C]

παντες] παντες εμαρτυρουν αυτω, και TR UBS³ ℵ A B
D L W Δ Θ Π Ψ Ω fam 1. 13 33 579 892 1241 a b;
cum viderent, testimonium illis reddebat et (=ειδοντες
εμαρτυρεν αυτοις και)   e

στοματος rell] corde (=καρδιας) e

Lac.: P⁷⁵ C

Luke 4:29

και ηγαγον αυτον...ε[ως ο]φρυος του ορους, ου η πολις
αυτων ωκοδομητο (GenT 180:22-24) [C]

εως UBS³ ℵ A B C L W Δ Θ Π Ψ Ω fam 1 33 579 892 1241]
εως της TR D (fam 13)

αυτων ωκοδομητο TR A C Δ Θ Π Ψ Ω fam 1 1241 b]
ωκοδομητο αυτων a e rell

αυτον rell] omit ℵ

ορους] ορους εφ' rell

ωκοδομητο rell] οικοδομηται D

Lac.: P⁷⁵

Luke 5:10

απο του νυν ανθρωπους εση ζωγρων (GenT 61:16-17) [C]

απο του νυν ανθρωπους εση ζωγρων TR UBS³ ℵ A B C L
W Δ Θ Π Ψ Ω fam 1. 13 33 579 892 1241 a b] ποιησω γαρ
υμας αλιεις ανθρωπων D e

Lac.: P⁷⁵

Luke 5:22

γνους δε ο Ιησους τους διαλογισμους αυτων (ZeT 178:16-17)
[C]

Luke 5:22 (cont.)

γνους] επιγνους TR UBS³ ℵ A B C D L W Δ Θ Π Ψ Ω
fam 1. 13 33 579 892 1241

Lac.: p⁷⁵

Luke 6:21

εν τω βιω τουτω οι κλαιοντες [γ]ελασωσιν μετα ταυτα ως
και μακαρισμου τυγχανειν (EcclT 72:1-2) [All]

μακαριοι οι κλαιοντες νυν (EcclT 72:2-3) [C]

μακαριοι οι κλαιοντες νυν, οτι γελασονται (JobT 228:
13-15) [C]

μακαριοι οι κλαιοντες νυν, οτι γελασονται (JobT 228:
20-21) [C]

μακαριοι...οι κλαιοντες νυν, οτι γελασονται (PsT 280:11)
[C]
_____

γελασονται (W) e] γελασετε TR UBS³ ℵ A B L Δ Θ Π Ψ
Ω fam 1. 13 33 (579) 892 1241 a b

μακαριοι...γελασονται] omit in toto D

Lac.: p⁷⁵ C

Luke 6:35

χρηστος εστιν επι τους αχαριστους και πονηρους
(PsT 251:11-12) [C]
_____

αχαριστους και πονηρους TR UBS³ p⁷⁵ ℵ A B D L W
Δ Θ Π Ψ Ω fam 13 33 579 892 a (b) e] πονηρους και
αχαριστους fam 1 1241

αχαριστους] gratos (=χαριστους) b

Lac.: C

Luke 6:36

και τοις αλλοις οικτιρμων γινομενος κατα τον εν τ[οις
ο]υρανοις (PsT 290:20-21) [All]

100/ Didymus and the Gospels

Luke 6:38

ω μετρω μετρειτε αντιμετρηθησεται υμιν (ZeT 83:7) [C]

ω (or τω) θ fam 13 a b] ω (or τω) γαρ TR UBS³ p⁷⁵ᵛⁱᵈ ℵ
A B C D L W Δ Π Ψ Ω fam 1 33 892 1241 e

ω (γαρ) μετρω UBS³ p⁷⁵ᵛⁱᵈ ℵ B D L W (fam 1) 33 892 1241 e]
τω (γαρ) αυτω μετρω ω rell

αντιμετρηθησεται rell] μετρηθησεται B 33 b e

Lac.: 579

Luke 6:45

ο...α[γ]αθος ανθρωπος εκ του αγαθ[ου] θησαυρου [της] καρδιας
προφ[ερε]ι το αγαθο[ν] (JobT 339:13-14) [C]

ο αγα[θ]ος ανθρωπος εκ του αγαθου θησαυρου της καρδιας
προφερει το αγαθον (PsT 331:16-17) [C]

ο αγαθος TR UBS³ p⁷⁵ ℵ A B C D L W Δ θ Π Ψ Ω
fam 1. 13 33 579 892 1241 e] bonus enim (= ο γαρ
αγαθος) a b

καρδιας UBS³ p⁷⁵ᵛⁱᵈ ℵ B 579] καρδιας αυτου (αυτου
ante της καρδιας D) rell

προφερει rell] προσφερει L Ω 579

το rell] omit D W

αγαθον rell] bona (= αγαθα) e

Luke 6:46

τι με λεγετε κυριε, κυριε, και ου ποιειτε α λεγω;
(EcclT 208:6) [C]

τι με λεγετε κυριε, κυριε, και ου ποιειτε α λεγω;
(PsT 204:12) [C]

τι με λεγετε κυριε, κυριε, και ου ποιειτε α λεγω;
(PsT 229:3) [C]

τι με λεγετε κυριε, κυριε, και ου [ποι]ειτε α λεγω;
(PsT 281:30) [C]

λεγετε D] καλειτε TR UBS³ p⁷⁵ ℵ A B C L W Δ θ Π Ψ Ω
fam 1. 13 33 579 892 1241 a b e

Text and Apparatus /101

Luke 6:46 (cont.)

    α rell] ο P^{75} B e

    τι] τι δε rell

Luke 6:48

    ουτως ο αγιος Ιωβ επι την σωτηριον πετραν εχων τον
    θεμελιον (JobT 27:20-22) [All]

    ...επει τον θεμελιον επι την σωτηριον πετραν τεθεικεν
    (ZeT 31:11-12) [All]

Luke 7:28

    μειζων εν γενν[ητοις γυν]αικων Ιωαννου ουδ[εις εστιν]
    (JobT 293:17-19) [C]

        γυναικων UBS^3 P^{75} ℵ B L W Π fam 1 33 579 a b e]
        γυναικων προφητης TR A D Δ Θ Ψ Ω fam 13 (892) 1241

        Ιωαννου UBS^3 P^{75} ℵ B L W Ψ fam 1 579 892] omit 1241;
        Ιωαννου του βαπτιστου (- του Δ) rell

        ουδεις εστιν rell] ουδεις ante μειζων D; ουκ εστιν
        1241

        Lac.: C

Luke 7:41

    δυο χρεοφειλεται ησαν δανειστη ενι· ο εις ωφειλεν δηναρια
    πεντηκοντα, ο ετερος πεντακοσια (PsT 106:28-29) [Ad]*

        ετερος TR UBS^3 ℵ A B L W Δ Θ Π Ψ Ω fam 1. 13 33 579
        892 1241 b e] ετερος δηναρια D a

        Lac.: P^{75} C

Luke 8:14

    οτε το [σπ]ερμα αυτου τελεσφορειται... (EcclT 324:13)
    [All]

Luke 8:15

    ...υπο εκεινης της λεγομενης αγαθης γης καλης καρδιας
    ενθα πεσων ο Ιησου σπορος εκαρποφορησεν (EcclT 320:
    17-20) [All]*

Luke 8:15 (cont.)

γη εστιν η αγαθη και καλη, ητις δεχομενη το σπερμα
το Ιησου ο βαλλει, καρποφορει   (PsT 21:25-26) [All]*

του κυριου εστιν η γη εκεινη η καρδια η καλη και αγαθη
η δεξαμενη ον εβαλεν Ιησους σπορον... (PsT 67:26-27)
[All]*

    καλη και   TR UBS^3 p^{75} ℵ A B L W Δ Θ Π Ψ Ω fam 1. 13
    33 579 892 1241] omit   D a b e

    καρποφορουσιν   rell] τελεσφορουσιν   L; φερουσιν   fam 13

    Lac.: C

Luke 9:23

ει τις θελει οπισω μου ελθειν, απαρνησασθω εαυτον και
αρατω τον σταυρον αυτου, και ακολουθειτω μοι καθ'
ημεραν   (ZeT 185:10)   [Ad]*

    καθ' ημεραν   TR UBS^3 p^{75} ℵ A B L W Θ Π Ψ fam 1. 13
    33 892 1241] omit   C D Δ Ω 579 a b e

Luke 9:30-31

...υιους δυο εκλαβειν παρεστηκοτας τω κυριω πασης της
γης, τους οφθεντας εν δοξη μετα Ιησου εν τω ορει
Μωυσεα και Ηλιαν   (ZeT 77:14-16)   [All]

Luke 9:62

ουδεις επιβαλων την χειρα επ' αροτρον και στραφεις εις
τα οπισω... (PsT 207:31)   [C]

    επιβαλων   TR UBS^3 ℵ B C Δ Π Ψ Ω fam 1. 13 33 579 892
    1241] επιβαλλων   p^{75} A D L W Θ

    χειρα   UBS^3 p^{75} B fam 1 a b] χειρα αυτου   e rell

    και στραφεις εις το οπισω   892] και βλεπων εις το
    οπισω   rell

    ουδεις επιβαλων...και στραφεις (or βλεπων) εις   rell]
    ουδεις εις τα οπισω βλεπων και επιβαλων   D a (b) e

Text and Apparatus /103

Luke 10:13

ει ε[ν] Τυρω και [Σιδων]ι εγενηθησαν αι δυνα[μεις] αι
γενομεναι, παλαι αν [εν σακ]κω [κα]ι σποδω καθημε[νοι
με]τε[νο]ησαν (JobT 346:12-16) [C]

εγενηθησαν UBS³ P⁷⁵ ℵ B D L θ fam 13 33 579 892
1241 a b] εγενοντο TR A C W Δ Π Ψ Ω fam 1 e

ει rell] omit L

γενομεναι] γενομεναι εν υμιν rell

καθημενοι rell] omit e

Luke 10:19

και εξουσιαν δοθη ημιν πατειν επανω οφεων και σκορπιων
(EcclT 81:23) [All]*

ο λαβων εξουσιαν πατειν επανω οφεων και σκορπιων και
επι πασαν την δυναμιν [το]υ εχθρου (EcclT 323:19-20)
[Ad]*

εξουσιαν ειληφασιν πατειν επανω οφεων και σκορπιων και
επι πασαν την δυναμιν...του εχθρου (GenT 61:18-20)
[Ad]*

και τοις αγιο[ις] δοθηνα[ι εξ]ουσιαν πατειν [επα]νω
οφεω[ν] και σκορπιων κα[ι ε]πι πασαν [τη]ν δυναμιν
του [εχθρο]υ (JobT 63:13-16) [Ad]*

[δεδ]ωκεν [ε]ξ[ουσιαν του πατειν επα]νω οφεω[ν] κ[αι
σκορπιων και επι] πασαν τ[ην] δ[υναμιν...]
(JobT 130:17-20) [Ad]*

δ[εδωκ]εν εξο[υσ]ιαν πατειν επα[νω οφ]εω[ν] κ[αι] σκορπιων
και [επι] πασαν την δ[υν]αμιν του εχθρ[ου] (JobT 143:
31-144:2) [Ad]*

εξουσιαν τοις αλλοις δεδωκεν πατειν απανω οφεων και
σκορπιων (PsT 5:23-24) [Ad]*

οι λαβοντες εξουσια[ν πατειν] επανω οφεων και σκορπιων
(PsT 297:8-9) [Ad]*

ειληφοτες εξουσιαν πατειν επανω οφεων και σκορπιων και
επι πασαν την δυναμιν του εχθρου...ουδεν υμας αδικησει
(ZeT 157:10) [Ad]*

δοθεισης εξουσιας πατειν επανω οφεων και σκορπιων και
πασης της δυναμεως του Σατανα (ZeT 217:16-18) [Ad]*

Luke 10:19 (cont.)

δεδωκα...υμιν πατειν επανω οφεων και σκορπιων και επι
πασαν την δυναμιν του εχθρου, και ουδεν υμας ου μη
αδικησει (EcclT 319:18-19) [C]

ιδου δεδωκα μεν υμιν εξουσιαν πατειν επανω οφεων και
σκορπιων, και επι πασαν την δυναμιν του εχθρου
(GenT 96:28-30) [C]

ιδου δεδωκα υμιν πατειν επανω οφεων και σκορπιων και
επι πασαν την δυναμιν...του εχθρου (PsT 78:11-12)
[C]

εδωκα υμιν εξουσιαν πατειν...επι πασαν την δυναμιν του
εχθρου, και ουδεν υμας αδικησει (ZeT 205:3) [C]

Reconstruction: ιδου δεδωκα υμιν εξουσιαν πατειν επανω
οφεων και σκορπιων, και επι πασαν την δυναμιν του
εχθρου, και ουδεν υμας [ου μη] αδικησει

δεδωκα   UBS³ P⁷⁵ ℵ B C L W fam 1 579 892 1241 b e]
διδωμι   TR A D Δ Θ Π Ψ Ω fam 13 33

πατειν   W fam 1] του πατειν rell

ου μη   Did^pt rell] omit Did^pt ℵ D

αδικησει   ℵ A D L Θ fam 1 579] αδικηση rell

εξουσιαν] την εξουσιαν rell

οφεων και σκορπιων   rell] των οφεων και των σκορπιων D

την] omit 579

δυναμιν   rell] δυναμιν την B

Lac.: (a)

Luke 10:20

εν η χαραττονται τα ονοματα των αποστολων εν τοις ουρανοις
(EcclT 329:5-6) [All]*

εν ο[υρ]ανω ενγραφωσιν   (JobT 48:21) [All]

των δε μαθητων τα ονοματα ενγεγραπται εν τοις ουρανοις
(PsT 264:11) [Ad]*

μη χαιρετε οτι τα δαιμονια υμιν υποτασσεται αλλ' οτι
τα ονοματα υμων εγγεγραπται εν τοις ουρανοις
(GenT 246:15-17) [C]**

Text and Apparatus /105

Luke 10:20 (cont.)

χαιρετε οτι τα ονοματα υμων ενεγραφησαν εν τοις ουρανοις
(ZeT 149:4-5)   [C]

τα δαιμονια   D fam 1 (e)] τα πνευματα   TR UBS³ P⁷⁵ ℵ
A B C L W Δ Θ Π Ψ Ω fam 13   33 (579) 892 1241 a b

εγγεγραπται   UBS³ P⁷⁵ ℵ B L fam 1 33 579 1241]
γεγραπται   θ; εγραφη   rell

τοις ουρανοις   rell] τω ουρανω   D a b e

υμιν υποτασσεται   rell] υποτασσεται υμιν   L

αλλ'] αλλα χαιρετε δε μαλλον   TR; αλλα χαιρετε δε   rell

Luke 10:30

ουτω γουν και ο καταβας απο της Ιερουσαλημ τουτεστιν
εις Ιεριχω   (PsT 202:5-6)   [All]

Luke 11:13

ει ουν υμεις πονηροι υπαρχοντες οιδατε αγαθα δοματα
διδοναι... (EcclT 5-6)   [Ad]*

δωσει πνευμα αγιον   (PsT 109:16)   [C]

υπαρχοντες   TR UBS³ P⁷⁵ A B C L W Δ Θ Ψ Ω fam 1.13
33 579 891 1241] οντες   ℵ D Π

πνευμα αγιον   rell] αγαθον δομα   D b; πνευμα αγαθον   L;
δοματα αγαθα   θ

Lac.: a e

Luke 11:15

εν βεεζεβουλ τω αρχοντι των δαιμονιων εκβαλλει τα δαιμονια
(PsT 145:28)   [C]

εν βεεζεβουλ τω αρχοντι των δαιμονιων εκβαλλει τα δαιμονια
(PsT 147:29)   [C]

εν βεεζεβουλ τω αρχοντι των δαιμονιων εκβαλλει τα δαιμονια
(PsT 369:32-34)   [C]

εν βεεζεβουλ τω αρχοντι των [...]   (PsT 304:19)   [C]

Luke 11:15 (cont.)

βεεζεβουλ ℵ B (579)] βεελζεβουλ TR UBS³ P⁷⁵ A C
D (L) W Δ Θ Π Ψ Ω fam 1. 13 33 892 1241 b

τω rell] omit TR D Δ Ω fam 1

τα rell] omit 579

Lac.: a e

Luke 11:33

ουδεις...αψας λυχνον εις κρυπτην τιθησιν... (ZeT 65:
12-13) [Ad]*

εις κρυπην UBS³ P⁷⁵ ℵ A B C D L W Δ Θ Π fam 13 33 892
1241 (a b e)] εις κρυπτον TR Ψ Ω fam 1 (a b e); omit 579

Luke 11:50

ζη[τηθησεται π]αν αιμα δικαιον εκκεχυμενον επι της γης
απο τ[ης γενεας] ταυ[της] (GenT 181:17-19) [Ad]*

παν αιμα δικαιον εκκεχυμενον επι της γης εκδικηθησεται
απο της γενεας ταυτης (PsT 70:14-15) [Ad]*

απο της γενεας TR UBS³ P⁷⁵ ℵ A B C L W Δ Θ Π Ψ Ω
fam 1. 13 33 579 892 1241] εως της γενεας D a b;
omit e

Luke 12:7

υμων δε αι τριχες της κεφαλης ηριθμηνται (JobT 120:27-28)
[Ad]*

ηριθμηνται TR UBS³ P⁷⁵ ℵ A B L W Δ Π Ψ Ω fam 1. 13
33 892 1241] ηριθμημενας εισιν D Θ 579

Lac.: C

Luke 12:8

πα[ς ος α]ν ομολογηση εν εμοι εμπροσθεν των ανθρωπων...
(GenT 176:10-11) [C]

πας...ος εαν ομολογηση εν εμοι ενπροσθεν των ανθρωπων
(PsT 210:34-35) [C]

Text and Apparatus /107

Luke 12:8 (cont.)

εαν Did^pt θ Ψ 579] αν Did^pt TR UBS³ p⁷⁵ ℵ A B
D L W Δ Π Ω fam 1. 13 33 892 1241

ομολογηση TR UBS³ p⁷⁵ ℵ L W θ] ομολογησει rell

Lac.: C

Luke 12:18

καθελω μου τας αποθηκας και μειζονας οικοδομησω
(JobT 101:17-19) [C]

καθελω μο[υ]τας αποθη[κ]α[ς και] μειζονας ο[ικο]δομησω
(JobT 396:14-16) [C]

μου TR UBS³ p⁷⁵ ℵ A B D L Δ θ Π Ψ Ω fam 1. 13 33 579
   892 1241 b e] omit W a

μειζονας οικοδομησω rell] ποιησω αυτας μειζονας D e;
   maiora faciam (=μειζονας ποιησω) b

οικοδομησω rell] ανοικοδομησω

Lac.: C

Luke 12:19

ψυχη, εχεις αγαθα πολλα, φαγε, π[ι]ε (EcclT 37:6) [Ad]*

ψυχη, εχεις αγαθα εις ετη πολλα, φαγε και πιε (EcclT 278:11)
   [Ad]*

[και ερω] τη ψυχη· ψυ[χη,] εχεις αγα[θα πολ]λα, φαγε,
   πιε, [ευφ]ραινου   (JobT 396:15-17) [Ad]*

ψυχη⁽²⁾ TR UBS³ p⁷⁵ ℵ A B D L Δ θ Π Ψ Ω fam 1. 13 33
   579 892 1241] συ ψυχη W; omit a b e

φαγε, πιε rell] omit D a b e

αγαθα πολλα] πολλα αγαθα rell

Lac.: C

Luke 12:20

αφρων, ταυτη τη νυκτι απαιτουσιν την [ψυχ]ην σου απο σου.
   α δε ητοιμασας, τινι εσται (EcclT 168:22-23) [C]

Luke 12:20

αφρων, ταυτη τη νυκτι απαιτουσιν την ψυχην σου απο σου.
α δε ητοιμασας, τινι εσται (EcclT 196:19-20) [C]

αφρων, ταυτη τη νυκτι την ψυχην σου αιρουσιν απο σου
(JobT 101:19-21) [C]

αφρων, ταυτη τη νυκτι αιρουσιν την ψυχην απο σου. α δε
ητοιμασας τινι εσται (JobT 108:12-14) [C]

αφρων, ταυτη τη νυκτι αφαιρουσιν την ψυχην σ[ου] απο
σου (JobT 375:30-376:1) [C]

ο κυριος αυτω λεγε[ι· α]φρων, ταυτη [τη] νυκτι απαιτ[ουσ]ιν
την ψυχ[ην] σου απο σου. α δε ητοιμασας, τ[ινι] εσται
(JobT 396:17-21) [Ad]*

αφρων, [ταυ]τη τη νυκτι την ψυχην σου απαιτουσ[ι]ν απο
σου (PsT 238:34) [C]

απαιτουσιν Did^{pt} TR UBS^3 ℵ A D W Δ Θ Π Ψ Ω fam 1. 13
892 1241, (reposcunt) a^{vid}, (repetunt) b] αφαιρουσιν
Did^{pt} (auferetur e); αιρουσιν Did^{pt}; αιτουσιν P^{75}
B L 33 579

(απαιτουσιν) την ψυχην οσυ Did^{pt} D 579] την ψυχην σου
(απαιτουσιν) Did^{pt} rell

δε$^{(2)}$ rell] ουν D a e

τινι rell] τινος D a b e

Lac.: C

Luke 12:49

του φωτος του ουρανιου...ου ηλθεν Ιησους επι γης βαλειν
θελων ηδη αυτο εξαφθηναι (GenT 47:1-2) [All]*

πυρ ηλθον βαλειν επι την γην, ειθε ηδη ανηφθη (ZeT 207:2)
[Ad]*

πυρ ηλθον βαλειν επι την γην και ειθε ηδη ανηφθη
(ZeT 358:24-25) [Ad]*

πυρ ηλ[θον β]αλειν επι την γην και ειθε ηδη αν[ηφθ]η
(ZeT 371:4-5) [Ad]*

πυρ [ηλθ]ον βαλειν επι ην γην και [τι θε]λω, ει ηδη
ανηφθη (JobT 346:18-20) [C]

Luke 12:49 (cont.)

 επι UBS³ P⁷⁵ ℵ A B L W θ Π Ψ fam 1.13 33 579 892 1241]
 εις TR D Δ Ω

Lac.: C a

Luke 13:11

 αυτικα γουν εκεινην την εχουσαν πνευμα ασθενειας οκτωκαιδεκα
 ετεσιν λεγει οτι συνκυψασα ην και μη ανανευουσα εις το
 παντελες (PsT 264:6-7) [All]

Luke 13:27

 ουκ οιδα υμας ποθεν εστε· αποχωρειτε εργαται ανομιας
 (GenT 194:17-18) [Ad]*

  ουκ οιδα (υμας) ποθεν εστε Did TR UBS³ P⁷⁵ ℵ A B L W
  Δ θ Π Ψ Ω fam 1.13 33 579 892 1241 a b] ουδεποτε
  ειδον υμας D e

  υμας rell] omit P⁷⁵ B L 1241 b

 Lac.: C

Luke 13:32

 πορευ[θεν]τες ειπατε τη αλωπεκι ταυτη (EcclT 96:1-2)
 [C]

  ταυτη TR UBS³ P⁷⁵ ℵ A B D L W Δ θ Π Ψ Ω fam 1.13
  33 579 892 1241 a e] illi (= εκεινη) b

 Lac.: C

Luke 14:26

 ει τι[ς θε]λει οπισω μου ελθειν και μισει τον πατερα
 εαυτου (EcclT 81:14) [Ad]*

 ει τις θελει οπισω μου ελθειν και ου μισει τον πατερα
 αυτου και τους αδελφους και τας αδελφας ετι δε και
 την γυναικα και τεκνα, ου δυναται ειναι μου μαθητης
 (GenT 209:13-16) [Ad]*

 στραφεις...ο Ιησους ειπεν τοις οχλοις· ει τις θελει
 οπισω μου ελθειν, εαν μη τις μισηση τον πατερα αυτου
 και την μητερα αυτου και την γυναικα και τους αδελφους
 και τα τεκνα, ου δυναται μου ειναι μαθητης (PsT 112:
 14-16) [Ad]*

110/ Didymus and the Gospels

Luke 14:26 (cont.)

ετι δε και την εαυτου ψυχην μισησει (PsT 112:24) [Ad]*

πατερα εαυτου Did^pt TR UBS³ P^75 B L 892 (a b)] πατερα αυτου Did^pt ℵ A D W Δ Θ Π Ψ Ω fam 1.13 33 1241 (a b); πατερα 579 e

μητερα αυτου D] μητερα rell

ετι δε και rell] ετι τε και UBS³ B L Δ 33; ετι και P^75 a b e

εαυτου ψυχην rell] ψυχην εαυτου UBS³ P^75 ℵ B 579 (1241) a b e

ειναι μου μαθητης Did^pt UBS³ ℵ B L 33 579 892 1241] μου ειναι μαθητης Did^pt P^75 Π Ψ fam 13; μαθητης μου ειναι e; μου μαθητης ειναι rell

την μητερα rell] μητερα 579

τα τεκνα rell] τεκνα 579

Lac.: C

Luke 14:28

τις εξ υμων ος θελει πυργον οικοδομησαι ο[υ καθ]ι[σα]ς πρωτον ψηφισει ει εχει τα προς απαρτισμον (ZeT 388:7-9) [Ad]*

τα προς TR Θ Π fam 1] εις UBS³ P^75 B D L W Ψ 579 1241; τα εις ℵ A Δ Ω fam 13 33 892

ει rell] omit L

Lac.: C

Luke 14:29

μ[η ποτε θε]ντος αυτου θεμελιον και μη ισχυσαντος εκτε[λε]σαι, αρξωνται οι θεωρουντες εμπαιζειν αυτω (ZeT 388:9-11) [Ad]*

και μη ισχυσαντες (or ισχυοντες) εκτελεσαι TR UBS³ P^75 ℵ A B L W Δ Θ Π Ψ Ω fam 1.13 33 579 892 1241 a b] μη ισχυση οικοδομησαι και D e

ισχυσαντος L Δ fam 1] ισχυοντος rell

Luke 14:29 (cont.)

αρξωνται...λεγοντες (v. 30) (a b) rell] μελλουσιν λεγειν D e

θεωρουντες rell] θεωρουντες αυτον θ 892

αυτω εμπαιζειν rell] εμπαιζειν αυτω TR Δ Ω fam 13 33;
εμπαιζειν Ψ 892; omit D a b e

ισχυσαντος (or ισχυοντος) rell] ισχυοντος αυτου θ

Lac.: C

Luke 14:30

λε[γο]ντες, ουτος ο ανθρωπος ηρξατο οικοδομειν, και
ουκ ισχυσεν εκτελεσαι (ZeT 388:11-13) [Ad]*

οικοδομειν TR UBS³ P⁷⁵ ℵ A B D L W Δ Θ Π Ψ Ω fam 1.13
33 892 1241] οικοδομησαι 579

Lac.: C

Luke 14:34

εαν το αλας μωρανθη, εν τινι αρτυθησεται (EcclT 305:13)
[C]

αλας TR UBS³ A B L Δ Θ Π Ψ Ω fam 1.13 33 579 892
1241] αλα P⁷⁵ ℵ D W

αρτυθησεται rell] αλισθησεται fam 1 33; αρτυσεται θ

εαν] εαν δε TR P⁷⁵ A W Δ Π Ω fam 1 892 b e; εαν δε και a
rell; ουν fam 13

τινι rell] τινι αυτου θ

Lac.: C

Luke 15:8

η εκ των δεκα δρ[α]χμ[ων] μιαν απολεσασα γυνη εξεβαλεν
τα κοπρια εκ της οικι[ας και] η[υ]ρεν [τ]ο κρυβεν
νομισμα (ZeT 404:9-10) [All]

Luke 15:17

εις εαυτον δε ελθων (PsT 226:15) [C]

Luke 15:17 (cont.)

εαυτον TR UBS³ p⁷⁵ ℵ A B D W Δ Θ Π Ψ Ω fam 1. 13 33 579 892 1241 a b e] αυτον L

Lac.: C

Luke 15:22

εξενεγκατ[ε αυ]τω την πρωτην στολην (JobT 262:18) [Ad]*

εξενεγκατε TR UBS³ ℵ B D L W Δ Θ Π Ψ Ω fam 1. 13 33 892 a b e] ενεγκατε p⁷⁵ 579 1241; εξεναγκαντες A την πρωτην στολην 579] την στολην την πρωτην TR p⁷⁵ Δ Ω fam 1. 13 33 892 1241 (a b e); στολην την πρωτην (a b e) rell

Lac.: C

Luke 16:8

υιοι του αιωνος το[υ]του φρονιμωτεροι εισιν των υιων του φωτος εν τη γενεα τη εαυτων (GenT 163:24-26) [Ad]*

φρονιμω[τεροι] ειναι οι υιοι του αιωνος τ[ουτου] εν τη εαυτων γενεα (JobT 76:27-29) [Ad]*

φρονιμω[τε]ρους τους υιους του αιωνος τουτου εν τη γενεα [αυ]των υπερ τους υιους του φωτος (ZeT 385: 20-22) [Ad]*

φρονιμωτεροι οι υιοι Did^pt ℵ] οι υιοι...φρονιμωτεροι Did^pt TR UBS³ p⁷⁵ A B D L W Δ Θ Π Ψ Ω fam 1. 13 33 (579) 892 (1241) a b e

οι rell] omit 579 1241

γενεαν την εαυτων (Did) rell] γενεαν ταυτην εαυτων ℵ ; gente hac (a), hac generatione (b) (= γενεαν ταυτην) a b

Lac.: C

Luke 16:15

υμεις...εστε [οι δικαιουντες] εαυτους ενπροσθεν των ανθρωπων, ο δε θεος γιγνωσκει τας καρδιας υμων [οτι το εν ανθρωποι]ς υψηλον βδελυγμα παρα θεω εστιν (EcclT 297:7-9) [C]

Text and Apparatus /113

Luke 16:15 (cont.)

υμεις εστε οι δικαιουντες εαυτους εμπροσθεν των ανθρωπων,
ο δε θεος γινωσκει τας καρδιας υμων, οτι το εν ανθρωποις
υψηλον, βδελυγμα παρα τω θεω εστιν   (ZeT 178:11-14) [C]**

παρα τω θεω   579] ενωπιον του θεου   TR UBS^3 p^{75} ℵ A
  (B) D L W Δ Θ Π Ψ Ω fam 1.13 33 892 1241

εστιν TR Ω fam 13 579 (892) (a) (b) (e)] omit rell

εμπροσθεν] ενωπιον rell

ανθρωποις rell] ανθρωπω B

υψηλον rell] ισχυρον 579

του θεου (τω θεω) rell] κυριου B

Lac.: C

Luke 16:19-23

αλλα και Λαζαρος κ[αι ο πλου]σιος--μεν κακοπαθων [ο δε
ζων με]τα πλειστης ευπαθειας--το των απορρητων θεου
κριμ[ατων ακρι]βες εκφερουσιν (JobT 68:19-23) [All]

τουτου παραδειγμα Λαζαρος ενταυθα μεν κλαιων δια της
κακοπαθειας, εν δε τοις κολποις Αβρααμ αναπαυομενος,
ο δε πλουσιος γελων δι' ηδονης εκαυσεν εν κολασει
βασανιζομενος πικρως επι τω ειρημενω γελωτι
(JobT 228:28-32) [All]

Luke 16:19

ο συν Λαζαρω μνημονευομενος ευφραινομενος [καθ' η]μεραν
λαμπρως βυσσον και πορφυραν ενδιδυσκαμενος (EcclT 106:
24-25) [Ad]*

ο συν τω Λαζαρω πλουσιος καθ' [η]μεραν ευφραινομενος
λαμπ[ρω]ς βυσσον τε κα[ι] πορφυραν εν[δ]ιδυσκομενος
(JobT 108:4-7) [Ad]*

πλουσιος TR UBS^3 ℵ A B D L W Δ Θ Π Ψ Ω fam 1.13 33
  579 892 1241 a b (e)] πλουσιος ονοματι Νευης p^{75}

και βρυσσον (Did) rell] omit b

Lac.: C

Luke 16:20

(Λαζαρος) προς τω πυλωνι αυτου εβεβλητο   (JobT 178:15-16) [Ad]

Luke 16:22

ο με[ν Λαζα]ρος εις κολ[πον Αβ]ραμ α[νατε]ιλεν, ο δε
π[λουσιο]ς τη κολ[ασ]ει παραδεδο[ται] (JobT 175:
10-11) [All]*

ερεις δε και περι του Λαζαρου του ειλκωμενου εχοντος
σωμα οτι, οτε μετηνεχθη εντευθεν υπο των αγ[γελ]ων...
εις κολπους γο[υν του] Απρααμ λοιπον διετριβεν
(PsT 292:5-6) [All]

απεθανεν δε ο πτωχος και απηνεχθη υπο των αγγελων εις
κολπους Αβρααμ (PsT 238:32-33) [Ad]*

εγ[ενε]το δε ε[ν] τω αποθανειν το[ν πτ]ωχον, [κ]αι
απενεχθηνα[ι υπ]ο των αγγελων εις κολπο[ν Α]βρααμ
(JobT 376:3-6) [Ad]*

εν τω αποθανειν p^{75}] αποθανειν TR UBS^3 ℵ A B D L
W Δ Θ Π Ψ Ω fam 1. 13 33 579 892 1241

Αβρααμ rell] του Αβρααμ TR W fam 13

εγενετο δε a b e rell] και εγενετο 579; εγενετο fam 13

αποθανειν rell] αποθανειν Λαζαρον b

υπο των αγγελων...Αβρααμ rell] Αβρααμ υπο των αγγελων D

Lac.: C

Luke 16:22-23

αυτικα γουν ο πλουσιος και ο Λαζαρος αμφοτεροι γεγονασιν
εκ του βιου, εξω του σωματος γεγενηται. και ο μεν
πλουσιος, ατε δη μολιβδου πεπληρωμενος, κατω ηνεχθη
εις τον τοπον της κολασεως, ο δε Λαζαρος ανω εχωρησεν,
ενθα ο Αβρααμ (EcclT 92:1-5) [All]

Luke 16:23

ουτω γουν και εν τοις κολποις Απρααμ ανεπαυετο την
αυτην... (PsT 217:5-6) [All]*

τοις κολποις TR UBS^3 p^{75} ℵ A B L W Δ Θ Π Ψ Ω fam 1. 13
33 579 892 1241] τω κολπω D a b e

αναπαυομενον (ανεπαυετο) (Did) D Θ b e] omit rell

Lac.: C

Text and Apparatus /115

Luke 16:24-28

και γαρ ο πλουσιος ο μετα Λαζαρου ονομαζομενος [λογιζο]μενος ελεγεν α ειρηκεν. ου λογισαμενος οτι χρηζει καταψυχαδος τινος [δια την αληδο]να τη γλωττη αυτου παρεκαλει περι ταυτα; ου λογιζομενος οτι εχει πεντε [αδελφους] εν τω βιω τα αυτα αυτω πραττοντας; και λογιζομενος ουκ ειπεν· Λαζαρον [πεμψον εις αυτου]ς; (EcclT 280: 5-9) [All]

Luke 16:25

απελαβες τα αγαθα σου (EcclT 85:27) [C]

απελα[βες τα] αγαθα σου εν τη ζω[η] σου (EcclT 106:26-27) [C]

απελαβες τα αγαθα σου [εν] τη ζωη σου, και Λαζαρος ομιοως τα κακα (GenT 98:2-3) [C]

απελαβες τα αγαθα σου (PsT 60:26-27) [C]

απελαβες UBS³ P⁷⁵ ℵ B D L θ fam 13 579 a e] απελαβες σu TR (A) W Δ Π Ψ Ω fam 1 33 892 1241 b

σου⁽¹⁾ rell] omit a b e

Lac: C

Luke 16:26

χασμα μεταξυ μεγα εστηρικται (GenT 20:24-25) [Ad]

Luke 17:5

προσθες ημιν πιστιν (GenT 162:13) [C]

Text: TR UBS³ (P⁷⁵) ℵ A B D L W Δ θ Π Ψ Ω fam 1. 13 33 579 892 1241 a b e

Lac.: C

Luke 17:10

οταν παντα ποιησητε, ειπατε· δουλοι αχρειοι εσμεν, ο οφειλο[μεν ποιησαι, πεποι]ηκαμ[ε]ν (JobT 341:34-342:1) [Ad]*

Luke 17:10 (cont.)

παντα, α ωφειλαμεν ποιησαι, πεποιηκαμεν   (PsT 96:21)
[Ad]*

παντα   TR UBS³ p⁷⁵ A B L W Δ Θ Π Ψ Ω fam 1. 13 33 892
1241] omit   579 a b e

δουλοι   A W Π fam 1 a b e] οτι δουλοι ℵ D rell

ο rell] οτι ο   TR W Δ Θ Π Ω fam 13 33

δουλοι αχρειοι rell]   αχρειοι δουλοι   892 1241

οταν (παντα) ποιησατε   rell] ποιησατε οσα λεγω   D;
omit   ℵ

παντα (rell)] παντα ταυτα   A

αχρειοι εσμεν   rell] εσμεν αχρειοι   D

ο οφειλομεν   rell] omit   a

Lac.: C

Luke 17:21

η βασιλεια των ουρανων εντος υμων εστιν   (JobT 141:22-23) [Ad]

η βασιλεια του θεου εντος υμων εστιν   (JobT 370:27-28)   [C]

Text: TR UBS³ p⁷⁵ ℵ A B D L W Δ Θ Π Ψ Ω fam 1. 13
33 579 892 1241 a b e

Lac.: C

Luke 18:2

τινα κριτη[ν] μηδε τον θεον φοβουμενον μηδε ανθρωπ[ο]ν
εντρεπομ[ενο]ν (EcclT 314:9)   [Ad]*

ανθρωπον   TR UBS³ p⁷⁵ ℵ A B D L Δ Θ Π Ψ Ω fam 1. 13
33 579 892 1241 a b e] ανθρωπους   W

Lac.: C

Luke 18:3, 5

εκδικ[η]σω αυτην απο του αντιδ[ικου αυ]της, οπως μη ερχηται
εις το παντελες και επωπιαζη με   (EcclT 314:11-12)   [All]

Text and Apparatus /117

Luke 18:6

[ακουσα]τε τι ο κριτης τη[ς] αδικιας λεγει   (EcclT 314:13) [C]

ακουσατε   TR UBS³ p⁷⁵ A B D L W Δ Θ Π Ψ Ω fam 1.13 33 579 892 1241 a b e] omit ℵ

Lac.: C

Luke 18:7

των βοωντων προς αυτον ημ[ε]ρας και νυκτος   (EcclT 314: 14-15) [C]

προς αυτον   TR A W Δ Θ Π Ω fam 1.13 33] αυτω   UBS³ p⁷⁵ ℵ B L Ψ 579 892 1241 e; αυτων   D; omit   a b

ημερας και νυκτος   rell] νυκτος και ημερας   D 1241

των   rell] omit   D

Lac.: C

Luke 18:8

αρα ελθων ο υιος του ανθρωπου ευρησει την [π]ιστιν επι τ[ης γ]ης   (GenT 187:23-24)   [C]

ευρησει   TR UBS³ p⁷⁵ ℵ A B D L W Δ Θ Π Ψ Ω fam 1.13 33 579 892 1241 b] putas inveniet (inveniet putas   a) (= νομιζεις ευρησει?)   a b

αρα ελθων ο υιος του ανθρωπου] αρα ο υιος του ανθρωπου ελθων   D a b e; ο υιος του ανθρωπου ελθων αρα   rell

την   rell] omit   D

Lac.: C

Luke 18:14

κατεβη ουτος δεδικ[αιω]μ[ενος] παρ' εκεινον   (JobT 284:1-2) [C]

παρ' εκεινον   UBS³ ℵ B L fam 1 33 579] η εκεινος   TR W Θ; η γαρ εκεινος   A Δ Π Ψ Ω fam 13 892 1241; μαλλον γαρ εκεινον τον Φαρισαιον   D a b e

δεδικαιομενος] δεδικαιομενος εις τον οικον αυτου   rell

Lac.: p⁷⁵ C

118/ Didymus and the Gospels

Luke 19:10

ο σωτηρ γουν εληλυθεν ζητησαι και σωσαι το απολωλος
(PsT 267:18) [Ad]*

εληλυθεν ζητησαι και σωσαι το α[πολω]λος (PsT 286:25-26)
[Ad]*

εληλυθοτος ζητησαι και σωσαι το απολωλος (ZeT 96:25)
[Ad]*

...ζητησαι και σωσαι το απολωλος (ZeT 38:21) [C]

ηλθεν ο υιος του ανθρωπ[ο]υ ζητησαι και σωσαι το απολωλος
(ZeT 220:9) [C]

ηλθεν] ηλθεν γαρ   TR UBS³ ℵ A B D L W Δ Θ Π Ψ Ω fam 1.13
33 579 892 1241 a b e

απολωλος   rell] αποαπολωλος ℵ

Lac.: C

Luke 19:12

ανθρωπος τις ευγενης επορευθη εις χωραν μακραν, λαβειν
εαυτω βασιλειαν (EcclT 47:2) [C]

τις   TR UBS³ ℵ A B D L Δ Θ Π Ψ Ω fam 1.13 33 579
892 1241 a] τις ην W b e

επορευθη   rell] επορευετο D 579

εαυτω   rell] omit D a b e

ευγενης   rell] ευγενης και W

Lac.: P⁷⁵ C

Luke 19:17, 19

η παραβολη η εν τοις ευαγγελιοις· [γινου ε]πανω δεκα
πολεων η πεντε (JobT 71:8-9) [All]

Luke 19:21

οτι ανθρωπος αυστηρος ει αιρων ο ουκ εθηκας, θεριζων
ο ουκ εσπειρας (PsT 251:22-23) [Ad]*

Text and Apparatus /119

Luke 19:21 (cont.)

οτι ανθρωπος   TR UBS³ ℵ A B L W Δ Θ Π Ψ Ω fam 1.13
33 579 892 1241 a b] ανθρωπος γαρ   D e

αυστηρος ει   rell] ει αυστηρος   D W e

Lac.: P⁷⁵ C

Luke 19:23

παντως ελαμβανον το εμον, ει ης αυτο δεδωκως επι τραπεζης
ινα πολυπλασιασθη   (PsT 251:24-25)   [All]

Luke 19:42

ει εγνως και συ τα προς ειρηνην. νυν δε εκρυβη απο
οφθαλμων σου   (ZeT 326:4-5)   [Ad]*

και συ   TR UBS³ ℵ A B D L W Δ Θ Π Ψ Ω fam 1.13 33 579
892 1241] συ   a e

ειρηνην UBS³ ℵ B L Θ Ψ 579]   ειρηνην σοι   D fam 13 e ;
ειρηνην σου   rell

νυν δε   rell] omit   a e

σου   rell] omit   ℵ a

νυν δε...σου   rell] omit in toto   A

οφθαλμων   rell] των οφθαλμων   Ω

Lac.: P⁷⁵ C b

Luke 19:43

επελευσομε[νο]ι γαρ εχθροι σου συνεξουσιν σε, χαρακα σοι
περιβαλοντες   (ZeT 326:5)   [Ad]*

και συνεξουσιν σε   (Did) TR UBS³ A B C D L Δ Θ Π Ψ Ω
fam 1.13 33 579 892 1241 a] και συνεξουσιν   ℵ ; omit   W e

σοι   rell] omit   D a e

περιβαλουσιν   (Did) TR A B W Δ Π Ω fam 1.13 892]
βαλουσιν (επι σε)   D; παρεμβαλουσιν   rell

Lac.: P⁷⁵ b

120/ Didymus and the Gospels

Luke 20:24

τινος εχει εικονα και επιγραφην (ZeT 309:11) [C]

    επιγραφην TR UBS³ ℵ A B C L W Δ Θ Π Ψ Ω fam 1.13 33 579 892 1241] την επιγραφην D

    Lac.: p^{75} b

Luke 20:25

τοινυν αποδοτε τα καισαρος καισαρι και τα του θεου τω θεω (ZeT 309:13) [C]

    τοινυν αποδοτε UBS³ ℵ B L fam 13 579 892 1241]
    αποδοτε τοινυν TR A C W Δ Θ Π Ψ Ω fam 1 33;
    αποδοτε D a e

    καισαρι rell] τω καισαρι C D L fam 13 1241

    καισαρος rell] του καισαρος D

    Lac.: p^{75} b

Luke 20:35

οι μετα αναστασιν εις αγγελοι γινομενοι, ουκετι γαμουντες η γαμιζομενοι (ZeT 53:23) [All]*

ουτε γαμ[ου]σι[ν ουτε γαμιζονται] (EcclT 66:12-13) [C]

    γαμιζονται UBS³ ℵ D L Δ fam 1 33 579 892] γαμισκονται
    B 1241; εκγαμισκονται TR Π Ψ Ω; εκγαμιζονται A W
    Θ fam 13

    Lac.: p^{75} C b

Luke 20:36

...ουκετι αποθανεν δυναμενοι (ZeT 53:24) [All]*

[...ουδε γαρ αποθαν]ειν ετι δυνανται (EcclT 66:13) [C]

    ετι TR UBS³ ℵ A B D L W Δ Θ Π Ψ Ω fam 13 33 579 892 1241 a] omit fam 1 e

    δυνανται rell] μελλουσιν D W Θ a e

    ουδε rell] ου 892

    Lac.: p^{75} C b

Luke 21:20

οταν γαρ...ιδητε την Ιερουσαλημ κυκλουμενην υπο στρατοπεδων, γιγνωσκετε οτι ηγγισεν η ερημωσις αυτης   (ZeT 326:8)
[Ad]*

    την   TR A L Δ Θ Π Ψ Ω fam 1. 13 33 892 1241] omit   UBS³
            א B D W 579

    (την) Ιερουσαλημ] post κυκλουμενην D 579; post
    στρατοπεδων rell

    γινωσκετε   W fam 1] γνωσεσθε   D e; γνωτε   rell

    ηγγισεν   A fam 1] ηγγικεν   rell

    Lac.: P^{75} C b

Luke 21:26

...εν ημερα μια συμβησεται ψυχη και παγος αποψυχοντων τω [ν ανθρωπ]ων προσδοκια των ελευσομενων σκυθρωπω[ν τε και] επιπονων, ω[ς το Ευ]αγγελιον διαγορευει
(ZeT 377:1)   [All]

Luke 22:15

επιθυμια επεθυμησα τουτο το πασχα φαγειν μεθ' υμων
(PsT 9:12)   [C]

    Text: TR UBS³ P^{75} א A B C D L W Δ Θ Π Ψ Ω fam 1. 13
          33 579 892 1241 a b e

Luke 22:30

επι της τραπεζης μου εν τη βασιλεια των ουρανων
(JobT 87:18)   [Ad]*

    εν τη βασιλεια των ουρανων] εν τη βασιλεια μου   TR UBS³
    P^{75} א A B L W Δ Θ Π Ψ fam 1. 13 33 579 892 1241 a b;
    εν τη βασιλεια   D e; omit   Ω

    Lac.:   C

Luke 22:31

ιδου ο σατανας εξητησατο ημας   (PsT 43:29)   [Ad]*

Luke 22:31 (cont.)

ιδου εξητησατο υμας ο σ[ατα]νας του σινιασαι ως τον σιτον
(JobT 7:24-26) [C]

ιδου εξητησατο υμ[ας] ο σατανας του σινιασαι ως τον σιτον
(JobT 90:17-19) [C]

ιδου εξητησατο υμας ο σατανας του σινιασαι ως τον σιτον
(ZeT 43:18) [C]

εξητησατο υμας ο σατανας Did^pt] ο σατανας εξητησατο υμας Did^pt TR UBS³ p⁷⁵ ℵ A B D L W Δ Θ Π Ψ Ω fam 1. 13 33 579 892 1241 a b e

ιδου rell] omit b

Lac.: C

Luke 22:32

καγω εδεηθην υπερ υμων...ινα μη εκλιπη η πιστις σου
(ZeT 43:19-20) [Ad]*

εκλιπη UBS³ ℵ B D L Θ Π Ψ fam 1 579] εκλειπη TR A W Δ Ω fam 13 33 892 1241

Lac.: p⁷⁵ C

Luke 22:33

ετοιμος ειμι μετα σου και εις φυλακην (PsT 148:17) [C]

ετοιμος ειμι μετα σου] μετα σου ετοιμος ειμι TR UBS³ p⁷⁵vid ℵ A B D L (W) Δ Θ Π Ψ Ω fam 1. 13 33 579 892 1241 a b e

ετοιμος rell] omit W

Lac.: C

Luke 23:21

σταυρου, σταυρου αυτον (PsT 290:30) [C]

σταυρου, σταυρου UBS³ p⁷⁵ ℵ B D] σταυρωσον, σταυρωσον TR A L Δ Θ Π Ψ Ω fam 1. 13 579 892 1241; σταυρωσον W a b e

Lac.: C 33

Luke 23:43

σημερον μετα μου εση εν τω παραδεισω (ZeT 26:20) [Ad]
σημερον εση μετα μου εν τω παραδεισω (ZeT 368:29) [Ad]
σημερον μετ' εμου εση εν τω παραδεισω (EcclT 92:9) [C]
σημερον μετ' εμου εση εν τω παραδεισω (GenT 108:9) [C]
σημερον μετ' εμου εση [ε]ν τω παραδεισω (GenT 110:12-13) [C]
σημερον μετ' εμου εση εν τω παραδεισω (GenT 117:5-6) [C]
σημερον μετ' εμου εση εν τω παραδεισω (PsT 221:1) [C]

    μετ' εμου εση TR UBS^3 p^{75} ℵ A B D L W Δ Θ Π Ψ Ω fam 1. 13
    33 579 892 1241 a b e] εση μετ' εμου C

Luke 24:32

ουχι η καρδια ημων καιομενη ην, οτε διηνοιγεν ημιν τας
γραφας (GenT 196:3-4) [Ad]*

ουχι η καρδια ημων ην καιομενη εν τη οδω, ηνικα διηνοιγεν
ημιν τας γραφας (PsT 274:10) [Ad]*

    ημων καιομενη ην TR UBS^3 p^{75} ℵ A B L W Δ Θ Π Ψ Ω
    fam 1. 13 33 579 892 1241 a b] ην ημων κεκαλυμμενη
    D (nostrum fuit exterminatum) e

    διηνοιγεν rell] ηνοιγεν D

    Lac.: C

Luke 24:49

υμεις δε καθησεσθε εν τη πολει, εως ενδυσησθε εξ υψους
δυναμιν (ZeT 67:21) [C]

    πολει UBS^3 p^{75} ℵ B C D L a b e] πολει Ιερουσαλημ
    TR A W Δ Θ Π Ψ Ω fam 1. 13 33 579 892 1241

    εως] εως οτου D fam 1; εως ου rell

    εξ υψους δυναμιν UBS^3 p^{75} ℵ B C L 33 579] δυναμιν
    εξ υψους rell

    καθησεσθε] καθισατε rell

124/ Didymus and the Gospels

John 1:1

...] τον θεον ην ο λογος   (PsT 302:27)   [Ad]*

ουτος...ην προς τον θεον, θεος λογος ων   (ZeT 94:22)   [Ad]*

εν αρχη ην ο λογος   (EcclT 355:27)   [C]

και ην...ο λογος προς τον θεον   (PsT 187:19-20)   [C]

Reconstruction: εν αρχη ην ο λογος και ο λογος ην προς τον θεον και θεος ην ο λογος

    θεος   TR UBS^3 p$^{66, 75}$ ℵ A B D Δ Θ Π Ψ fam 1. 13 33 579 892 1241] ο θεος   L

    Lac.: C W Ω

John 1:2

ο ων εν αρχη προς τον θεον   (ZeT 253:13)   [Ad]

John 1:3

δι' ου τ[α] πα[ντα]   (JobT 14:9)   [All]

παντα δι' αυτου εις ουσιαν εληλυθεν   (PsT 134:3-4)   [All]

δι' αυτου γεγονε τα παντα   (ZeT 253:13)   [All]

πα[ν]τα δι' αυτου εγενετο και χωρις αυτου εγενετο ουδεν   (JobT 281:15-17)   [C]

παντα δι' αυτου εγενετο   (PsT 110:28)   [C]

    ουδεν   p^{66} ℵ D fam 1] ουδε εν   TR UBS^3 p^{75} A B C^{vid} L Δ Θ Π Ψ fam 13 33 579 892 1241

    Lac.: W Ω

John 1:4

η ζωη ην το φως των ανθρωπων   (PsT 98:26)   [C]

    ην   TR UBS^3 p$^{66, 75}$ ℵ A B C D L Δ Θ Π Ψ fam 1. 13 33 579 892 1241 a e] est (=εστιν) e

    των ανθρωπων   rell] omit   B

    Lac.: W Ω

John 1:5

[κ]αι το φω[ς ε]ν τη σκοτια φαιν[ει] και η σκο[τια α]υτο
ου κατελα[βεν] (JobT 352:3-4) [C]

Text: TR UBS³ p⁶⁶·⁷⁵ ℵ A B C D L Δ Θ Π Ψ fam 1.13
33 579 892 1241 a (b) (e)

Lac.: W Ω

John 1:6

εγενετο ανθρωπος, απεσταλμενος παρα θεου, ονομα αυτω
Ιωαννης (PsT 30:9) [C]

εγενετο ανθρωπος, απεσταλ[με]νος παρα θεου, ονομα αυτω
Ιωαννης (PsT 321:7-8) [C]

ονομα TR UBS³ p⁶⁶·⁷⁵ A B C L Δ Θ Π Ψ fam 1.13 33 579
892 1241] ην ονομα ℵ D

θεου a b e rell] κυριου D

Lac.: W Ω

John 1:7

Ιωαννης εληλυθεν ινα μαρτυρηση περι του φωτος (PsT 82:2-3)
[Ad]

ουτος ηλθεν εις μαρτυριαν, ινα μαρτυρηση περι του φωτος
(PsT 321:8) [C]

Text: TR UBS³ p⁶⁶·⁷⁵ ℵ A B C D L Δ Θ Π Ψ fam 1.13
33 579 892 1241 a b e

Lac.: W Ω

John 1:9

η[ν] το φως το αληθινον, ο φωτιζει παντα ανθρωπων
(EcclT 330:9-10) [C]

ην το φως το αληθινον (EcclT 356:1) [C]

ην...το [φω]ς το [αληθινο]ν, ο φωτιζει παντα ανθρωπον
ερχομενο[ν εις] τον κο[σμον] (GenT 6:4) [C]

[φω]τιζει παντα αν[θρωπον] (JobT 333:6-7) [C]

ην το φως το αληθινον (PsT 305:22) [C]

John 1:9 (cont.)

ην TR UBS³ p⁶⁶·⁷⁵ ℵ A B C D L Δ Θ Π Ψ fam 1.13 33 579 892 1241 a b] est (= εστιν) e

φωτιζει rell] inlumnabat (= εφωτιζε) b

Lac.: W Ω

John 1:14

οταν θεασωμεθα την δοξαν αυτου, δοξαν ως μονογενους παρα πατρος, πληρης χαριτος και αληθειας (PsT 48:22-25) [Ad]

γεναμενος δε ο λογος σαρξ και εσκηνωσεν εν ημιν, και εθεασαμεθα την δοξαν αυτου (PsT 63:14) [Ad]

οταν δε τις θεασηται την δοξαν αυτου, δοξαν ως μονογενους παρα πατρος (PsT 63:18-19) [Ad]

τον λογον κατα μεταβολην ουσιας σαρκα γεγενησθαι (PsT 73:13) [Ad]

θεασηται τη[ν δοξ]αν αυτου, δοξαν ως μονογενους παρα πατρος (PsT 131:8-9) [Ad]

εθεασαμεθα αυτον, δοξαν ως μονογενους παρα πατρος (PsT 185:13-14) [Ad]

οταν θεασωμεθα την δοξαν αυτου, δοξαν ως μονογενους παρα πατρος, πληρης χαριτος κ[αι] αληθειας (PsT 327:17-18) [Ad]

θεασαμενοι γαρ την δοξαν αυτου δοξαν ως μενογενους (PsT 328:16) [Ad]

ινα μετα ταυτα οφθη η δοξα [του υιου] παρα πατρος, πληρης χαριτος και αληθειας (ZeT 33:6-7) [All]

θεασασθαι ημας την δοξαν αυτου, ως μονογενους παρα πατρος (ZeT 40:16-17) [Ad]

θεασω[ν]ται την δοξαν αυτου, δοξαν ως μονογενους παρα πατρος, πληρης χαριτος και αληθειας (ZeT 315:6) [Ad]

πηγη αγαθοτητος και πληρης χαριτος και αληθειας τυγχανων (ZeT 366:12-13) [All]

και εθεασαμεθα την δοξαν αυτου, δοξαν ως μονογενους παρα πατρος (PsT 86:23) [C]

εθεασαμεθα την δοξαν αυτου, δοξαν ως μονογενους παρα πατρος πληρης χαριτος και αληθειας (PsT 103:16-17) [C]

Text and Apparatus /127

John 1:14 (cont.)

και ο λογος σαρξ εγενετο και εσκηνωσεν εν ημιν, και εθεασαμεθα την δοξαν αυτου, δοξαν ως μονογενους παρα πατρος (PsT 149:28-29) [C]

ο λογος σαρξ εγενετο...και εθεασαμεθα την δοξαν αυτου, δοξαν ως μονογενους παρα πατρος (PsT 153:30-31) [C]

εθεασαμεθα την δοξαν αυτου, δοξαν ως μονογενους παρα πατρος (PsT 221:19-20) [C]

μονογενους παρα πατρος, πληρης χαριτος και αληθειας (ZeT 32:13) [C]

ο λογος σαρξ εγενετο κ[αι ε]σκηνωσεν εν ημιν, και εθεασαμεθα την δοξαν α[υτ]ου, δοξαν ως μονογενους παρα πατρος, πληρης χαριτος [κ]αι αληθειας (ZeT 249:17) [C]**

και TR UBS³ P⁶⁶·⁷⁵ ℵ A C D L Δ Θ Π Ψ Ω fam 1. 13 33 579 892 1241 a b e] omit B

πληρης rell] πληρη D

Lac.: W

John 1:16

ουτω και το χαριν αντι χαριτος νοησομεν... (GenT 162:22-23) [All]*

εκ του πληρωματος αυτου λαμβανουσιν...αλλα παντες εκ το πληρωμα αυτου (PsT 327:2-3) [All]

εκ του πληρωματο[ς ο]υν [λα]μβανουσιν οι αγιοι (PsT 327:18) [All]

εκ του πληρωματος αυτου ημεις παντες ελαβομεν (PsT 134:16) [C]

εκ του πληρωματος ημεις παντες ελαβομεν (ZeT 70:24) [C]

Reconstruction: εκ του πληρωματος αυτου ημεις παντες ελαβομεν...χαριν αντι χαριτος

Text: TR UBS³ P⁶⁶·⁷⁵ ℵ A B C D L Δ Θ Π Ψ Ω fam 1. 13 33 579 892 1241 a b e

Lac.: W

128/ Didymus and the Gospels

John 1:17

η χαρις γαρ και η αληθεια παραγινεται δια Ιησου Χριστου
(PsT 155:26)   [Ad]*

η χαρ[ι]ς γαρ και η αληθεια δια Ιησου Χριστου εγενετο
(PsT 3:20)   [C]

γαρ (autem a b e)] δε P^{66} (a b e); omit TR UBS^3 P^{75} ℵ
A B C L Δ Θ Π Ψ Ω fam 1.13 33 579 892 1241

Χριστου rell] omit ℵ

Lac.:   D Ω

John 1:18

μονογενης θεος ο ων εις κολπον   (EcclT 356:1)   [C]

θεον ουδεις εωρακεν πωποτε   (GenT 216:22)   [C]

θεον ουδεις εωρακεν πωποτε· μονογενης θεος ο ων εις τον
κολπον του πατρος εξηγησατο   (ZeT 365:16-18)   [C]**

πωποτε TR UBS^3 P$^{66.75}$ ℵ A B C L Δ Θ Π Ψ Ω fam 1.13
33 579 892 1241] umquam nisi (=πωποτε ει μη) a b e

μονογενης UBS^3 P^{66} ℵ B C L] ο μονογενης rell

θεος UBS^3 P$^{66.75}$ ℵ B C L 33] υιος rell

ο ων rell] omit ℵ a

εωρακεν πωποτε rell] πωποτε εωρακεν P^{75}

(θεος) υιος rell] filius suus (=υιος αυτου) a

εις rell] omit a

πατρος] πατρος εκεινος rell

Lac.:   D W

John 1:29

δια την αφαιρεσιν της αμαρτιας του κοσμου   (PsT 5:2)   [All]

αμνος εστιν του θεου αιρων την αμαρτιαν του κοσμου
(PsT 286:1)   [Ad]

γεγονεν χρησιμος η προδοσια επι τω αρθηναι την αμαρτιαν
του κοσμου   (PsT 315:2)   [All]

John 1:29 (cont.)

ετυθη υπερ του αραι την αμαρτιαν του κοσμου ο του θεου αμνος
(ZeT 252:10-11) [Ad]*

αιρων την αμαρτιαν του κοσμου (ZeT 60:8) [C]

ιδε ο αμνος του θεου ο αιρων την αμαρτιαν του κοσμου
(ZeT 148:22-23) [C]

ιδε ο αμνος του θεου ο αιρων την αμαρτιαν του κοσμου
(ZeT 252:10-11) [C]

θεου TR UBS^3 p$^{66.\ 75}$ ℵ A B C L Δ Θ Π Ψ Ω fam 1.13 33
579 892 1241 e] Dei ecce (= θεου ιδε) a b

την αμαρτιαν rell] peccata (= τας αμαρτιας) e

Lac.: D W

John 1:30

οπισω μου ερχεται ανηρ (Ecc1T 73:5) [C]

οπισω μου ερχεται ανηρ ος εμπροσθεν μου γεγονεν
(ZeT 23:15-16) [C]**

ερχεται οπισω μου ανηρ ος εμπροσθεν μου γεγονεν
(ZeT 105:12) [C]

Text: TR UBS^3 p$^{66.\ 75}$ ℵ A B C L Δ Θ Π Ψ Ω fam 1.13 33
579 892 1241 a b e

Lac.: D W

John 1:47

ιδε ανθρωπος Ισραηλιτης, εν ω δολος ουκ υπαρχει (GenT
219:10-11) [Ad]

ανθρωπος] αληθως TR UBS^3 p$^{66.\ 75}$ ℵ A B L Δ Θ Π Ψ Ω
fam 1.13 33 579 892 1241 a b e

ουχ υπαρχει] ουκ εστιν rell

ιδε rell] ιδε ει 579

Lac.: C D W

John 2:19

λυσατε τον ναον τουτον   (PsT 238:20)   [C]

λυσατε τον ναον τουτον και εν τρισιν ημεραις εγερω αυτον
(ZeT 16:23)   [C]

   εν   TR UBS³ p⁶⁶·⁷⁵ ℵ A L Δ Θ Π Ψ Ω fam 1. 13 33 579
   892 1241 a b e] omit   B

Lac.: C D W

John 2:21

ναος γαρ του σωτηρος ειρηται το σωμα   (PsT 73:24)   [All]

τουτο δε ελεγεν περι του ναου του σωματος   (PsT 238:21)   [C]

ελεγεν περι του ναου του σωματος αυτου   (ZeT 16:25)   [C]

Reconstruction: τουτο δε ελεγεν περι του ναου του σωματος
   αυτου

   τουτο] εκεινος   TR UBS³ p⁶⁶·⁷⁵ ℵ A B L Δ Θ Π Ψ Ω
   fam 1. 13 33 579 892 1241 a b e

αυτου   rell] omit ℵ

Lac.: C D W

John 3:4

μη δυναται τις γερων ων γεννηθηναι η δευτερον εις την κοιλιαν
της μητρος εισελθειν   (JobT 104:8-10)   [Ad]*

πως δυναται ανθρωπος γεννηθηναι γερων ων   (GenT 243:22)   [C]

   ανθρωπος γεννηθηναι γερων ων   TR UBS³ p⁷⁵ A B L Δ Θ Π Ψ
   Ω fam 1. 13 33 579 892 1241 a b] γεννηθηναι ναι
   ανθρωπος γερων ων   p⁶⁶; ανθρωπος γερων ων γεννηθηναι
   ℵ ; homo denuo renasci cum sit senex (= ανθρωπος
   ανωθεν γεννηθηναι γερων ων) e

την κοιλιαν   rell] κοιλιαν   fam 13

Lac.: C D W

John 3:5

τω τεχθησομενω εξ υδατος και πνευματος (PsT 56:23) [All]

ωστε αλλην αυτοις δουναι γενεσιν την εξ υδατος και πνευματος
(PsT 225:11-12) [All]

John 3:7

δει υμας γεννηθηναι ανωθεν (GenT 243:21) [C]

δει υμας γεννθηθναι ανωθεν (JobT 104:6-7) [C]

Text: TR UBS³ $p^{66.75}$ ℵ A B L Δ Θ Π Ψ Ω fam 1. 13 33
579 892 1241 a b e

Lac.: C D W

John 3:13

ουδεις αναβεβηκεν εις τον ουρανον ει μη ο εκ του ουρανου
καταβας, ο υιος του ανθρωπου (PsT 153:8-9) [C]

ουδεις αναβεβηκεν εις τον ουρανον ει μη ο εκ του ουρανου
καταβας, ο υιος του ανθρωπου (PsT 234:23) [C]

Text: TR UBS³ $p^{66.75}$ ℵ A B L Δ Θ Π Ψ Ω fam 1. 13 33
579 892 1241 a b e

Lac.: C D W

John 3:16

ουτω γαρ ηγαπησεν ο θεος τον κοσμον αυτου ως τον υιον αυτου
μονογενη (PsT 221:21) [Ad]*

ουτως ηγαπησεν ο θεος τον κοσμον ωστε τον υιον αυτου τον
μονογενη (PsT 86:24-25) [C]

ουτως ηγαπησεν ο θεος τον κοσμον ωστε τον υιον αυτου τον
μονογενη εδωκεν, ινα πας ο πιστευων εις αυτον εχη ζωην
αιωνιον (ZeT 337:13-15) [C]**

τον υιον αυτου TR A L Δ Θ Π Ψ Ω fam 1. 13 33 579 892
a b e] τον υιον UBS³ $p^{66.75}$ ℵ B

εδωκεν rell] εδωκεν εις τον κοσμον 33 (e)

εις αυτον rell] επ' αυτον p^{75} (L) Ψ

John 3:16 (cont.)

εδωκεν rell] omit ℵ

ο πιστευων rell] πιστευων θ

αυτον] αυτον μη απολπται αλλ' rell

omit in toto 1241

Lac.: C D W

John 3:18

ο δε μη πιστευων ηδη κεκριται, οτι μη πεπιστευκεν εις το ονομα του μονογενους υιου του θεου (PsT 87:1-2) [C]

οτι μη πεπιστευκεν εις το ονομα του μονογενους υιου του θεου (PsT 221:22) [C]

ο δε TR UBS³ P⁶⁶˙⁷⁵ A L Δ Θ Π Ψ Ω fam 1.13 33 579 892 1241 a b e] ο ℵ B

Lac.: C D W

John 3:19

ηγαπησαν οι ανθρωποι μαλλον το σκοτος η το φως (EcclT 47:29) [C]

ηγαπησαν οι ανθρωποι μαλλον το σκοτος TR UBS³ P⁷⁵ A B L Δ Θ Π Ψ Ω fam 13 33 579 892 1241 a b] ηγαπησαν μαλλον οι ανθρωποι το σκοτος P⁶⁶ fam 1 e; οι ανθρωποι ηγαπησαν το σκοτος μαλλον ℵ

Lac.: C D W

John 3:20

πας ο πονηρευομενος μισει το φως (EcclT 48:3) [Ad]

John 3:29

ο εχων την νυμφην νυμφιος εστιν. ο δε φιλος του νυμφιου χαρα χαιρει δια την λαλιαν του νυμφιου (ZeT 105:13) [Ad]

ο εχων...την νυμφην νυμφι[ος εσ]τιν (EcclT 76:13) [C]

Text and Apparatus /133

John 3:29 (cont.)

ο εχων την νυμ[φην] νυμφιος [εστι]ν   (EcclT 66:29-67:1)   [C]

ο εχων την νυμφην νυμφιος εστιν   (EcclT 76:13)   [C]

ο εχων την νυμφην νυμφιος εστι[ν]   (EcclT 325:18)   [C]

Text: TR UBS³ p⁶⁶·⁷⁵ ℵ A B D L Δ Θ Π Ψ Ω fam1.13
       33 579 892 1241 a b e

Lac.: C W

John 4:13

ο πινων...εκ τ[ου υ]δατος τουτου διψησει παλιν   (EcclT 148:2)   [C]

Text: TR UBS³ p⁶⁶·⁷⁵ ℵ A B C D L Δ Θ Π Ψ Ω fam1.13
       33 579 892 1241 a b e

Lac.: W

John 4:14

πινων εκ της πηγης και του υδατος, ου Ιησους διδωσιν και μ[ενει αυτω. εχ]ε[ι] γαρ εν εαυτω γενομενην εις ζωην αιωνιον πηγην   (EcclT 164:26-27)   [All]

ο εχων εν εαυτω την πηγην του υδατος του ζωντος...   (EcclT 361:26   [All]

πινοντες εκ του υδατος [ου] Ιησους παρεχει των δικαιων, ο και [ε]ν αυτοις γινεται πηγη υδα[το]ς αλλομενου εις ζωην αιω[νι]ον   (JobT 140:8-12)   [Ad]*

(ο πιστευων εις εμε, ποταμοι εκ της κοιλιας αυτου ρευσουσιν) υδατος αλλομενου εις ζωην αιωνιον   (JobT 371:24-25)   [Ad]*

ο πινων...εκ του υδατος ου εγω δωσω, εξει πηγην αλλομενην εις ζωην αιωνιον   (PsT 58:23-24)   [Ad]*

ποταμοι δε εισιν οι προφηται σχοντες απο [της πηγης του υ]δατος του αλλομεν[ου εις ζ]ωην αιωνιον   (PsT 310:15)   [All]*

134/ Didymus and the Gospels

John 4:14 (cont.)

ινα και εκ των αυτου πρακτικων δυναμεων πηγη ζωης αναβη
υδατος αλλομενου εις ζωην αιωνιον (ZeT 122:3-4) [All]

[ος δε] αν πιη εκ του υδατος ου εγω δ[ωσ]ω αυτω, γενησεται
εν αυτω [πηγη] υδατος ζωντος αλλομε[νο]υ εις ζωην αιωνιον
(ZeT 381:4-6) [Ad]*

ος δε αν πιη TR UBS³ $p^{66 \cdot 75}$ A B C L Δ Θ Π Ψ Ω fam 1.13
33 579 892 1241] ο δε πινων ℵ D

εν αυτω πηγη a b e rell] πηγη εν αυτω p^{66}

αλλομενου rell] αλλομενου ζωντος fam 13

Lac.: W

John 4:20-24

φανερον δ' οτι τοις κατα το νοητον Ιουδαιοις τοις εν
πνευματι και αληθεια προσκυνουσι τω θεω, ουκ εν
Ιεροσολυμοις η τω Σαμαριτων ορει (ZeT 196:19-21)
[All]

John 4:20

...εν Ιεροσολυμοις ην· ο τοπος οπου προσκυνειν εδει...
(ZeT 162:10) [Ad]*

προσκυνειν δει (Did) UBS³ $p^{66 \cdot 75}$ ℵ A B C D L Ψ 33
892 b] δει προσκυνειν TR Δ Θ Π Ω fam 1.13 579
1241 a e

ο τοπος rell] omit ℵ

Lac.: W

John 4:23

ει γαρ προσκυνηται γινονται οι πνευματι και αληθεια
προσερχομενοι θεω... (PsT 55:15-16) [All]*

...προσκυνουσιν αυτον εν πνευματι και αληθεια τοις
αγγελοις (ZeT 103:29-30) [All]*

ου[τω] γαρ δυνατον προσκυνησαι πνευματι και αληθεια
[τω βα]σιλει κυριω παντοκρατορι (ZeT 405:5-6) [All]*

Text and Apparatus /135

John 4:23 (cont.)

    πνευματι   TR UBS³ p⁶⁶·⁷⁵ ℵ A B C D L Δ Θ Π Ψ Ω fam 13
    33 579 892 1241] τω πνευματι fam 1

    Lac.: W

John 4:24

    πνευμα ο θεος (GenT 88:20) [C]

    Text: TR UBS³ p⁶⁶·⁷⁵ ℵ A B C D L Δ Θ Π Ψ Ω fam 1.13
    33 579 892 1241 a b e

    Lac.: W

John 4:28

    ουτως ευρισκεις κ[αι] περ[ι] της Σαμαριτιδος γεγραμμενον
    [οτι και] εκεινη αφηκεν την υδριαν, εν η ει[λ]ηλυθει
    αρυσασθαι υδωρ, και α[πηλθεν τοις] πολιταις εαυτης
    ειπειν... (EcclT 361:12-14) [All]*

    αφηκεν TR UBS³ p⁶⁶·⁷⁵ ℵ A B C L Δ Θ Π Ψ Ω
    fam 1.13 33 579 892 1241 a] αφηκεν η γυνη
    D b e

    την υδριαν rell] υδριαν Δ

    Lac.: W

John 4:29

    δευτε ιδετε ανθρωπον, ος ειπεν μοι παν το αμ[αρτημα] μου
    (EcclT 361:14-15) [Ad]

John 4:32

    εγω βρωσιν εχω φαγειν ην υμεις ουκ οιδατε (PsT 315:25)
    [C]

    Text: TR UBS³ p⁶⁶·⁷⁵ ℵ A B C D L Δ Θ Π Ψ Ω fam 1.13
    33 579 892 1241 a b e

    Lac.: W

John 4:34

λεγει τουτο θελημα αυτου ειν[α]ι το τελειωσαι το
θ[ε]λημα του πατρος (PsT 286:30) [All]

ινα τις ποιηση το θελημα του πατρος μου (PsT 315:24)
[Ad]

John 4:35

επαρατε τους οφθαλμους υμων και θεασασθε οτι λευκαι εισιν
αι χωραι (Ecc1T 40:24) [Ad]

[ιδου λεγω υμιν, επαρατε τ]ους οφθαλμους υμων και
θεασασθε [τας χωρας, οτι λευκαι ει]σιν προς θερισμον
ηδη (ZeT 18:23) [C]

ιδου λεγω υμιν Did^{vid} TR UBS^3 P$^{66.\ 75}$ ℵ A B C D L
Δ Θ Π Ψ Ω fam 13 33 579 892 a b e] omit fam 1 1241

Lac.: W

John 4:36

...αμα χαιρει σπειρων και θεριζων (Ecc1T 324:12-13) [All]

ινα ο σπειρων αμα χαιρη και ο θεριζων (Ecc1T 324:7-8) [C]

ινα ο σπειρων ομου χαιρη και ο θεριζων (Ecc1T 328:3) [C]**

ινα UBS^3 P$^{66.\ 75}$ B C L Ψ fam 1 33 1241 e] ινα και TR
ℵ A D Δ Θ Π Ω fam 13 579 892 a b

ο θεριζων rell] θεριζων P^{66} θ

ομου χαιρη και ο θεριζων rell] και ο θεριζων ομου
χαιρη D

και ο θεριζων rell] cum eo qui metit (= μετα του
θελοντος) e

Lac.: W

John 5:5

εχε τα περι [των παραλυ]τικων εν τοις ευαγγελιοις ειρημενα
εν κλινη οδυνης εμεινεν ο τριακοντα και οκ[τω] ενιαυτους
βεβλη[μενος] (PsT 291:15) [All]

Text and Apparatus /137

John 5:6

θελεις υγιης γενεσθαι; (PsT 132:15) [C]

Text: TR UBS³ p⁶⁶·⁷⁵ ℵ A B C D L Δ Θ Π Ψ Ω fam 1.13
33 579 892 1241 a b e

Lac.: W

John 5:8

εγειρε, αρον τον κραβακτον σου και περιπατει
(PsT 132:15-16) [C]

εγειρε, αρον τον κραβακτον σου και περιπατει
(PsT 292:10) [C]

εγειρε   TR UBS³ p⁶⁶·⁷⁵ ℵ B C L Δ Θ Ψ Ω fam 1.13
33 579 892 1241] εγειρε και A D Π a b e

κραβακτον ℵ] κραβαττον (or κραββατον) rell

τον κραβακτον σου rell] σου τον κραββατον 1241

Lac.: W

John 5:18

δια [του]το εζ[ητουν αποκτειναι] Ιησουν, ο[υ] μονον οτι
ελυεν το σαββατον, αλλ' οτι και πατερα [ιδιον ελεγεν]
τον [θ]εον, ισον εαυτον ποιων τω θεω   (GenT 9:5-7)
[Ad]*

εζητουν   TR UBS³ p⁶⁶·⁷⁵ ℵ A B D L W Δ Θ Π Ψ Ω fam 1.13
33 892 a b e] εδιωκον οι Ιουδαιοι τον Ιησουν και
εζητουν   579 1241

Lac.: C

John 5:19

α γαρ [αν εκεινος ποι]η, ταυτα και ο υιος ομοιως ποιει
(GenT 22:6-7) [C]

γαρ αν εκεινος ποιη   (Did) TR UBS³ p⁶⁶·⁷⁵ ℵ B W Δ Θ Ψ Ω
fam 1.13 33 (579) a] γαρ εκεινος ποιηση (Did) D;
γαρ εκεινος ποιει A (L) Π 892 1241 (b) e

138/ Didymus and the Gospels

John 5:19 (cont.)

ομοιως ποιει   rell] ποιει ομοιως   ℵ D a b; ποιει   e

α   rell] ο   W

α γαρ αν   rell] αν γαρ   579

Lac.: C

John 5:29

εξελευσονται οι τα αγαθα πραξ[α]ντες εις αναστασιν ζωης, οι δε τα φαυλα εις αναστασιν κρισεως   (PsT 146:16-17) [Ad]*

εξελευσονται   D W] εκπορευσονται   TR UBS^3 p$^{66.75}$ ℵ A B L Δ Θ Π Ψ Ω fam 1. 13 33 579 892 1241

οι δε   b rell] οι   B a e; και οι   p^{66} W

τα φαυλα   rell] φαυλα   D

Lac.: C

John 5:37

ουτε φω[ν]ην αυτου ακηκοατε ουτε [ει]δος αυτο[υ ε]ωρακατε...   (JobT 353:2-4) [Ad]*

ειδος αυτου   TR UBS^3 p$^{66.75}$ ℵ A B D L Δ Θ Π Ψ Ω fam 1. 13 33 579 892 1241 a e] ειδος   W b

Lac.: C

John 5:38

...ουτε τον λογον αυ[το]υ εχετε εν υμ[ιν] μενοντα   (JobT 353:5-6) [C]

ουτε τον λογον αυτου   e] και τον λογον αυτου ουκ   TR UBS^3 p$^{66.75}$ ℵ A B D L W Δ Θ Π Ψ Ω fam. 1. 13 33 579 892 1241 a b

εν υμιν μενοντα   UBS^3 p$^{66.75}$ ℵ B L W Ψ fam 1. 13 33 579 892 1241 b] μενοντα εν υμιν   rell

Lac.: C

John 5:39

    ως οστρακον αυτον ηγησασθαι τους εραυνωντας γραφας τας
    μαρτυρουσας περι του αυτας ειρηκοτος Σωτηρος
    (ZeT 308:23-25) [All]

    εραυνατε τας γραφας οτι αυται εισ[ιν] αι μαρτυρουσαι περι
    εμου (Ze 384:13) [Ad]*

        αυται W e] εκειναι TR UBS^3 p$^{66.75}$ ℵ A B D L Δ Θ Π
        Ψ Ω fam 1.13 33 579 892 1241 a b

        Lac.: C

John 5:45

    [μ]η [νο]μισητε οτι εγω κατηγορω υμων [π]ρ[ος] τον πατερα·
    εστιν ο κατηγορων υμων Μωυσης, εις ον υμεις ηλπικατε
    (EcclT 315:14-15) [Ad]*

    μη νομισητε οτι εγω κατηγορησω υμων προς τον πατερα· εστιν
    Μωυσης ο κατηγορων υμων εις ον υμεις ηλπισατε (EcclT
    351:5-7) [C]

        υμων$^{(1)}$ TR UBS^3 p^{66} ℵ A B W Δ Θ Π Ψ Ω fam 1.13 33 579 892]
        υμιν p^{75} L 1241; υμας D

        νομισητε] δοκειτε rell

        υμων$^{(2)}$ a b e] rell] υμων προς τον πατερα B

        Lac.: C

John 5:46

    ποιειν [τα εργα τ]ου Αβρααμ και πιστευειν εις Μωσεα
    (EcclT 274:24-25) [All]

    ει γαρ επιστευετε Μωσει, επιστευετε αν εμοι (EcclT 351:7)
    [C]

        αν εμοι TR UBS^3 p$^{66.75}$ ℵ A B D L W Δ Θ Π Ψ Ω fam 1.13
        33 579 892 1241] et mihi (= και αν εμοι) a b e

        Lac.: C

John 5:47

ει δε τοις εκεινου γραμμασιν ου πιστευετε πως τοις εμοις
ρημασι πιστευετε   (EcclT 351:7-8)   [C]
───────────────
πιστευετε$^{(2)}$ p^{66}, ^{75} B Π] πιστευσετε   TR UBS^3 ℵ A L Ψ Ω
33 892 a b e; πιστευσητε   D W Δ (θ) fam 1. 13 579 1241

Lac.:   C

John 6:27

ερωτα λαβειν της μη απολλυμενης βρωσεως μενουσης εις
ζωην αιωνιον   (EcclT 283:20)   [All]

τη ενεργαζομενη γουν ψυχη την μενουσαν εις αιωνιου [ζ]ωνην
βρωσιν   (ZeT 168:25-26)   [All]

εργαζεσθε [μη την βρωσιν την απο]λλυμε[ν]ην, αλλα την
βρωσιν την μενουσαν [...]   (EcclT 118:22-23)   [C]
───────────────
την βρωσιν$^{(2)}$ TR UBS^3 p^{75} A B D L W Δ Θ Π Ψ Ω fam 1. 13
33 579 892 1241 a b e] omit ℵ

Lac.:   p^{66} C

John 6:29

ινα [πιστ]ευητε εις ον απεστειλεν εκεινος   (EcclT 118:25)
[C]
───────────────
πιστευητε   UBS^3 p^{75} ℵ A B (L) Θ Ψ fam 1 33 579 a b e]
πιστευσητε   TR D W Δ Π Ω fam 13 892 1241

Lac.:   p^{66} C

John 6:38

καταβεβηκα απο του ουρανου ουχ ιν[α] ποιησω ανθρωπινον
θελημα, αλλα το του πεμψαντος με   (PsT 286:17)   [Ad]*

καταβεβηκα...απο του ουρανου ουχ ινα ποιω το θελημα το
εμον   (PsT 29:19-20)   [C]

καταβεβηκα απο του ουρανου ινα ποιω το θελημα του πεμψαντος
με   (ZeT 38:20-21)   [C]

Reconstruction: καταβεβηκα απο του ουρανου ουχ ινα ποιω
το θελημα το εμον αλλα το θελημα του πεμψαντος με
───────────────

John 6:38 (cont.)

απο του ουρανου UBS³ p⁶⁶ A B L W θ fam 13 33 1241]
    εκ του ουρανου TR ℵ D Δ Π Ψ Ω fam 1 579 892

καταβεβηκα απο του ουρανου ουχ a b rell] ου κατεβεβηκα απο
    του ουρανου ℵ (b) e

ποιω rell] ποιησω ℵ D L W

του πεμψαντος rell] του πεμψαντος πατρος D 892 a (b) e

καταβεβηκα rell] καταβη Δ

το εμον rell] εμον 579

το θελημα⁽²⁾ rell] omit a

Lac.: p⁷⁵ C

John 6:41

ο αρτος ο εκ του ουρανου καταβας (PsT 237:9) [C]
    ———————————————————
    εκ του ουρανου καταβας Ψ fam 13 b e] καταβας εκ του
        ουρανου TR UBS³ p⁶⁶.⁷⁵ ℵ A B C D L W Δ θ Π Ω fam 1
        33 (579) 892 1241 a

    ο εκ rell] εκ Π

    καταβας rell] καταβαινων 579

John 6:46

ουχ οτι τον πατερα εωρακεν τις (GenT 216:23) [C]**

ουχ οτι τον θεον εωρακεν τις, ει μη ο ων παρα του πατρος
    (ZeT 365:18-19) [C]
    ———————————————————
    εωρακεν τις UBS³ p⁶⁶ ℵ B C D L W θ Ψ 33 579 1241 a b e]
        τις εωρακεν TR A Δ Π Ω fam 1.13 892

    του πατρος ℵ] του θεου p⁷⁵ (B) rell

    παρα rell] εκ fam 1

    Lac.: (p⁷⁵)

142/ Didymus and the Gospels

John 6:47

    ο πιστευων εις εμε εχει ζωην αιωνιον (EcclT 171:7) [C]

    ο πιστευων εις εμε εχει ζωην αιωνιον (PsT 13:12-13) [C]

    ο πιστευων εις εμε εχει ζωην αιωνιον (ZeT 231:6) [C]

        εις εμε TR A D Δ Π Ψ Ω fam 1.13 33 579 1241 a b e]
        omit UBS³ P⁶⁶ ℵ B C L W Θ 892

        Lac.: P⁷⁵

John 6:51

    εα[ν] τις φαγη τον αρτον της ζ[ωης] του καρπ[ου] του [ξυλο]υ
    της [ζ]ωης και τας σ[αρκ]ας Ιησου... (EcclT 161:4-5)
    [All]

John 6:57

    ζω δια τον πατερα μ[ου] (PsT 2:7) [C]

    ζω...δια τον πατερα (PsT 147:13) [C]

    ως απε[στ]ειλεν με ο ζ[ων πατηρ καγω] ζω δια το[ν πατερα]
    (PsT 298:11-12) [C]

    ζω δια τον πατερα (PsT 305:12) [C]

        απεστειλεν TR UBS³ P⁷⁵ ℵ B C L W Δ Θ Ψ Ω fam 1 33 892]
        απεσταλκεν P⁶⁶ D Π fam 13 579 1241

        μου P⁷⁵] omit a b e rell

        ως] καθως rell

        Lac.: A

John 6:62

    εαν ουν ιδητε τον [υιο]ν του ανθρωπου αναβαινοντα οπου
    ην το προτερον (PsT 153:12-13) [C]

        ιδητε W] θεωρητε TR UBS³ P⁽⁶⁶⁾·⁷⁵ ℵ B C D L Δ Θ Π Ψ Ω
        fam 1.13 33 579 892 1241

        ουν rell] omit a b e

        οπου ‹rell] ου P⁶⁶ D Θ; που Δ

John 6:62 (cont.)

    ανθρωπου rell] omit 1241

    αναβαινοντα rell] ante τον υιον ℵ

    Lac.: A

John 6:63

    η σαρξ...ουκ ωφελει ουδεν, το πνευμα εστι το ζωοπ[οι]ουν
    (GenT 153:10-11) [Ad]*

        το πνευμα   TR UBS^3 p$^{66.\ 75}$ B C D L W Δ Θ Π Ψ Ω fam 1.13
        33 579 892 1241] πνευμα   ℵ

    Lac.: A

John 6:70

    ουχι τους δωδεκα υμας εξελεξαμην; (PsT 322:1) [C]

    ουχι τους δωδεκα υμας εξελεξαμην; και εις εξ υμων διαβολος
    εστιν (ZeT 44:19) [C]

        ουχι   ℵ] ουκ   TR UBS^3 p$^{66.\ 75}$ B C D L W Δ Θ Π Ψ Ω fam 1.13
        33 579 892 1241

        εις εξ υμων   D b (e)] εξ υμων   ℵ ; εξ υμων εις   a rell

        ουχι] (ουκ) εγω   rell

        τους   rell] omit   ℵ

        τους δωδεκα υμας] υμας τους δωδεκα   rell

        δωδεκα...εκελεξαμην   rell] εξελεξαμην δωδεκα   ℵ

        εξελεξαμην   rell] εξαλεξα   Δ

    Lac.: A

John 7:37

    εστως ο Ιησους εκεκραγεν λεγων· Ει τις διψα, ερχεσθω
    προς με και πινετω (ZeT 42:21) [Ad]*

        ει   W] εαν   TR UBS^3 p$^{66.\ 75}$ ℵ B D L Δ Θ Π Ψ Ω fam 1.13
        33 579 892 1241

144/ Didymus and the Gospels

John 7:37 (cont.)

προς με (a) rell] προς εμε P[75] B (a); omit P[66] ℵ D b e

Lac.: A C

John 7:38

ουτοι δε εισιν οι κατα πνευμα βιον εχοντες ων εκ της κοιλιας ρευουσιν ποταμοι ζωντες   (PsT 21:2)   [All]

ινα δεχωνται τους ποταμους τουτους τους εκ της κοιλιας εκαστου των πιστων ρεοντας   (PsT 68:14-15)   [All]

ο πιστευων εις εμε, ποταμοι εκ της κοιλιας αυτου ρευσουσιν υδατος   (JobT 371:21-23)   [C]

ο πιστευων...εις εμε, καθως ειπεν [η γραφη, ποταμο]ι εκ της κοιλιας [αυτου ρευ]σουσιν υδατος ζωντος   (PsT 310:15-16)   [C]**

ο πιστευων εις εμε, καθως ειπεν η γραφη, εκ της κοιλ[ιας αυτου] ρευσουσιν ποταμοι υδατος ζωντος   (ZeT 381:6-8)   [C]

ρευσουσιν   TR UBS[3] P[66.75] ℵ B D L W Θ Π Ψ Ω fam 1.13 33 579 892 1241 a b e] ρευσωσιν   Δ

Lac.: A C

John 7:39

τουτο δε ελεγεν περι του πνευματος ου [εμελλον λαμ]βανειν οι πιστευο[ντες]   (PsT 310:16-17)   [C]

ελεγεν   P[66] ℵ] ειπεν   TR UBS[3] P[75] B D L W Δ Θ Π Ψ Ω fam 1.13 33 579 892 1241

πνευματος ου   rell] πνευματος ο   UBS[3] P[75] B

οι πιστευοντες   rell] οι πιστευσαντες   UBS[3] P[66] B L W; omit   b

εμελλον λαμβανειν   a b e rell] ελαμβανον   W

Lac.: (P[75]) A C

John 8:3-11

φερομεν ουν εν τισιν ευαγγελιοις· γυνη φησιν, κατακριθη
υπο των Ιουδ[αι]ων επι αμαρτια και απεστελλετο λιθοβολη-
θηναι εις τον τοπον, οπου ειωθει γιν[εσθ]αι. ο σωτηρ,
φησιν, εωρακως αυτην και θεωρησας οτι ετοιμοι εισιν προς
το λιθ[οβολ]ησαι αυτην, τοις μελλουσιν αυτην καταβαλειν
λιθοις ειπεν· ος ουκ ημαρτεν, αι[ρε]τω λιθον και βαλετω
αυτον. ει τις συνοιδεν εαυτω το μη ημαρτηκεναι, λαβων
λιθον παισατω αυτην. και ουδεις ετολμησεν. επιστησαντες
εαυτοις και γνοντες, οτι και αυτοι υπε[υθυ]νοι εισιν
τισιν, ουκ ετολμησαν καταπταισαι εκεινην. (EcclT 223:6-13)
[All]

John 8:12

εγω ειμι το φως του κοσμου. ο ακολουθων εμοι ου περιπατησει
εν τη σκοτια, αλλ' εξει το φως της ζωης   (PsT 99:2-3) [C]

    εξει   TR UBS³ p⁶⁶·⁷⁵ B D L W Δ Θ Π Ψ Ω fam 1.13 33 579
    892 1241 (a) b] εχει ℵ e

    εγω ειμι το φως rell] φως ειμι   ℵ

    εμοι rell] μοι   B

    ου] ου μη   rell

    Lac.: A C

John 8:33

σπερμα Αβρααμ εσμεν (GenT 99:9) [C]

    Text: TR UBS³ p⁶⁶·⁷⁵ ℵ B D L W Δ Θ Π Ψ Ω fam 1.13 33
    579 892 1241 a b e

    Lac.: A C

John 8:34

ο...ποιων της [αμαρτ]ιας δουλος εστι της αμαρτιας (GenT
175:19-20) [Ad]*

    της αμαρτιας⁽²⁾ TR UBS³ p⁶⁶·⁷⁵ ℵ B C L W Δ Θ Π Ψ Ω
    fam 1.13 33 579 892 1241 a e] omit   D b

    Lac.: A

John 8:37

οιδα οτι σπερμα Αβρααμ εστε   (GenT 218:30)   [C]

Text: TR UBS³ p⁶⁶·⁷⁵ ℵ B C D L W Δ Θ Π Ψ Ω fam 1.13
33 579 892 1241 a b e

Lac.: A

John 8:39

ποιειν [τα εργα τ]ου Αβρααμ και πιστευετε εις Μωσεα
(EcclT 274:24-25)   [All]

ο γαρ ποιων αυτου τα εργα τεκνον αυτου εστιν   (GenT 234:
17-18)   [All]

ει τεκνα του Αβρααμ ητε, το εργα του Αβρααμ ποιειτε
(GenT 99:11-12)   [C]

ει τεκνα του Αβρααμ εστε, τα εργα του Αβρααμ ποιειτε
(GenT 218:27-28)   [C]

ει τεκνα του Αβ[ραα]μ εστε, τα εργα του Αβρααμ π[οιειτ]ε
(JobT 151:13-16)   [C]

ει τεκνα του Αβρααμ εστε, τα εργα του Αβρααμ ποιειτε
(ZeT 262:14)   [C]

εστε Did^pt UBS³ p⁶⁶·⁷⁵ ℵ B D L] ητε Did^pt TR C W Δ Θ Π Ψ Ω
fam 1.13 33 579 (892) 1241 a b e

ποιειτε p⁶⁶ B] επoιειτε UBS³ p⁷⁵ ℵ D W (Θ); εποιειτε αν
rell

Lac.: A

John 8:40

ζητει[τ]ε με αποκτειναι, ανθρ[ωπον οντ]α ος τ[ην α]ληθειαν
υμι[ν] λελαληκα, ην [ηκο]υσα παρα του θεου   (PsT 3:13-14)
[C]

υμιν λελαληκα   TR UBS³ p⁶⁶·⁷⁵ ℵ B C L W Δ Π Ψ Ω
fam 1 33 579 892 1241] λελαληκα υμιν   D Θ fam 13
a b e

ηκουσα rell] ηκουσεν   D e

John 8:40 (cont.)

του θεου rell] του πατρος μου   fam. 13 1241

με   rell] omit   e

αποκτειναι   rell] αποκτειναι και   579

οντα] omit rell

λελαληκα   rell] locutus est (=λελαληκεν)   e

ην   rell] ην ουκ   Δ

Lac.: A

John 8:42

εγω εκ θεου εξηλθον και ηκω   (ZeT 26:15)   [C]

εγω εκ του θεου εξηλθον και ηκω· ουδε γαρ απ' εμαυτου εληλυθα, αλλ' εκεινος με απεστειλεν   (ZeT 366:15)   [C]**

ουδε   TR UBS³ p^{75} ℵ B C L W Δ Π Ψ Ω fam 1.13 33 579 892 1241 a b] ου p^{66} D Θ e

εγω] εγω γαρ   rell

εκ   rell] παρα   579

εξηλθον   rell] εξεληλυθα p^{66}

και ηκω   rell] omit   e

εμαυτου   rell] εμαυτου ουκ   W

εληλυθα   rell] εληλυθον   D

απεστειλεν   rell] απεσταλκεν p^{66}

Lac.: A

John 8:44

η εκ του διαβολου γεννησαντος αυτους θελησαντες τας επιθυμιας αυτου ποιειν   (ZeT 234:18)   [C]

οταν λαλη το ψευδος εκ των ιδιων λαλει, οτι ψευστης εστιν και ο πατηρ αυτου   (GenT 94:22-23)   [C]

148/ Didymus and the Gospels

John 8:44 (cont.)

...τας επιθυμιας [τ]ου πατρος υμων θελετε   (JobT 151:21)   [C]

υμεις εκ του πατρος του διαβολου εστε και τας επιθυμιας του πατρος υμων θελετε ποιειν   (PsT 70:19)   [C]

υμεις...εκ του πατρος του διαβολου εστε και τας επιθυμιας του διαβολου θελετε ποιειν   (PsT 198:8-9)   [C]

...εν τη αληθεια ουκ εστηκεν   (PsT 198:14)   [C]

εκ του πατρος   UBS³ p⁶⁶·⁷⁵ ℵ B C D L W Δ Θ Π Ψ Ω fam 1. 13 33 579 1241] εκ πατρος   TR 892

του πατρος υμων   rell] πατρος υμων   892

οταν   a b rell] qui (= ος)   e

εκ των ιδιων λαλει   rell] omit   579

Lac.: A

John 8:45

εγ[ω δ]ε οτι την αληθειαν υμιν λεγω ου πιστευετε μοι   (PsT 3:15-16)   [C]

δε   TR UBS³ p⁶⁶·⁷⁵ ℵ B C L W Δ Θ Π Ψ Ω fam 1. 13 33 579 892 1241] omit   D a b e

υμιν λεγω] λεγω υμιν   C fam 13 1241 b; λεγω   rell

οτι   rell] ο   L

λεγω   rell] λαλω   D

μοι   rell] μοι υμεις   D

Lac.: A

John 8:48

ου καλως ελεγομεν ημεις οτι Σαμαριτης ει συ και δαιμονιον εχεις;   (PsT 145:26-27)   [C]

[ο]υ καλως ελεγομεν ημεις οτι Σαμ[αριτ]ης ει συ και δαιμονιον εχεις;   (PsT 294:10)   [C]

John 8:48 (cont.)

ελεγομεν p⁶⁶] λεγομεν TR UBS³ p⁷⁵ ℵ B C D (L) W
Δ Θ Π Ψ Ω fam 1.13 33 579 892 1241 a b e

(ε)λεγομεν ημεις rell] ημεις (ε)λεγομεν p⁶⁶ D L 892
1241

ημεις rell] omit a e

συ rell] omit ℵ fam 1.13

Lac.: A

John 8:56

ημερας δε εκεινης, ης ερωτα και ποθον ελαβεν ο Αβρααμ, ινα
ιδη, και δειχθη αυτω υπο του σωτηρος (EcclT 326:19-20)
[All]

Αβρααμ επεθυμησεν ιδειν την ημεραν [τ]ην εμην, και ειδεν και
εχαρη (GenT 214:29-215:1) [Ad]

ο Αβρααμ γουν [ου]τως ηγαλλιασατο [ινα ι]δη την ημεραν
την εμην, και ιδων εχαρη (PsT 300:9) [Ad]

...ην αγαλλιασαμενος ιδειν ο πατηρ των πιστευσαντων παντων
εθνων Αβρααμ εχαρη (ZeT 305:9) [All]

Αβρααμ ο πατηρ υμων ηγαλλιασατο ινα ιδη την ημεραν την
εμην, και ειδεν και εχαρη (GenT 221:9-11) [C]

Text: TR UBS³ p⁶⁶.⁷⁵ ℵ A B C D L W Δ Θ Π Ψ Ω fam 1.13
33 579 892 1241 a b e

John 9:1

τυφλον απο γενετης Ιησους ιασατο... (GenT 168:14) [All]

απο γενετης τυφλον εις οψιν ηγαγεν Ιησους (PsT 15:26)
[All]

John 9:2

ηρωτησ[α]ν τον Ιησουν οι μαθηται αυτου· α[υ]τ[ο]ς ημαρτεν
η οι γονεις αυτου, ινα τυφλος γεννηθη; (JobT 118:23-25) [Ad]*

μαθηται αυτου TR UBS³ p⁶⁶.⁷⁵ ℵ A B C L W Δ Θ Π Ψ Ω
fam 1.13 33 579 892 1241 a b] μαθηται D e

John 9:6

σημειον και τερας ην το εις οψιν αγαγειν τον απο γενετης
τηφλον, πηλου επιχρισθεντων των οφθαλμων αυτου
(ZeT 56:25)   [All]*

επεχρισεν   (Did) TR UBS³ p⁶⁶·⁷⁵ ℵ A C D L W Δ Θ Π
Ψ Ω fam 1. 13 33 579 892 1241 a b e] επεθηκεν B

John 9:16

αμαρτωλος εστιν οτι το σαββατον ου τηρει   (PsT 147:30) [Ad]

ει ην ουτος ο ανθρωπος παρα θεου, ουκ ελυεν το σαββατ[ο]ν
(PsT 294:9) [All]

John 9:28

του Μωυσεως μαθηται εσμεν   (EcclT 205:23-24)   [C]

μαθηται εσμεν a b] εσμεν μαθηται   TR UBS³ p⁶⁶·⁷⁵ ℵ A B
D L W Δ Θ Π Ψ Ω fam 1.13 33 579 892 1241 e

του rell] omit p⁶⁶

Lac.: C

John 9:39

εγω ηλθον ινα οι μη βλεποντες βλεπωσιν και οι βλεποντες
τυφλοι γενωνται   (GenT 81:23-24)   [Ad]*

εις κριμα εγω ηλθον εις τον κοσμον, ινα [ο]ι [μη βλε]ποντες
βλεψωσιν και οι βλεποντες τ[υφλ]οι γενωνται (ZeT 392:22-
393:1) [C]

ηλθον TR UBS³₇₅p⁶⁶ ℵ A B D L W Δ Θ Π Ψ Ω fam 1.13 33 1241]
εληλυθα p⁷⁵ 579 892

κοσμον p⁶⁶ 1241] κοσμον τουτον rell

ηλθον εις τον κοσμον p⁶⁶ D a b] εις τον κοσμον (τουτον)
ηλθον e rell

κριμα   rell] κρισιν Δ

εις κριμα εγω rell] εγω εις κριμα D

οι μη βλεποντες βλεπωσιν και rell] omit 1241

Text and Apparatus /151

John 9:39 (cont.)

βλεπωσιν και οι βλεποντες rell] omit 579

γενωνται rell] γενησονται fam 13

Lac.: C

John 10:9

Εγω ειμι η θυρα. Δι' εμου εαν τις εισελθη εισελευσεται
και εξελευσετ[α]ι και νομην ευρησει (ZeT 251:16) [C]

εαν TR UBS³ p⁶⁶ ℵ A B D L Δ Θ Π Ψ Ω fam 1.13 33 579 1241]
αν p75 W

και εισελευσεται b rell] omit W Δ a e

εισελθη] εισελθη σωθησεται και rell

Lac.: C 892

John 10:10

εγω ηλθον...ινα ζωην εχωσιν και περισσον εχωσιν (EcclT 46:2-3)
[C]

εγω ηλθον ινα ζωην εχωσιν και περισσον εχωσιν (EcclT 82:16-17)
[C]

εγω ηλθον ινα ζωην εχωσιν και περισσον εχωσιν (ZeT 303:11)
[C]

εγω TR UBS³ p⁶⁶·⁷⁵ ℵ A B L W Δ Θ Π Ψ Ω fam 1.13 33
579 1241 b e] εγω δε D a

και περισσον εχωσιν rell] omit p⁶⁶ D

περισσον rell] περισσοτερον p⁷⁵ Ψ 579, (abundantius) a b e

ζωην rell] ζωην αιωνιον ℵ

Lac.: C 892

John 10:11

...οια νομευς αρ[ι]στος την ψυχην εαυτου εθηκεν υπερ ων
εληλυθεν [σω]σαι προβατων (ZeT 253:18-19) [All]

152/ Didymus and the Gospels

John 10:11 (cont.)

ουτω και ποιμνη μια υπο ενα ποιμενα τον αληθινον τον την
ψυχην αυτου υπερ των προβατων τεθεικοτα   (ZeT 297:8-10)
[All]

πως γαρ ουκ αγαθοι νομεις ων αρχει ο την ψυχην εαυτου υπερ
των προβατων διδους, αγαθος ποιμην ων (ZeT 316:15-16)
[All]

...θανατον του ποιμενος του αληθινου τεθεικοτος την ψυχην
εαυτου υπερ των προβατων (ZeT 354:17-19) [All]

...κατα του αγαθου ποιμενος υπ[ερ τ]ων προβατων τεθ[ει]κοτος
ινα σωτηριαν εχωσιν την εαυ[το]υ ψυχην (ZeT 356:4-6)
[All]

εγω ειμι ο ποιμην ο καλος. Ο καλος ποιμην την ψυχην αυτου
τιθησιν υπερ των προβατων   (ZeT 102:30-103:2) [C]

τιθησιν   TR UBS³ p⁶⁶·⁷⁵ A B L W Δ Θ Π Ψ Ω fam 1.13 33
579 1241 a e] διδωσιν   ℵ D b

ο καλος ποιμην   rell] pastor enim (b)/autem (a) bonus
(= ο δε καλος ποιμην) a b

προβατων rell] ovibus suis (= προβατων αυτου) b e

ο καλος ποιμην] ο ποιμην ο καλος   rell

αυτου τιθησιν   rell] τιθησιν αυτου   θ

Lac.: C 892

John 10:14

εγω ειμι ο ποιμην ο καλος (ZeT 278:16) [C]

ο ποιμην ο καλος   TR UBS³ p⁶⁶·⁷⁵ ℵ A B L W Δ Θ Π Ψ Ω
fam 1.13 33 579 1241] ο καλος ποιμην   D

Lac.: C 892

John 10:15

...τιθεντος μου την ψυχην υπερ των προβατων (ZeT 303:12)
[Ad]

και την ψυχην μου τιθημι υπερ των προβατων (ZeT 278:16)
[C]

John 10:15 (cont.)

τιθημι   TR UBS³ A B L Δ Θ Π Ψ Ω fam 1. 13 33 579 1241
    a b e] διδωμι   p⁶⁶ ℵ D W

προβατων   rell] ovibus meis (= προβατων μου)   b e

μου   rell] omit   D

Lac.: p⁷⁵ C 892

John 10:16

ωστε μιαν ποιμνην και ενα ποιμενα υπαρξαι υπο του νομιμου
βασιλεως παντος του εθνους κρατουμενου   (ZeT 312:8-9)
[All]

και αλλα προβατα εχω α ουκ εισιν εκ της αυλης ταυτης·
κακεινα με δει συναγαγειν και της φωνης μου ακουσουσιν,
ινα γενωνται μια ποιμνη και ποιμην εις   (ZeT 297:11-14)
[C]

αλλα   TR UBS³ ℵ A B L W Δ Θ Π Ψ Ω fam 1. 13 33 579 1241
    b e] αλλα δε   p⁶⁶ D a

με δει   TR A Ω 579 1241] δει με   rell

συναγαγειν   p⁶⁶] αγαγειν   rell

ακουσουσιν   TR UBS³ p⁶⁶·⁷⁵ B D L Π Ω fam 1 b e] ακουουσιν
    Ψ; ακουσωσιν   rell

ινα γενωνται] και γενησεται   TR p⁶⁶ ℵ A Δ Π Ω fam 13 579
    1241 a b e; και γενησονται   rell

και ποιμην εις] και εις ποιμην   Δ a b e; εις ποιμην   rell

εισιν] εστιν   rell

Lac.: (p⁷⁵) C 892

John 10:17

τιθω την ψυχην μου, ινα παλιν λαβω αυτην   (PsT 238:22)   [Ad]

...ινα παλιν λαβη αυτην   (PsT 238:26-27)   [Ad]

ψυχη...ην ως ανθρωπος τελειος εχει, ην τιθεται ινα παλιν
λαβη αυτην   (ZeT 301:5)   [All]

154/ Didymus and the Gospels

John 10:17 (cont.)

...ινα παλιν λαβω αυτην· (PsT 148:10)   [C]

...ινα παλιν λαβω αυτην   (PsT 238:37)   [C]

Text: TR UBS³ p⁶⁶ ℵ A B D L W Δ Θ Π Ψ Ω fam 1.13 33 579 1241 a b e

Lac.: p⁷⁵ C 892

John 10:18

[ο]υδεις αιρει την ψυχην [μου απ'] εμου, αλλ' εγω τιθημι [αυτην] απ' εμαυτου (JobT 375:8-10) [Ad]*

και δυναται και περι της εαυτου ψυχης τουτο λεγειν ης εσχεν εξουσιαν θειναι και λαβειν αυτην (PsT 41:18-19) [All]

ουδεις αιρει την ψυχην μου απ' εμου· εγω τιθημι αυτην απ' εμαυτου (PsT 148:10) [Ad]*

ουδεις αιρει αυτην απ' αυτου, αλλ' αυτος εξουσιαν εχει θειναι και λαβειν αυτην (PsT 238:23-24) [Ad]*

ει δε ουδεις ηρεν την ψυχην, αλλ' αυτος αφ' εαυτου αυτην εθηκεν (PsT 238:26-27) [Ad]*

ουδεις ηρεν αυτην...απ' εμου· εγω εξουσιαν εχω θειναι αυτην (PsT 238:37) [Ad]*

Reconstruction: ουδεις αιρει/ηρεν αυτην απ' εμου, αλλ' εγω τιθημι αυτην απ' εμαυτου· εξουσιαν εχω θειναι αυτην και λαβειν αυτην

αιρει Did^pt TR UBS³ p⁶⁶·⁷⁵ A D L W Δ Θ Π Ψ Ω fam 1.13 33 579 1241 a b e] ηρεν Did^pt ℵ B

ουδεις rell] ουδεις γαρ Ψ

αλλ'...εμαυτου   rell] omit in toto   D

εμαυτου   rell] εμαυτου και   W; εμου   579

εξουσιαν   rell] potestatem autem (= εξουσιαν δε)   a

θειναι αυτην   rell] αυτην θειναι   θ

Lac.: (p⁷⁵) C 892

John 10:27

    τα προβατα τα εμα της εμης φωνης ακουουσιν και ακολοθουσιν
    μοι   (ZeT 302:20-21) [Ad]*

    τα προβατα τα εμα της εμης φωνης ακουουσιν (PsT 58:6-7)
    [C]

    τα προβατα τα εμα της εμης φωνης ακουουσιν (PsT 236:31)
    [C]

    τα προβατα τα εμα της εμης φωνης ακουουσιν (ZeT 278:15-16)
    [C]

    ακουουσιν UBS^3 P^{66} ℵ B L W θ fam 13 33 1241 a b e]
    ακουει   TR P^{75} A D Δ Π Ψ Ω fam 1; ακουσωσιν 579

    εμης φωνης] φωνης μου rell

    Lac.: C 892

John 10:28

    καγω διδωμι αυτοις ζωην αιωνιου, και ου μη απολωνται εις
    τον αιωνα (ZeT 302:21-303:1) [C]

    διδωμι αυτοις UBS^3 P^{75} ℵ B L W 33 1241] post αιωνιον
    TR P^{66} A D Δ θ Π Ψ Ω fam 1.13 579 a b e

    Lac.: C 892

John 10:29

    ουδεις γαρ αρπαζει εκ της χειρος του πατρος (PsT 148:26)
    [Ad]

    [ου]δεις δυνα[τ]αι αρ[πα]σαι εκ τη[ς χ]ειρος του πατ[ρος]
    μου (JobT 22:20-21) [C]

    [ου]δεις δυναται αρπασαι εκ [της] χ[ε]ιρος του πατρος μου
    (JobT 150:11-13) [C]

    ουδε[ι]ς δυν[αται] αρπασαι εκ της χε[ι]ρος τ[ου πατρος] μου
    (JobT 150:24-26) [C]

    ουδεις...δυναται αρπασαι εκ της χειρος του πατρος (PsT 148:
    31-149:1) [C]

156/ Didymus and the Gospels

John 10:29 (cont.)

αρπασαι θ fam 13] αρπαζειν TR UBS³ p⁶⁶ ℵ A B D L W
Δ Π Ψ Ω fam 1 33 579 1241

αρπασαι (αρπαζειν) rell] rapere illud (= αρπαζειν
αυτο) a b e

μου rell] omit UBS³ p⁶⁶·⁷⁵ ℵ B L

Lac.: (p⁷⁵) C 892

John 10:30

ωσπερ εγω και συ εν εσμεν   (JobT 266:19-21) [Ad]

ωσπερ εγω και συ εν εσμεν   (PsT 131:2) [All]

εγω και ο πατηρ μου εν εσμεν   (PsT 7:27-28) [C]

εγω και ο πατηρ εν εσμεν   (ZeT 35:5) [C]

εγω και ο πατηρ εν εσμεν   (ZeT 185:16) [C]

πατηρ TR UBS³ p⁶⁶·⁷⁵ ℵ A B D L Θ Π Ψ Ω fam 1. 13 33
579 1241 a b] πατηρ μου Did^pt W Δ e

Lac.: C 892

John 10:32

πολλα καλα εργα εδειξα υμιν εκ του πατρος μου· δια ποιον
αυτων ου πιστευετε (EcclT 87:20) [Ad]*

καλα εργα εδειξα υμιν TR p⁶⁶ D L Δ Ω fam 13 579]
εργα καλα εδειξα υμιν UBS³ ℵ A Θ Π Ψ fam 1 33 1241
a e; εργα εδειξα υμιν W b; εργα εδειξα υμιν καλα B;
εδειξα υμιν εργα καλα p⁷⁵vid

μου TR p⁶⁶ A L W Δ Π Ψ Ω fam 1. 13 33 579 1241 a b]
omit UBS³ ℵ B D Θ e

αυτων p⁷⁵ rell] ουν W; ουν αυτων p⁶⁶; omit e

Lac.: (p⁷⁵) C 892

John 10:33

συ ανθρωπος ων ποιεις σεαυτον θεον   (GenT 9:3-4)   [C]

συ ανθρωπος ων [ποιεις σεαυτον] θεον   (GenT 45:20-21)   [C]

συ TR UBS^3 p^{66} א A B L W Δ Θ Ψ Ω fam 1. 13 33 579 a b] omit D Π 1241 e

σεαυτον p^{75} rell] εαυτον p^{66} 1241

θεον rell] τον θεον p^{66}

Lac.:   (p^{75}) C 892

John 10:35

αλλα θεοι γινομεθα κατ' εκεινους τους π[ρο]ς ους ο λογος του θεου εγενετο   (PsT 328:17)   [All]*

εκεινους...θεους ειπεν, προς ους ο λογος του θεου εγενετο   (EcclT 41:2)   [C]

εκεινους θεους ειπεν προς ους [ο λογο]ς του θεου εγε[νετο]   (GenT 159:3-4)   [C]

εκεινους...θεους ειπεν προς ους ο λογος του θεου εγενετο   (GenT 246:11-12)   [C]

εκεινους...θεους ειπεν προς ους ο λογος του θεου εγενετο   (PsT 187:21)   [C]

εκεινους...θεους ειπεν προς ους ο λογος του θεου εγενετο   (PsT 279:24-25)   [C]

ει εκεινους θεους ειπεν προς ους ο λογος του θεου εγενετο   (ZeT 94:27-28)   [C]

εκεινους θεους ε[ι]πεν προς ους ο λογος του θεου εγενετο   (ZeT 279:24-25)   [C]

του θεου εγενετο TR UBS^3 p$^{66, 75}$ א A B L W Δ Θ Π Ψ Ω fam 1. 13 33 579 1241] εγενετο του θεου D a b e

θεους ειπεν] ειπεν θεους   rell

Lac.: C 892

John 10:36

ον ο πατηρ ηγιασεν και απεστειλεν εις τον κοσμον...υμιν
λεγετε οτι βλασφημει οτι ειπον· Υιος του θεου ειμι
(ZeT 94:29-95:2) [C]

βλασφημει a b e] βλασφημεις TR UBS³ p⁶⁶·⁷⁵ ℵ A B D
L W Δ Θ Π Ψ Ω fam 1.13 33 579

του θεου 1241 rell] θεου p⁶⁶ ℵ D W

ηγιασεν και] omit 579

υμιν] υμεις rell

υμιν (υμεις) λεγετε οτι βλασφαμει(ς) rell] τουτο υμεις
ου πιστευετε 1241

Lac.: C 892

John 11:26

και πας ο ζων και πιστευων ου μη αποθανη εις τον αιωνα
(PsT 134:27-28) [C]

πιστευων W] πιστευων εις εμε TR UBS³ p⁶⁶·⁷⁵ ℵ A B C
D L Δ Θ Π Ψ Ω fam 1.13 33 579 1241 a b e

Lac.: 892

John 11:39

ο σωτηρ Λαζαρον ηγειρεν τεταρταιον ηδη εν τω θανατω οντα
και εγγυς του διαλυθηναι και ηδη εις το οζειν εφθακεναι
(PsT 15:24-25) [All]

John 11:43

Λαζαρε, δευρο εξω (PsT 270:20) [C]

Text: TR UBS³ p⁶⁶·⁷⁵ (ℵ) A B C D L W Δ Θ Π Ψ Ω fam 1.13
33 579 1241 a b e

Lac.: 892

Text and Apparatus /159

John 12:2

Λαζαρος εις ην των ανακειμενων   (PsT 270:21-22)   [C]

ην   TR A D W Δ Θ Π Ψ Ω fam 1.13 33 579 1241] ην εκ
UBS³ p⁶⁶ ℵ B L

ανακειμενων   rell]   συνανακειμενων   TR 33

Lac.: p⁷⁵ C 892

John 12:24

εαν μη ο κοκ[κ]ος του σ[ιτου] πεσων εις την γην αποθαν[η
αυ]τος μονος μενει. εαν δε α[πο]θανη, πλειονα κα[ρ]πον
[φε]ρει   (JobT 156:4-7)   [C]

πλειονα] πολυν   TR UBS³ p⁶⁶·⁷⁵ ℵ A B D L W Θ Π Ψ Ω
fam 1.13 33 579 892 1241 a b e; πολυ Δ

Lac.: C

John 13:2

περι του Ιουδα τοιαυτα ειρηται· προτερον εβ[αλ]εν εις την
καρδιαν αυτου ινα παραδω τον κυριον   (EcclT 294:15-16)
[All]

εβαλεν εις την καρδιαν [Ιουδα ο σατανα]ς παραδουναι τον
διδασκαλον (EcclT 295:11-12)   [All]

ουτω γαρ και κατ' ιδιαν προθε[σιν ε]ις την καρδιαν Ιουδα
(JobT 245:9-10) [All]

εβαλεν εις την καρδιαν αυτου προδουναι τον εκλεξαμενον
(ZeT 43:9)   [All]

John 13:13

υμεις...φωνειτε με ο κυριος και ο διδασκαλος, και καλως
λεγετε· ειμι γαρ   (PsT 58:9)   [C]

υμεις φωνειτε με ο κυριος και ο διδασκαλος, και καλως
λεγετε· ειμι γαρ   (PsT 236:34)   [C]

φωνειτε με ο κυριος και ο διδασκαλος, και καλως λεγετε·
ειμι γαρ   (ZeT 28:3-4)   [C]

160/ Didymus and the Gospels

John 13:13 (cont.)

υμεις φωνειτε με ο κυριος και ο διδασκαλος, και καλως λεγετε· ειμι γαρ   (ZeT 182:21-22)   [C]

κυριος και ο διδασκαλος fam 13 33 892 1241] διδασκαλος και ο κυριος TR UBS³ p⁶⁶ ℵ A B C D L W Δ Θ Π Ψ Ω fam 1 579 a b e

Lac.: p⁷⁵

John 13:25

δια [τουτο] και ο [Ιωαννης] επι το στηθος του Ιησου ανακλιθεις... (EcclT 15:20-21) [All]

John 13:27

[Ιουδα] ουκ εφυλαξεν το· μη δωτε τοπον τω διαβολω, και ου παρεληλυθεν αυτον· εις αυτον γαρ εισηλθεν (PsT 42:3) [All]

και εισηλθεν μετα το ψωμιον ο δι[αβολ]ος εις αυτο[ν] (PsT 293:22) [Ad]*

μετα το ψωμιον εισπ[λ]θεν [εις εκεινον ο σ]ατανας (EcclT 294:17) [C]

ο ποιεις, ποιησον εν ταχει (PsT 293:17) [C]

μετα το ψωμιον εισηλθεν εις αυτον ο σατανας (ZeT 43:13) [C]**

μετα το ψωμιον TR UBS³ p⁶⁶ ℵ A B C L W Δ Θ Π Ψ Ω fam 1. 13 33 579 892 1241 (a) (b)] omit D e

ψωμιον ℵ D L 579 a b] ψωμιον τοτε rell

εις αυτον 1241 a b e] εις εκεινον rell

ο σατανας rell] σατανας D Δ

εις rell] omit Ψ

εν ταχει] ταχιον rell

Lac.: p⁷⁵

John 13:30

εξηλθεν εξω· νυξ γαρ ην   (PsT 149:3)   [Ad]

John 13:37

υπερ σου την ψυχην θησω   (John 375:25-26)   [Ad]*

θειναι ψυχην μου υπερ σου   (PsT 148:17)   [Ad]*

  την ψυχην μου υπερ σου Did^pt TR UBS³ A B C D L Δ Θ
  Π Ψ Ω fam 1.13 33 892 1241 a (b) e] υπερ σου την ψυχην
  μου Did^pt p66 ℵ W 579

  Lac.: p75

John 13:38

υπερ εμου την ψυχην θησεις;   (JobT 375:27-28)   [Ad]

John 14:2

πολλαι γαρ μοναι παρα τω πατρι   (GenT 232:4)   [All]

John 14:6

εγω ειμι η οδος, η αληθεια   (EcclT 43:5)   [Ad]

εγω ειμι η αληθεια   (PsT 4:4)   [Ad]

εγω ειμι η αληθεια   (PsT 79:24)   [Ad]

εγω...ειμι η αληθεια   (PsT 155:16)   [Ad]

εγω ειμι η οδος   (PsT 138:27)   [C]

εγω ειμι η οδος   (PsT 252:24)   [C]

  Text: TR UBS³ p66 ℵ A B C D L W Δ Θ Π Ψ Ω fam 1.13
  33 579 892 1241 a b e

  Lac.: p75

John 14:9

ο γαρ τουτον ιδων εωρακεν τον πατερα   (GenT 89:19)   [All]

John 14:9 (cont.)

ο εωρακως τον υιον ορα τον πατερα   (PsT 131:9) [Ad]*

ο...εωρακως τον υιον εωρακεν τον πατερα   (PsT 240:2) [Ad]*

ο εωρακος εμε...εωρακεν τον πατερα   (EcclT 331:10) [C]

ο εωρακως εμε εωρακεν τον πατερα   (GenT 58:6) [C]

ο...εωρακως εμε εωρακεν τον πατερα   (PsT 18:30-31) [C]

ο εωρακως εμε   (PsT 147:6) [C]

ο...εωρακως εμε εωρακεν τον πατερα   (PsT 151:21) [C]

ο εμε εωρακως εωρακεν τον πατερα   (ZeT 185:16) [C]

ο...εμε εωρακως εωρακεν τον πατερα   (ZeT 194:10) [C]

ο εωρακως εμε εωρακεν τον πατερα   (ZeT 259:11) [C]**

    εωρακεν TR UBS^3 p^{66} ℵ A B D L W Δ Θ Π Ψ Ω fam 1. 13
    33 579 892 1241 e] εωρακεν και p^{75} a b

    Lac.: C

John 14:10

ο πατηρ ο μενων εν εμοι ποιει τα εργα αυτου (EcclT 87:19)
[Ad]*

εγω εν τω [πατρ]ι και ο πατηρ εν εμοι εστιν (GenT 176:21) [C]

εγω εν τω πατρι και ο πατηρ εν εμοι (PsT 7:27) [C]

εγω εν τω πατρι, και ο πατηρ εν εμοι εστιν (ZeT 185:15-16)
[C]

    ο εν εμοι μενων   (Did) TR ℵ A D W Δ Θ Π Ω fam 1.13 33
    579 892 1241 a] εν εμοι μενων   UBS^3 p$^{66.75}$ B L Ψ b e

    ποιει τα εργα αυτου UBS^3 p^{66} ℵ B D] ποιει τα εργα αυτος
    p^{75} L W 33 579; αυτος ποιει τα εργα TR A Δ Θ Π Ψ Ω
    fam 1.13 892 1241; ipse loquitur et opera, quae ego
    facio, ipse facit (=αυτος λαλει και εργα α ποιω αυτος
    ποιει) a b; facit facta (= ποιει τα εργα) e

    Lac.: C

John 14:12

ο πιστευων εις εμε τα εργα α εγω ποιω εκεινος ποιησει,
και μειζονα τουτων ποιησει   (PsT 15:20-21)   [C]

    εκεινος] κακεινος   TR UBS³ p⁶⁶·⁷⁵   ℵ A B D L W Δ Θ Π
    Ψ Ω fam 1.13 33 579 892 1241 a b e

    τουτων   rell] omit p⁶⁶

    και...ποιησει   rell] omit in toto   e

    Lac.: C

John 14:21

ο εχων τας εντολας μου και τηρων αυτας, εκ[ει]νος εστιν ο
αγαπων με· ο δε αγαπων με αγαπηθησεται υπο του πατρος
μου, και εμφ[α]νισω αυτω εμαυτον   (EcclT 331:5-7)   [C]

ο εχων τας εντολας μου και τηρων αυτας, εκεινος εστιν α
αγαπων με· ο δε αγαπων με αγαπηθησεται υπο του πατρος
μου, καγω αγαπησω αυτον και εμφανισω αυτω εμαυτον
(ZeT 192:22)   [C]**

    ο δε αγαπων με   TR UBS³ p⁶⁶·⁷⁵   ℵ A B D L W Θ Π Ψ Ω
    fam 1.13 33 579 892 1241 a b] omit   Δ e

    με$^{(2)}$ rell] εμε   θ 892

    αυτω εμαυτον   rell] εμαυτον αυτω   579 e; αυτω εμαυτω   fam 13

    μου   rell] του πατρος μου   Ψ

    αγαπηθησεται   rell] τηρηθησεται   p⁷⁵

    εμφανιζω   rell] ενφωνησω   D

    αυτω   rell] αυτων   θ

    Lac.: C

John 14:23

[εαν τις αγαπα] με, ελευσομεθα εγω [και ο πα]τηρ και μονην
παρ' αυτω π[οιησομε]θ[α]   (JobT 224:10-12)   [Ad]*

ελευσομαι εγω και ο πατηρ μου και μονην παρ' αυτω ποιησομεθα
(PsT 131:1)   [Ad]*

164/ Didymus and the Gospels

John 14:23 (cont.)

εαν τις αγαπα με, τον λογον τον εμον τηρησει, καγω αγαπησω αυτον, και ελευσομεθα και εγω και ο πατηρ μου και μονην παρ' αυτω ποιησομεθα (ZeT 16:30-33) [C]

εαν τις αγαπα με, τον λογον τον εμον τηρησει, και ο πατηρ μου αγαπησει αυτον και ελευσομεθα εγω και ο πατηρ μου, και μονην παρ' αυτω ποιησομεθα (ZeT 166:14-16) [C]**

ελευσομεθα TR UBS³ p⁷⁵ ℵ A B L W Δ Θ Π Ψ Ω fam 1.13 33 579 1241 a b] ελευσομαι D e; εισελευσομεθα p⁶⁶

ποιησομεθα (a b) rell] ποιησομεν TR A Δ Θ Π Ψ Ω 1241 (a b); ποιησομαι D e

τον εμον] μου rell

και⁽²⁾] και προς αυτον rell

εγω και ο πατηρ μου] omit rell

μονην παρ' αυτω rell] προς αυτον μονην D

Lac.: C 892

John 14:27

ειρηνη την εμην διδωμι υμιν, ειρηνην την εμην αφ[ι]ημι υμιν (ZeT 158:16-17) [Ad]*

ειρηνην την εμην αφιημι υμιν (ZeT 15:2) [C]

ειρηνην την εμην δι[δ]ωμι υμιν (ZeT 171:22-23) [C]

Reconstruction: ειρηνην την εμην αφιημι υμιν, ειρηνην την εμην διδωμι υμιν

την εμην⁽¹⁾ a e] omit TR UBS³ p⁷⁵ ℵ A B D L Δ Θ Π Ψ Ω fam 1.13 33 579 1241 b

Lac.: p⁶⁶ C W 892

John 14:31

εγειρεσθε, αγωμεν εντευθεν (GenT 110:1) [C]

[εγειρεσ]θε, αγωμεν εντευθεν (ZeT 398:4) [C]

Text and Apparatus /165

John 14:31 (cont.)

 Text: TR UBS³ ℵ A B D L Δ Θ Π Ψ Ω fam 1.13 33 579 1241
  a b e

 Lac.: p⁶⁶·⁷⁵ C W 892

John 15:1

 και ο οινος ουτος τρυγαται απο της αμπελου της αληθινης
 (EcclT 42:21-22) [All]

 ...τον τρυγωμενον της αμπελου της αληθινης (EcclT 312:12)
 [All]

 και πινουσιν ουτοι τον οινον τον απο της αληθινης αμπελου
 τρυγωμενον (PsT 238:17-18) [All]

 και πιη τον τρυγωμενον απο της αμπελου της αληθινης οινον
 (PsT 331:15) [All]

John 15:1-2

 οι γεναμενοι κληματα της αμπελου της αληθινης και αυτο
 τουτο αμπελος καρποφορος γεναμενοι επι τω φερειν καρπον
 θειον (EcclT 36:20-21) [All]

 ως λαβειν την σταφυλην την τρυγωμενην απο τη[ς α]μ[πελου
 τ]ης αληθινης κ[αι] των κ[αρ]ποφορουντων [κλη]μα[των
 αυτ]ης (ZeT 389:1-3) [All]

John 15:2

 παν κλημα μενον εν εμοι πλειονα καρπον φερει (ZeT 61:13-14)
 [Ad]*

 παν κλημα μενον εν εμοι, καθαιρει αυτο ο πατηρ, ινα πλειονα
 καρπον φερη (ZeT 172:7) [Ad]*

  πλειονα καρπον TR A D Δ Θ Π Ω fam 1.13 1241] καρπον
   πλειονα UBS³ (ℵ)B L Ψ 33 579 a b e

  πλειονα rell] πλειω ℵ

  Lac.: p⁶⁶·⁷⁵ C W 892

John 15:2, 6

 παν κλημα μη μενον εν εμοι εκκοπτεται και εις πυρ βαλλεται
 (ZeT 343:17-18) [All]

John 15:5

εγω ειμι η αμπελος, υμεις δε τα κληματα   (ZeT 61:13)   [C]

εγω ειμι η αμπελος, υμεις τα κληματα   (ZeT 172:7)   [C]

εγω   TR UBS³ P⁶⁶ ℵ A B L Δ Θ Π Ψ Ω fam 1. 13 33 579 1241 b e]   εγω γαρ   D a

Lac.:   P⁷⁵ C W 892

John 15:14

υμεις φιλοι εστε   (PsT 198:12)   [C]

υμεις   TR UBS³ P⁶⁶ A B L Δ Θ Π Ψ Ω fam 1. 13 33 1241 a b e] υμεις γαρ   ℵ D 579

φιλοι] φιλοι μου   rell

Lac.:   P⁷⁵ C W 892

John 15:15

οτι παντα τα του πατρος εγνωρισα υμιν   (PsT 198:12)   [Ad]*

πατρος   fam 1] πατρος μου   TR UBS³ P⁶⁶ ℵ A B D L Δ Θ Π Ψ Ω fam 13 33 579 1241 a b e

Lac.:   P⁷⁵ C W 892

John 15:16

δια τουτο εθηκα υμας...ινα υπαγητε και πλειονα καρπον φερητε   (ZeT 263:18-20)   [Ad]*

εθηκα υμας   TR UBS³ ℵ A B D L Θ Π Ψ Ω fam 1. 13 33 579 1241 a b e] εθηκα   P⁶⁶;   omit   Δ

Lac.:   P⁷⁵ C W 892

John 15:19

ουκετι εκ του κοσμου τουτου [εσ]τε, εγω δε εξελεξαμην υμας   (GenT 149:9-10)   [Ad]*

Text and Apparatus /167

John 15:19 (cont.)

ουκετι εστε εκ του [κο]σμου τουτου, αλλ' εγω εξελε[ξα]μην
υμας   (JobT 66:29-31) [Ad]*

ουκετι εστε εκ του κοσμου τουτου   (JobT 137:4-5)   [Ad]*

Reconstruction: ουκετι εστε εκ του κοσμου τουτου, αλλ'
εγω εξελεξαμην υμας

  ουκετι εστε] ουκ εστε   TR UBS^3 P^{66} ℵ A B L Δ Θ Π Ψ Ω
  fam 1.13 33 579 1241 a b e; ει ητε D

  κοσμου τουτου] τουτου κοσμου   P^{66}; κοσμου rell

  αλλ' rell] et (= και) e

  Lac.: P^{75} C W 892

John 16:13

ου δυναται αφ' εαυτο[υ λ]αλησαι   (PsT 334:24-25)   (Ad)

John 16:33

θαρσειτε εφη, εγω νενικηκα τον κοσμον   (ZeT 158:18)   [Ad]*

  εγω   TR UBS^3 ℵ A B C D L W Δ Θ Π Ψ Ω fam 1.13 33 579
  1241 b] quia ego (= οτι εγω) a e
  Lac.: P$^{66, 75}$ 892

John 17:3

αυτη δε εστιν η αιωνιος ζωη, ινα γιγνωσκουσιν σε τον μονον
αληθινον θεον και ον απεστειλας Ιησουν Χριστον   (EcclT
171:8-9) [C]**

αυτη δε εστιν η αιωνιος ζωη, ινα γιγνωσκουσιν σε τον μονον
αληθινον θεον και ον απεστειλας Ιησουν Χριστον   (PsT
13:11-12) [C]

αυτη δε εστιν η αιωνιος ζωη, ινα γιγνωσκουσιν σε τον μονον
αληθινον [θεον]   (PsT 240:6-7) [C]

αυτη δ' εστιν η αιωνιος ζωη, ινα γινωσκουσιν σε τον αληθινον
θεον, και ον απεστειλας Ιησουν Χριστον   (ZeT 231:6-8) [C]

168/ Didymus and the Gospels

John 17:3 (cont.)

ινα γινωσκουσιν   A D L W Δ 33 579 1241] ινα γινωσκωσιν
TR UBS³   א B C Θ Π Ψ Ω fam 1. 13 a b e

τον μονον αληθινον   rell]   solum et verum (= τον μονον
και τον αληθινον) b e

δε   rell] omit   L

σε   rell] omit   W

απεστειλας   rell] απεστειλεν   W; απεπεμψας   p⁶⁶vid
Lac.:   p⁽⁶⁶⁾. 75 892

John 17:5

ωστε φθασαι επι την δοξαν εκεινην, ην ειχεν προ του κοσμου
ο σωτηρ   (EcclT 322:7-8)   [All]

John 17:11

πατερ αγιε, τηρησον αυτους   (GenT 100:28)   [C]

πατερ αγιε, τηρ[ησον αυτο]υς   (PsT 246:26)   [C]

Text: TR UBS³ p⁶⁶ א A B C D L W Δ Θ Π Ψ Ω fam 1. 13 33 579
1241 a b e
Lac.:   p⁷⁵ 892

John 17:12

οτε ημην μετ αυτων, εγω ετηρουν αυτους   (PsT 246:26)   [C]

αυτων   UBS³ p⁶⁶ א B C D L W fam 1 a b e] αυτων εν τω
κοσμω   TR A Δ Θ Π Ψ Ω fam 13 33 579 1241
Lac.:   p⁷⁵ 892

John 17:21

ωσπερ εγω και συ εν εσμεν ινα και ουτοι εν ημιν εν ωσιν
(JobT 266:19-21)   [Ad]*

ιν' ωσπερ εγω και συ εν εσμεν...και ουτοι εν ημιν εν ωσιν
(PsT 131:2)   [Ad]*

John 17:21 (cont.)

ιν' ωσπερ εγω και συ εν εσμεν, πατερ, ουτω εν ημ[εις ωμεν παντες] (PsT 179:4) [All]

ημιν εν TR ℵ A L Δ Θ Π Ψ Ω fam 1. 13 33 579 1241] ημιν UBS³ p⁶⁶vid B C D W a b e

ουτοι] αυτοι rell

Lac.: p⁽⁶⁶⁾. 75 892

John 18:4-5

τινα ζητειτε...Ιησουν τον Ναζαρ[η]νον (PsT 148:13) [C]

Ναζαρηνον D a] Ναζωραιον TR UBS³ ℵ A B C L W Δ Θ Π Ψ Ω fam 1. 13 33 579 1241 b e

Lac. p⁶⁶. 75 892

John 18:6

εγω ειμι...απηλθαν εις τα οπισω και επεσαν χαμαι (PsT 148:13) [C]

Text: TR UBS³ ℵ A B C D L W Δ Θ Π Ψ Ω fam 1. 13 33 579 1241 a b e

Lac.: p⁶⁶. 75 892

John 18:7

και δευτερον παλιν· τινα ζητειτε (PsT 148:14) [Ad]

John 18:8

αφετε τουτους υπαγειν (PsT 148:15) [C]

τουτους TR UBS³ p⁶⁶vid ℵ A B C D L W Δ Θ Π Ψ Ω fam 1. 13 33 579 a b (e)] αυτους 1241

Lac.: p⁽⁶⁶⁾. 75 892

John 19:14

τη γαρ εκτη ωρα της παρασκ[ευη]ς εσταυρωθη (GenT 189:23-24) [All]

John 19:15

αιρε, αιρε, σταυροι αυτον· ουκ εχομεν βασιλεα ει μη καισαρα (PsT 32:27-28) [Ad]*

ουκ εχομεν βασιλε[α] ει μη κα[ι]σαρα (Ecc1T 205:23) [C]

ουκ εχομεν βαιλεα ει μη καισαρα (PsT 290:31) [C]

ουκ εχομεν βασ[ιλ]εα ει μη καισαρα (ZeT 161:25) [C]

    αρον, αρον (Did) TR UBS³ ℵ A B L W Δ Θ Π Ψ Ω fam 1.13 33 579 1241 a b e] αρον p⁶⁶

    Lac.: p$^{(66).75}$ C D 892

John 19:23-24

το μερισθηναι αυτους τα ιματια αυτου και βαλειν κληρον περι του υφαντου δι' ολου χιθωνος (PsT 39:11-12) [All]

John 19:30

κλινας...την κεφαλην παρεδωκεν το πνευμα (PsT 238:25-26) [C]

    παρεδωκεν TR UBS³ p⁶⁶vid ℵ A B L Θ Π Ψ Ω fam 1.13 33 579 1241 a b e] παρεδεδωκεν W

    Lac.: p$^{(66).75}$ C D Δ 892

John 19:37

αλλα μ[αλλ]ον αισχυνην οφλισκανουσιν και φοβον υφιστανται θεωρησα[ντες ον] εφεκεν[τησαν] (PsT 295:12) [All]

οψ[ονται εις ο]ν εξεκεντησαν (PsT 295:4-5) [C]

οψονται εις ον εξεκεντησαν (ZeT 341:11) [C]

    Text: TR UBS³ p⁶⁶vid ℵ A B L W Δ Θ Π Ψ Ω fam 1.13 33 579 1241 (a) b (e)

    Lac.: p⁷⁵ C D 892

John 19:38-40

αυτικα γουν οι αμφι τον Ιωσηφ και Νικοδημον εσμυρνισαν το κατενεχ[θ]εν απο του σταυρου σωμα του Ιησου (ZeT 268: 6-8) [All]

John 20:19

ως παλιν μετα αναστασιν τα ιδιωματα του φθαρτου φερειν το εγειρομενον σωμα, θυρων κεκλεισμενων εισηλθεν (PsT 71: 25-26) [All]

Indeterminable References and Complex Conflations

Matt. 3:3; Mark 1:3; Luke 3:4; John 1:23

ελεγομεν και τον Ιωαννην φωνην [βοω]ντος ειναι εν τη ερημω (EcclT 38:23-24)

Matt. 3:9; Luke 3:8

ο Σωτηρ γουν λεγει τοις ειπουσιν οτι πατερα εχομεν τον Αβρααμ (GenT 218-26-27)

Matt. 3:10; Luke 3:9

οταν δε το [δενδρον] μη καλον καρπον ετι αγαγη...εχει ηδη τη[ν αξινη π]ρος την ριζαν προς το εκτεμειν αυτο (EcclT 68:15-16)

ηδη η αξινη προς την ριζαν των δενδρων κειται· παν δενδρον μη ποιουν καρπον καλον εκκοπτετα[ι] και εις πυρ βαλλεται (JobT 369:13-16)

ηδη η αξινη προς την ριζαν των δενδρων κειται· παν ουν δενδρον μη ποιουν καρπον καλον εκκοπτεται και εις πυρ βαλλεται (ZeT 79:24-26)

Matt. 3:10; 7:19; Luke 3:9

του ακαρπου ξυλου εκκοπτομενου και παραδιδομενου εξω πυρι (ZeT 27:3-4)

τα γαρ δενδρα μη ποιουντα καλον καρπον εκκοπτομενα και εις πυρ βαλλομενα ξυλα εισιν κολασει παραδιδομενα (ZeT 331:13-15)

παν δενδρον μη ποιουν καλον καρπον εκκοπτεται και εις πυρ βαλλεται (ZeT 342:18-19)

Matt. 3:11; Mark 1:8; Luke 3:16

εγω ηλθον βαπτιζων εν υδατι εις μετανοια...εκεινος υμας βαπτισει εν πνευματι αγιω και πυρι (ZeT 358:27-29)

Matt. 3:12; Luke 3:17

ειρηται γαρ εν Ευαγγελιω οτι διακαθαραντος του Ιησου την αλωνα εν ω εχει εν τη χειρι πτυω, ο μεν σιτος εις αποθηκην των επαγγελιων εισαγεται--ουτοι δ' εισιν οι δικαιοι ανδρες--το δ' αχυρον ασβεστω πυρι κατακαησεται (ZeT 331:17-21)

Text and Apparatus /173

Matt. 4:8; Luke 4:5

και δειξας πασας τας βασιλειας της οικουμενης και τας
δοξας αυτων   (ZeT 44:25-45:1)

Matt. 4:23; 9:35; 10:1

πασης νοσου και μαλιακας ιασις παρ' αυτου επετελειτο
(JobT 3:33-34)

Matt. 5:12; Luke 1:47; Rev. 19:7

αλλα τη νικη τη κατα των αναντιων χαιροντες και αγαλλιω-
[μενοι εν] θεω   (JobT 72:6-9)

Matt. 5:18; 24:35; Mark 13:31; Luke 16:17; 21:33

η γη αυτη...μενει...εως αν παρελθη μετα του ουρανου
(EcclT 12:21-22)

τοτε γενησεται, οταν ο ουρανο[ς] και η γη παρελθη
(EcclT 340:19-20)

παρελευσεται ουν η γη μετα του ουρανου   (PsT 245:29)

Matt. 5:29; 5:30; 18:8; 18:9

[ει] η χειρ σου η δεξια σκανδαλιζει σε [η ο οφθα]λμος, εξελε
και βαλε απο σου   (EcclT 69:1-2)

Matt. 5:37; James 5:12

...αρκουμενος τω ναι ναι και τω ου ου   (PsT 69:6)

εστω υμων το ναι ναι και το ου ου   (PsT 199:1)

αλλ' εστω υμων το ναι ναι, και το ου ου   (ZeT 185:28)

Matt. 5:44; Luke 6:27

αγαπατε τους εχθρους υμων   (PsT 77:5-6)

Matt. 5:44; Luke 6:27-28

προστοττομεθα τους εχθρους αγαπαν και τους μισουντ[α]ς εχειν
ουτως, ωστε και προσευχην περι αυτων αναπεμπειν   (EcclT 81:8-9)

Matt. 5:44; Luke 6:27-28 (cont.)

ευχεσθε περι των μισουντων υμας, αγαπατε τους μισουντας υμας (PsT 89:16-17)

Matt. 6:2, 5, 16

απεχουσιν...τον μισθον εαυτων (EcclT 124:7)

Matt. 6:4, 6

ο βλεπων εν τω [κρυ]πτω αποδωσει σοι (JobT 37:21-22)

ο πατηρ ο βλεπων εν τω κρυπτω αποδωση (PsT 201:15)

Matt 6:9; Luke 11:2

αγιασθητω το ονομα σου (PsT 183:18, 20)

αγιασθητω το ονομα σου (PsT 190:16)

αγιασθητω το ονομα σου (PsT 205:21)

αγιασθητω το ονομα σου (ZeT 383:15)

Matt. 6:9-10; Luke 11:2

πατερ ημων ο εν τοις ουρανο[ις α]γιασθητω το ονομα σου... ελθατω η βασιλεια σου (PsT 280:4-5)

Matt. 6:10; Luke 11:2

γενεθητω το θελημα σου ως εν ουρανω και επι της γης (GenT 104:25-26)

ελθατω η βασιλεια σου· γενηθητω το θελημα σ[ου] (PsT 205:22)

Matt. 6:13; Luke 11:4

και μη εισενεγκης ημας εις πειρασμον (JobT 167:8-9)

μη εισενεγκης [η]μας εις πειρασμον (JobT 286:18-19)

μη εισενεγκης ημας εις πειρασμον (PsT 28:2)

μη εισενεγκης ημας εις πειρασμον (PsT 62:5)

Matt. 6;13; Luke 11:4 (cont.)

ρυσαι ημας (ουκ απο πονηρου, αλλα) απο του πονηρου
(PsT 78:12-13)

ρυσαι ημας απο του πονηρου και μη εισενεγκης ημας εις
πειρασμον (PsT 141:21-22)

μη εισενεγκης ημας εις πειρασμον (PsT 210:21)

μη εισενεγκης ημας εις πειρασμον (PsT 219:24-25)

ρυσαι ημας απο του πονηρου (PsT 305:7)

Matt. 6:21; Luke 12:34

οπου γα[ρ ο θησα]υρος, εκει και [η καρδια εστα]ι   (EcclT 44:16)

Matt. 6:24; Luke 16:13

ωσπερ ου πεφυκεν δουλευειν μαμωνα ο θεω δουλευων (PsT 84:8)

Matt. 7:7; Luke 11:9

επει προσταττει κρουειν ινα ανοιγη (EcclT 350:19-20)

κρουετε και ανοιγησεται υμιν (ZeT 284:4)

Matt. 7:11; Luke 11:13

ει ουν υμεις πονηροι υπαρχοντες [οι]δατε αγαθα δοματα
δι[δο]ναι τοις τεκνοις υμω[ν], ποσω μαλλον ο πατηρ ο ουρανι[ο]ς
δωσει αγαθ[α] τοις αιτουσιν αυτον (EcclT 314:5-7)

Matt. 7:12; Luke 6:31

παντα οσα θελετε, ινα ποιωσιν [υμιν οι ανθρωποι, και αυτοις
πο]ιειτε (EcclT 223:21)

παντα οσα θελετε ινα ποιω[σιν υμιν οι] ανθρωποι, και υμεις
ποιειτε ομοιως (GenT 183:6-7)

Matt. 7:17-18; 12:33; Luke 6:43

εαν δε τουτων τινες μεταβ[α]λ[οντε]ς καρπους φερουσιν ου
καλους σαπρα δενδρα γεναμενοι... (EcclT 69:8-9)

176/ Didymus and the Gospels

Matt. 7:24; Luke 6:47-48

οταν ακουσας τους Ιησου λογους εις εργα μεταβαλη και οικιαν οικοδομηση (EcclT 352:18-19)

εαν ποιηση τους Ιησου λογους ο ακουσας αυτους, οικοδομει την οικιαν εαυτου (PsT 108:12-13)

ο προς εμε ερχομενος και ακουων τους λογους μου και ποιων αυτους ομοιωθησεται ανδρι φρονιμω (ZeT 183:21-23)

Matt. 7:24-25; Luke 6:47-48

οι τους Ιησου λογ[ου]ς ακουσαντες και ποιησαντες επι την πετραν οικοδομουσιν τους θεμελιους (EcclT 35:29-36:3)

Matt. 8:2; Mark 1:40; Luke 5:12

εαν θελης δυνασαι με καθαρισαι (GenT 54:11-12)

εαν θελης δυνασαι με καθαρισαι (PsT 132:13)

εαν θελης δυνασαι με καθαρισαι (PsT 286:25)

Matt. 8:3; Mark 1:41; Luke 5:13

θελω, καθαρισθητι (PsT 132: 13-14)

θελω, καθαρισθητι (PsT 292:10)

Matt. 8:12; 13:42, 50; 22:13; 24:51; 25:30; Luke 13:28

εκει εσται ο κλαυθμος και ο βρυγμος των οδοντων (EcclT 72: 7-8)

[ε]κει γαρ εστιν ο κλαυθμος και ο βρυγμος των οδοντων (EcclT 199:5-6)

Matt. 9:6; Mark 2:10; Luke 5:24

εξουσιαν εχει ο υιος του ανθρωπου αμαρτιας αφιεναι (PsT 158:19)

Matt. 9:20; Mark 5:25-27; Luke 8:43-44

προς τουτοις και η αιμορροουσα γυνη ολοις ετεσι δωδεκα, εξω γεγονεν της φορας του ακαθαρτου αιματος δι' ην εκωλυετο τικτειν εκ του αψασθαι του κρασπεδου Ιησου (ZeT 57:5-7)

Matt. 9:22; Mark 5:34; Luke 8:48

[θυγ]ατερ, η πιστις σου σεσωκεν σε   (ZeT 413:17)

Matt. 10:22; 24:13; Mark 13:13

ο υπομεινας γαρ εις τελος σωθησεται   (PsT 90:12)

ο υπομεινας εις τελος, ουτος σωθησεται   (PsT 282:1)

Matt. 10:30; Luke 12:7

ηριθμημεναι εισιν πασαι αι τριχε[ς της καφαλης υμων]
(EcclT 122:19-20)

Matt. 10:32; Luke 12:8

πας...ος εαν ομολογηση εν εμοι ενπροσθεν των ανθρωπων...
καγω ομολογησω αυτον   (PsT 210:34-35)

Matt. 11:3; Luke 7:19

συ ει ο ερχομενος, [η ετερ]ον προσδοκωμεν   (PsT 133:7-8)

Matt. 11:7; Luke 7:24

τι εξηλθατε εις την ερημον θεασασθαι; καλαμον υπο ανεμου
σαλευομενον;   (JobT 357:26-28)

Matt. 11:9; Luke 7:27

ο βαπτιστης περισσοτερον εχων προφητου...   (ZeT 252:13)

Matt. 11:11; Luke 7:28

εν γεννητοις γυναικων ουδεις μειζων εγηγερται   (ZeT 105:11)

και ο μεγας Ιωαννης ου μειζων ουδεις εν γεννητοις γυναικων
ηγερθη   (ZeT 358:26-27)

ο βαπτιστης Ιωαννης ου μειζων ουδεις εν γεννητοις γυναικων
γεγονεν   (ZeT 368:15-16)

Matt. 11:15; 13:9: 13:43; Luke 8:8; 14:35

ο εχων ωτα ακουειν ακουετω   (PsT 308:12)

Matt. 11:16-17; Luke 7:32

παιδιοις καθημενοις εν αγορα και φωνουσιν ετερον προς το ετερον εθρηνησαμεν υμιν και ουκ εκοψασθε, ηυλησαμεν υμιν και ουκ ορχησασθε (EcclT 73:1-2)

Matt. 11:16-18; Luke 7:31-32

τινι ομοιωσω την γενεαν ταυτην;...ομοια εστιν παιδιοις εν αγορα καθημενοις, α προσφωνει ετερα προς ετερα λεγοντες· ηυλησαμεν υμιν και ουκ ωρχησασθε, εθρηνησαμεν υμιν και ουκ εκοψασθε...ηλθεν Ιωαννης μητε εσθιων μητε πινων (EcclT 358:26-359:2)

Matt. 11:19; Luke 7:34

οτε δε ηλθεν Ιησους, ον ειρηκαν· φαγον και οινοποτην... (EcclT 73:13-14)

εδικαιωθη γαρ [η σοφι]α απο των τεκνων αυτης (EcclT 159:1-2)

Matt. 11:21; Luke 10:13

οτι ει εν Τυρω και Σιδονι αι δυναμεις εγινοντο, παλαι αν εν σακκω και σποδω καθημενοι μετενοησαν (PsT 136:18-19)

ουαι σοι Χοραζιν. ουαι σοι Βησσαιδα. οτι ει εν Τυρω και Σιδωνι εγενοντο αι δυναμεις αι γενομεναι εν υμιν, παλαι αν εν σακκω και σποδω κ[αθημ]ενοι μετενοησαν (PsT 236:5-7)

Matt. 11:23; Luke 10:15

Καφαρναουμ η εως ουρανου αναβηση; εως αδου καταβιβασθηση (JobT 313:23-25)

και συ, Καφαρναου, η εως ουρανου υψωθηση, εως αδου καταβιβασθηση (PsT 150:3-4)

Καφαρναου, η εως ουρανου υψωθηση, εως αδου καταβιβασθηση (PsT 201:30)

Matt. 11:25; Luke 10:21

εξομολογουμαι σοι πατερ κυριε του ουρανου και της γης (GenT 223:10-11)

εξομολογησομαι σοι,[πατερ], κυριε του ουρανου και της γης, οτ[ι εκρυψ]ας τα θεια απο σοφων και συνετων, και απεκαλυψας αυτα [νηπιο]ις (PsT 300:16-18)

Matt. 11:25; Luke 10:21 (cont.)

εξομολογησομαι σοι, οτι εκρυψας ταυτα [απο σοφων] και
συν[ετ]ων και ανε[κα]λυψας αυτα νηπιοις   (PsT 312:21-22)

Matt. 12:41-42; Luke 11:31-32

...καθα και Νινευι[ται] τους Ιουδαιους κατακρι[νου]σι μη
πεισθεντας τω σωτηρι, αυτοι π[επ]εισμενοι τω κηρυματι Ιω[να]
περι μετανοιας καταγγειλα[ντο]ς. αλλα και το περι της
βασιλι[δος] Σαβα λεγομενον της αυτη[ς] διανοιας εστι παραστατικον
(JobT 3:7-14)

Matt. 12:45; Luke 11:26

πνευματα ετερα επτα πονηροτερα αυτου, εισερχεται και
κατοικει, και γινεται τα εσχατα του ανθρωπου εκεινου χειρονα
των πρωτων   (ZeT 88:2-5)

Matt. 13:5-6; Mark 4:6-7

κατα τους εν τη παραβολη] μη εις βαθος τον σπορο[ν απ]οδεξα-
μενους και υ[ποπεσον]τας τω φλογμω της αμ[αρτιας]   (JobT 80:17-20)

Matt. 13:8, 23

ο σπορος ο πεσων ει[ς καλην γη]ν, ον εβαλεν Ιησους ωστε
εκατονταπλασιονα γενεσθαι και εκατον και εξηκοντα και τριακοντα
(PsT 233:28-29)

μονον ενα των καρπων της γης της αγιας φερων· ο μεν γαρ
εκατον, ο [δε εξηκοντα,] ο δε τριακοντα   (PsT 259:33-34)

Matt. 13:31; Luke 13:19

ομοια εστιν τω κοκκω του σιναπεως   (PsT 318:28-319:1)

Matt. 16:24; Mark 8:34; Luke 9:23

ει τι[ς θε]λει οπισω μου ελθειν...   (EcclT 81:14)

ει τις θελει οπισω μου ελθειν...   (GenT 209:13)

ει τις θελει οπισω μου ελθειν...   (PsT 112:14)

εἰ τις θελει οπισω μου ελθειν, αρνη[σασθ]ω εαυτον και αρατω
τον σταυρον αυτου και ακολουθειτω μοι   (PsT 198:21-22)

Matt. 16:24; Mark 8:34; Luke 9:23 (cont.)

ει τις θελει οπισω μου ελθειν, απαρνησασθω εαυτον, και αρατω τον σταυρον αυτου, και ακολουθειτω μοι   (ZeT 133:8-10)

Matt. 16:25; Mark 8:35; Luke 9:24

ο θελων την ψυχην αυτου ευρειν, απολεσει αυτην. ο δε ευρισκων αυτην, απολλυσιν αυτην   (EcclT 77:25-26)

Matt. 16:28; Mark 9:1; Luke 9:27

[Σ]ωτηρος περι των θανατου μη γευομενων· Εισι τινες των ωδε εστηκοτων   (GenT 136:17-18)

εισιν τινες των ωδε εστ[η]κοτων, οι ου μη γευσωνται θ[ανα]του (JobT 148:21-23)

εισιν τινες των ωδε εστηκοτων   (ZeT 53:11-12)

εισι τινε[ς των ωδε ε]στηκοτων οιτινες ου μη γευσωνται θα[νατου]   (ZeT 392:9-10)

Matt. 19:27: Mark 10:28

ιδου ημεις αφηκαμεν παντα και ηκολουθηκαμεν σοι   (GenT 209:19)

Matt. 20:28; Mark 10:45

τεθειται μεν ουν αυτην λυτρον αντι πολλων αυτην δεδωκως (ZeT 301:5-6)

θεις την ψυχην μου και δους αυτην λυτρον αντι πολλων (ZeT 308:15-16)

σταυρω τε γαρ και μαστιξιν περιεβαλον τον δοντα την ψυχην αυτου λυτρον...   (ZeT 324:23-24)

την ψυχην εαυτου...δοθεισαν λυτρον αντι πολλων   (ZeT 354:18-19)

Matt. 21:2; Mark 11:2; Luke 19:30

ο υπο των αποσταλεντων προς του κυριου μαθητων εις την κατεναντι κωμην ονος λυ[ο]μενος...   (GenT 52:6-7)

εν τοις Ευαγγελιοις γραφεται περι του απο της κατεναντι κωμης λυθεντος πωλου ινα προς τον Ιησουν ελθη, εξημερωθησομενου επιβαντος αυτω του Σωτηρος· ειρηται γαρ οτι ουπω τοτε εκαθισεν επ' αυτον ανθρωπων τις   (ZeT 221:21-24)

Matt. 22:21; Mark 12:17; Luke 20:25

    αποδοτε τα του θεου τω θεω   (PsT 155:11)

Matt. 22:29; Mark 12:24

    πλαν[α]σθε μη ειδοτες τας γραφας μηδε την δυναμιν το[υ] θεου   (PsT 1:23-24)

Matt. 22:32; Mark 12:27; Luke 20:38

    ο θεος ουκ εστιν νεκρων αλλα ζωντων   (EcclT 199:7)

    ο θεος...ουκ εστιν νεκρων αλλα ζωντων   (EcclT 312:17-18)

    ουκ εστιν...ο θεος νεκρων αλλα ζωντων   (PsT 276:2)

Matt. 22:39; Mark 12:31, 33; Luke 10:27; Rom. 13:9; Gal. 5:14 James 2:8; Lev. 19:18

    ...τους δ' αδικους και πονηρους, μη αγαπησαντας τον πλησιον ως εαυτους, αποπεμψη εις κολασιν   (ZeT 178:5-6)

Matt. 23:25; Luke 11:39

    ...το εξω[θ]εν του ποτηριου καθαριζοντες   (GenT 125:19)

Matt. 23:35; Luke 11:50-51

    ζη[τηθησεται π]αν αι[μα δ]ικαιον εκκεχυμενον επι της γης απο τ[ης γενεας] ταυ[της]   (GenT 181:17-19)

    παν αιμα δικαιον εκκεχυμενον επι της γης εκδικηθησεται απο της γενεας ταυτης...απο Αβελ του δικαιου   (PsT 70:14-15)

Matt. 23:37; Luke 13:34

    ποσακις ηθελησα, και ουκ ηθελησατε   (PsT 134:2)

Matt. 23:37-38; Luke 13:34-35

    Ιερουσαλημ η αποκτεινασα τους προφητας...ιδου αφιεται υμιν ο οικος υμων   (PsT 186:28-29)

Matt. 23:38; Luke 13:35

    ιδου αφιεται υμιν ο οικος υμων   (EcclT 345:11)

Matt. 23:38; Luke 13:35 (cont.)

   ιδου αφιεται υμιν ο οικος υμων   (ZeT 237:16)

   ιδου αφιεται υμιν ο οικος υμων ερημος   (ZeT 325:11-12)

   ιδου αφιεται υμιν ο οικος υμων   (ZeT 367:10)

Matt. 24:3; Mark 13:4; Luke 21:7

   ειρηται δε και· οτε ταυτα ειναι   (PsT 12:7)

Matt. 24:19; Mark 13:17; Luke 21:23

   ουαι ταις εν γαστ[ρι εχο]υσαις και τα[ι]ς θ[ηλα]ζουσαις (EcclT 173:25)

   ουαι δε ταις εν γαστρι εχουσαις και ταις θηλαζουσαις εκεινη τη ημερα   (GenT 245:19-20)

Matt. 24:29; Mark 13:24; Isa. 13:10

   ο ηλιος...σκοτισθησεται και η σεληνη ου δωσει το φως αυτης   (EcclT 340:20-21)

   ο ηλιος σκοτισθησεται και η σελη[νη ου] δωσει φως αυτης (PsT 16:14-15)

Matt. 24:31; Mark 13:27

   δυνατον ειπειν τεκτονας τεσσαρας τους αποσταλεντας αγγελους συναγαγειν τους εκλεκτους του θεου εκ των τεσσαρων ανεμων... (ZeT 21:19-21)

   αποστελλεσθαι τους αγγελους συναγαγειν τους εκλεκτους εκ των τεσσαρων ανεμων   (ZeT 30:25-26)

Matt. 24:35; Mark 13:31; Luke 21:33

   ως γαρ οι λογοι αυτου ου παρερχονται καν ο ουρανιος και η γη παρελθη   (EcclT 87:22-23)

   κ[α]ν ο ουρανος ουν [και η γη παρ]ελθη μενουσιν οι Ιησου λογοι...   (PsT 160:3-4)

   καν γαρ ο ουρανος και η γη παρελθη, μενουσιν αυτου οι λογοι   (PsT 337:8-9)

   μενοντων των λογων αυτου καν ο ουρανος και η γη παρελθωσιν (ZeT 55: 26-27)

Matt. 24:35; Mark 13:31; Luke 21:33 (cont.)

ου παρερχονται οι του Ιησου λογοι, καν παρελθη ο ουρανος και η γη   (ZeT 128:23-24)

Matt. 24:42, 43; 25:13; Mark 13:35; Luke 12:39

γρηγορειτ[ε] οτι ουκ οιδατε ποια ωρ[α] ο κλεπτης ερχεται (JobT 88:15-16)

Matt. 24:45; Luke 12:42

[τις αρα ε]στιν ο πιστος και φρονιμος   (EcclT 46:29)

Matt. 25:21, 23

εισερχε[ται] εις την χαραν του κυριου εαυτου   (EcclT 72:5)

εισερχομε[νος] εις την χαραν του κυριου εαυτου   (EcclT 199:4)

εισελθε εις την χαραν του κυριου σου   (JobT 86:1-2)

επ'ολιγων πιστος γινομενος, εις την χαραν του πλησιου και του θεου εισερχεται   (PsT 6:20-21)

εισελθε εις την χαραν του κυριου σου   (ZeT 260:8)

Matt. 25:26; Luke 19:22

ανθρωπε δουλε πονηρε, η ηδεις οτι αιρω ο ουκ εθηκα... θεριζω οπου ουκ εσπειρα   (PsT 251:23-24)

Matt. 26:13; Mark 14:9

ουτω και το ευαγγελιον εν ολω τω κοσμω [κεκηρυκ]ται... (GenT 183:14)

Matt. 26:24; Mark 14:21

καλον [ην] αυτω, ει ουκ εγ[εννηθη]   (EcclT 172:24)

καλον [ην αυτω ει ου] γεγε[ν]νητο   (EcclT 175:22)

καλον ην αυτ[ω ει ου]κ εγγενηθη ο ανθρωπος ε[κεινο]ς (JobT 62:7-8)

καλον ην αυτ[ω ε]ι ουκ [εγεννηθ]η   (JobT 289:14-15)

Matt. 26:31; Mark 14:27

παντες υμεις σκανδαλισθησεσθε   (PsT 33:12)

Matt. 26:34; Mark 14:30

πριν αλεκτορα φωνησαι, τρις με απαρνησει   (JobT 375:27-28)

πριν αλεκτορα φωνησαι, τρις με απαρνηση   (PsT 148:18)

Matt. 26:48; Mark 14:44

...ελθουσιν επι συνλημψει του Ιησου οτι ουτος εστιν, κρατησατε αυτ[ο]ν   (PsT 293:28)

Matt. 26:49; Mark 14:45; Luke 22:47

οτε ελεγ[ε]ν οτι ραββι και εφιλησεν αυτ[ο]ν   (PsT 293:16)

Matt. 27:40; Mark 15:29

ουα ο καταλυων τον ναον και εν τρισιν ημεραις οικοδομων αυτον   (PsT 29:5)

ουα ο καταλυων τον ναον του θεου κ[αι] δια τριων ημερων εγειρων αυτον   (ZeT 341:6-7)

Matt. 27:42; Mark 15:31

αλλους εσωσεν, εαυτον ου δυναται σωσαι   (ZeT 341:7)

Mark 1:7; Luke 3:16; John 1:27

ουκ ειμι ικανος, ινα λυσω τον ιμαντα των υποδηματων αυτου   (PsT 130:18)

Mark 2:9: John 5:8, 11

αλλ' αυτος λοιπον αιρει τον κραβακτ[ο]ν και περιπατει   (PsT 291:21)

Mark 5:30; Luke 8:46

ως εν τω υπο του Ιησου λεγ[ομενω]· ηψατο μου τις   (ZeT 34:7-8)

Text and Apparatus /185

Mark 8:38; Luke 9:26

ος εαν επαισχυνθη με και τους λογους μου... (PsT 93:18)

εαν ουν επαισχυνθη τον Ιησουν και τους λογους αυτου... (PsT 288:7)

Luke 3:6; Isa. 40:5

και οψεται πασα σαρξ το [σω]τηριον του θεου   (GenT 153:8-9)

και οψεται πασα [σ]αρξ το σωτηριον του θεου   (GenT 198:23-24)

Luke 8:16; 11:33

ουδεις...αψας λυχνον εις κρυπτην τιθησιν η υπο σ[κευος η] κλινην, αλλ' επι την λυχνιαν, ινα παντες οι εν τη οικια ορ[ω]σιν το φως (ZeT 65:12-14)

Luke 14:11; 18:14

ο γαρ ταπεινων εαυτον υψωθησεται και [ο υ]ψων εαυτον ταπεινωθησεται   (JobT 121:18-20)

ο ταπεινων εαυτον υψωθησεται και ορα γε πας ο υψων εαυτον ταπεινωθησεται   (PsT 201:32-33)

πας...ο ταπεινων εαυτον υψωθησεται   (PsT 264:29-30)

Luke 15:23; 15:27, 30

οστις και σιτευτος εν τη [παραβολη του ευαγγελιου ειρηται... (JobT 12:11-13)

John 5:24; 1 John 3:14

...μεταβωμεν εκ του θανατου εις την ζωην   (ZeT 105:22)

John 6:33, 35, 41, 48, 50, 51, 58

αρτος ουτος ουκ εστιν ο αισθητος, αλλα περι ου λεγεται οτι εξ ουρανου καταβεβηκεν αρτος της ζωης   (EcclT 316:14-15)

...παρεχων αυτοις τον αρτον της ζωης τον ουραν[οθεν κα]ταβαινοντα, τας σαρκας αυτου τυγχανουσας βρωσις αληθινη (PsT 182:10-11)

186/ Didymus and the Gospels

John 6:33, 35, 41, 48, 50, 51, 58 (cont.)

οι αποστρεφομενοι την χρησιν του αρτου της ζωης και των σαρκων Ιησου αι εισιν αρτος ζωης, αρτος αληθειας εκ του ουρανου καταβας... (ZeT 119:13-15)

John 6:35, 48

εστιν γαρ και αρτος ζωης (PsT 50:14)

...απεστραφησαν τον αρτον της ζωης (PsT 196:16)

εσθιει τον αρτον της ζωης (PsT 220:3)

ο αρτος της ζωης (PsT 237:9)

οταν ουν αγιος τραφη τον αρτον της ζω[ης] (PsT 331:13-14)

John 10:3, 16, 27

τα γαρ συναγομενα ποιμνια εκ τω[ν προ]βατων των ακουοντων της φωνης αυτου... (EcclT 38:10-11)

ουτοι προβα[τα] εισιν μονης φωνης Ιησου ακουοντες. μονον ακουουσιν των γραφων (EcclT 38:19)

κτηνη δε σωζομενα τα την φωνην Ιησου ακουοντα προβατα (ZeT 27:29-30)

ωσπερ δε ποιμην αρ[ιστ]ος...ανεστη επι τω νεμειν [τα] προβατα τα της φωνης Ιησου ακουοντα (ZeT 103:11-13)

John 11:25; 14:6

εγω ειμι η ζωη (GenT 106:2-3)

εγω ειμι η ζωη (PsT 147:12)

εγω ειμι η ζωη (PsT 239:32)

John 17:21, 22

δος αυτοις ινα ωσιν εν εν ημιν, καθως εγω και συ εν εσμεν (ZeT 268:19-20)

Chapter IV

The Gospel Text of Didymus: Quantitative Analysis

For over two hundred years textual critics analyzed and classified NT MSS by tabulating their agreements whenever they varied from the TR. Although used from the inception of the discipline, this practice did not find an adequate theoretical rationale until Karl Lachmann popularized his dictum that "identity of reading implies identity of origin."[1] Lachmann's position was eventually buttressed by Westcott and Hort's understanding of the history of the NT text[2]: in 1902 Kirsopp Lake[3] argued that since the Byzantine text (Westcott and Hort's "Syrian") came to dominate the tradition in the Middle Ages, earlier forms of text were partially preserved in documents not completely conformed to the Byzantine standard. For this reason, to ascertain the true lineage of a MS, one need only remove the Byzantine corruptions and compare the remaining portions of text. This is readily done by collating against the TR and comparing variants.[4] B. H. Streeter gave an eloquent exposition of this method as late as 1936.[5]

By the middle of the present century, textual critics came to recognize the insurmountable deficiencies of the tra-

---

[1]For a more detailed account of the rise of this traditional method of MS analysis and the development of contemporary methods as reactions against it, see my article "Methodological Developments in the Analysis and Classification of New Testament Documentary Evidence," NovT, forthcoming.

[2]Introduction and Appendix, vol. II, The New Testament in the Original Greek (Cambridge: Macmillan, 1881).

[3]Codex 1 of the Gospels and Acts (Cambridge: University Press, 1902) xxiii.

[4]In that same year, but quite independently of Lake, Edgar Goodspeed applied a similar principle in his analysis, The Newberry Gospels (Chicago: University Press, 1902).

[5]The Four Gospels: A Study of Origins, 5th impression (London: Macmillan, 1936) 25-76, esp. 39-45. Streeter's straightforward statement of his methodological conclusion is worth citing: this "is a canon of first importance. Of MSS, whether Greek or Latin, later than the fifth century, only those readings need be noted which differ from the standard text (p. 44, emphasis his).

ditional method of MS analysis and classification.[6] The method <u>may</u> provide a "rough and ready" measure of textual consanguinity. But overlooking documentary agreements in readings <u>shared</u> with the TR--readings that often prove to be very ancient, if not genuine--can seriously skew the picture of textual alignments. For this reason, the traditional method of classification has given way to a more sophisticated method of quantitative analysis, originally devised by E. C. Colwell, former professor of NT at the University of Chicago.[7] Instead of counting agreements in variation from an extrinsic norm, such as the TR, the newer method tabulates a witness's proportional agreements with carefully selected textual representatives in <u>all</u> units of variation judged to be genetically

---

[6] The death knell for the method was sounded in 1945 by Bruce M. Metzger, "The Caesarean Text of the Gospels," reprinted in his <u>Chapters in the History of New Testament Textual Criticism</u> (Leiden: E. J. Brill, 1963) 42-72. Subsequent research confirmed Metzger's findings. In addition to the articles of E. C. Colwell cited in the following note, see esp. Harold Murphy, "Eusebius' New Testament Text in the <u>Demonstratio Evangelica</u>," <u>JBL</u> 78 (1954) 162-68; Gordon D. Fee, "Codex Sinaiticus in the Gospel of John: A Contribution to Methodology in Establishing Textual Relationships," <u>NTS</u> 15 (1968-69) 23-44; Idem, "The Text of John in Origen and Cyril of Alexandria: A Contribution to Method in the Recovery and Analysis of Patristic Citations," <u>Bib</u> 52 (1971) 357-94. It should be noted that even in the earliest period of research not everyone was oblivious to the methodological flaws of the traditional system of classification. See, e.g., the scathing assessment of Griesbach's <u>Symbolae criticae</u> (2 vols., Halle, 1785) by Archbishop Richard Laurence, <u>Remarks on the Systematic Classification of Manuscripts Adapted by Griesbach in his Edition of the New Testament</u> (Oxford, 1814), reprinted in the <u>Biblical Repertory</u> 2 (1826) 33-95.

[7] See his revised and updated essays in <u>Studies in Methodology in Textual Criticism of the New Testament</u> (Grand Rapids: Eerdmans, 1969), esp. "Method in Locating a Newly Discovered Manuscript," 26-44; and "Method in Establishing Quantitative Relationships Between Text-Types of New Testament Manuscripts," (with Ernest W. Tune), 56-62. The superiority of Colwell's methods was demonstrated by several subsequent studies, most notably Gordon D. Fee, "Codex Sinaiticus," and Larry Hurtado, <u>Text-Critical Methodology and the Pre-Caesarean Text</u> (Grand Rapids: Eerdmans, 1981). The analysis used in this chapter essentially follows the quantitative method as outlined by Fee and Hurtado.

significant.[8]

In a pioneering article on the quantitative method of analysis, Colwell, in collaboration with Ernest Tune, observed that closely related MSS, such as Vaticanus and Sinaiticus, agree in approximately 70% of all instances of genetically significant variation, while being separated from their next closest textual relations by about 10%.[9] Colwell and Tune reasoned by extrapolation that MSS belonging to the same textual group would normally stand in comparable proximity both to one another (at least a 70% agreement) and to witnesses of other groups (a 10% gap).

A thorough testing of Colwell's method in recent years has effected several modifications. The most significant breakthrough came in W. L. Richard's demonstration that no set rate of agreement among MSS of a group can be anticipated at the outset of an analysis; the different textual groups must be allowed to set their own levels of agreements, and these will vary.[10] In his careful study of the MSS of the Johannine Epistles, for example, Richards showed that members of most of the Byzantine subgroups agree in the vicinity of 90% of all variation. Nevertheless, subsequent research has supported one important aspect of Colwell's conclusions. Several studies, including Richards's, have shown that <u>Alexandrian</u> witnesses do tend to agree together in about 70% of all instances of variation.[11] This conclusion proves significant for the

---

[8]Variants are "genetically significant" when they indicate textual relationship. Thus a quantitative analysis does not consider variants that are readily attributed to scribal error (e.g. nonsense readings) or to common scribal predilection (e.g. nu-movable, itacism, οὕτω/οὕτως, etc.). For a demonstration of the genetic insignificance of these kinds of variation, see W. L. Richards, <u>The Classification of the Greek Manuscripts of the Johannine Epistles</u> (SBLDS 35. Missoula: Scholars Press, 1977) 33-41. Furthermore, a quantitative analysis does not take singular readings into account, since these also do not demonstrate a MS's affinities with other MSS.

[9]"Method in Establishing Quantitative Relationships," 59.

[10]Richards, <u>Classification</u>, 43-68.

[11]Gordon D. Fee, in an important methodological study, ("The Text of John in Origen and Cyril of Alexandria: A

analysis of a witness, such as Didymus, who could be suspected on a priori grounds to preserve an Alexandrian text. And the suspicion receives a remarkable confirmation when Didymus's text is subjected to a thorough-going quantitative analysis.

Didymus's Affinities in Matthew

Didymus quotes Matthew more extensively than the other Synoptic Gospels. When these quotations (and usable allusions)[12] are collated against the MSS representing the major textual groupings in Matthew, 163 units of genetically significant variation are uncovered. A rank ordering of the representative witnesses according to their proportional agreements with Didymus in these readings results in the alignments set forth in Table I (p. 191).

A close examination of these data reveals that this list requires a minor adjustment before it accurately reflects Didymus's textual affinities in Matthew. Codex A is simply too fragmentary here to be construed as evidence that Didymus's text stood in close proximity to an early strand of the Byzantine tradition--a conclusion that otherwise would have to be drawn. It should seem obvious that since A does not preserve even one-eighth of the total number of readings under consideration (20/163), its testimony must be discounted. This assumption is borne out by considering the alignments of the other Byzantine witnesses (TR, E, Δ, W, Π, Ω), witnesses that normally agree extensively with A. These documents align themselves with Didymus ±20% _less_ than does A.

Contribution to the Methodology in the Recovery and Analysis of Patristic Citations," Bib 52 [1971] 357-94) showed that although the "primary Alexandrian" witnesses can agree with one another in excess of 80%, the 70% level of agreement holds true for the "secondary Alexandrians." These findings were confirmed in his subsequent study, "P75, P66, and Origen: The Myth of Early Textual Recension in Alexandria," in New Dimensions in New Testament Studies, ed. Richard N. Longenecker and Merrill C. Tenney (Grand Rapids: Zondervan, 1974) 19-45. Similarly, Richards demonstrated that the Alexandrian witnesses have their highest level of agreements at 70% in the Johannine Epistles, despite the fact that members of other textual groups agree among themselves at higher levels (Classification, 43-129).

[12] See pp. 13-15 above.

Table I

Witnesses Ranked According to Proportional Agreement With Didymus in Genetically Significant Variation in Matthew
(163 units of variation)

1.	A	16/20	(80.0%)
2.	UBS³	111/163	(68.1%)
3.	33	108/163	(66.3%)
4.	L	104/157	(66.2%)
5.	892	106/161	(65.8%)
6.	ℵ	106/162	(65.4%)
7.	C	80/123	(65.0%)
8.	B	105/163	(64.4%)
9.	Π	102/163	(62.6%)
10.	Ω	100/162	(61.7%)
11.	fam 13	100/163	(61.3%)
12.	E	100/163	(61.3%)
13.	TR	99/163	(60.7%)
14.	fam 1	98/163	(60.1%)
15.	Δ	97/163	(59.5%)
16.	Θ	88/159	(55.3%)
17.	W	88/161	(54.7%)
18.	1241	72/134	(53.7%)
19.	e	24/46	(52.2%)
20.	D	62/132	(47.0%)
21.	a	60/130	(46.2%)
22.	b	54/127	(42.5%)
23.	k	32/76	(42.1%)

For these reasons, A cannot be used to determine Didymus's textual affinities in Matthew.

This procedure of eliminating from consideration largely fragmentary witnesses raises an inevitable question: exactly what length of text is required for an analysis of this sort? No hard and fast rule has emerged for deciding the issue. Each instance must be considered individually. One should

192/ Didymus and the Gospels

probably question, for example, whether the Old Latin MS k can be used for the analysis of Matthew, since it contains fewer than half of the readings under consideration. But it should be noted that the relationship of this MS to Didymus corresponds closely to that of the other representatives of the Western group (D, a, b, e). Apparently, then, k preserves enough text to be used for the analysis.

After the testimony of A is discounted, Table I is seen to contain clear blocks of witnesses in close agreement. In general, the seven leading Alexandrian witnesses (excluding 1241) top the list, while the five Western documents come at the end. Between these two blocks stand representatives of the Byzantine and Caesarean texts, in no clear-cut pattern. Equally noticeable, however, is the absence of major breaks between these blocks of witnesses. Leaving the TR and UBS[3] out of consideration for the moment, the clearest breaks occur between B and Π (1.8% difference), Δ and Ω (4.2% difference), 1241 and e (1.5% difference), and e and D (5.2% difference). The last of these breaks holds no great significance since MS e is so fragmentary in Matthew (containing only 46/164 units of variation under examination). The amount of text preserved in MS e is adequate to establish a basic alignment: it joins the other Western witnesses at the bottom of the list. But the sparsity of its attestation should caution against making too much of its distance from D and the others.

Thus one is left with three groupings of witnesses: (1) Alexandrian documents which vary from one another only ±1.9% in relationship to Didymus, (2) a group of Byzantine and Caesarean documents which split into two groups, the first varying among themselves ±3.1% and the second ±1.6%, and (3) a group of Western witnesses which vary among themselves ±10.1%. This comparative disparity among the Western sources derives, no doubt, from the widely recognized uncontrolled character of the text-type.

One witness requiring special attention at this juncture is codex 1241, a document commonly assigned to the Late-Alexandrian group. Why is it that 1241 exhibits such a low proportion of agreement with Didymus (53.7%), falling to the bottom of the Byzantine and Caesarean block of witnesses? Here it can only be pointed out that no thorough analysis of the document has been published, and its text of Matthew has occasionally been linked to the Byzantine tradition.[13] In view of the ambiguity of its witness, it should not be used to define more carefully Didymus's textual alignments in Matthew.

The breakdown of witnesses into groups, which may at first appear unconvincing in view of the absence of major gaps between representatives of the different text-types, becomes more compelling when the aggregate relationships of known group members are tabulated. Here the work of earlier critics in establishing the textual consanguinity of these representatives must be assumed.[14] Furthermore, witnesses which have been shown to be unusually fragmentary or aberrant (A, 1241) cannot be used for the tabulation. The role of the modern editions is more ambiguous, since, on the one hand, UBS^3 and TR are not, strictly speaking, Early Alexandrian and Byzantine documents, but, on the other hand, do represent eclectic texts drawn primarily from these traditions. For this reason, two sets of tabulations will be provided, one with and the other without the testimony of the editions.

The aggregate relationships of all the representative witnesses with Didymus in Matthew is set forth in Table II (pp. 194-95).

Here the breakdown of witnesses is much clearer than when the documents were considered individually. Didymus's text of Matthew stands closest to the Alexandrian witnesses. When the testimony of UBS^3 is taken into account, Didymus stands equally close to the earlier and later strands of this tradition (66.0% and 65.9% respectively). Without the text of UBS^3, however, Didymus's agreement with the earlier strand drops a full percentage point, making him more closely aligned

---

[13] Thus Kirsopp Lake and Silva New, <u>Six Collations of New Testament Manuscripts</u> (HTS, xvii; Cambridge, Mass.: Harvard University Press, 1932) 95. See further, pp. 205, 212 below.

[14] See e.g. Metzger, <u>The Text of the New Testament: Its Transmission, Corruption, and Restoration</u>, 2nd ed. (New York: Oxford University Press, 1968) 36-66; 213-19.

Table II

Proportional Relationship of All Witnesses With Didymus Arranged by Textual Group in Matthew

	Agreements	Disagreements	% Agreement
EARLY ALEXANDRIAN:			
UBS^3	111	52	
ℵ	106	56	
B	105	58	
Totals	322	166	66.0%
Totals w/o UBS^3	211	114	64.9%
LATE ALEXANDRIAN:			
C	80	43	
L	104	53	
33	108	55	
892	106	55	
Totals	398	206	65.9%
(Average Alexandrian)	720	372	65.9%
(Average Alexandrian w/o UBS^3)	609	320	65.6%
CAESAREAN:			
θ	88	71	
fam 1	98	65	
fam 13	100	63	
Totals	286	199	59.0%
BYZANTINE:			
TR	99	64	
E	100	63	
W	88	73	
Δ	97	66	
Π	102	61	
Ω	100	62	
Totals	586	389	60.1%
Totals w/o TR	487	325	60.0%

Table II (cont.)

	Agreements	Disagreements	% Agreement
WESTERN:			
D	62	70	
a	60	70	
b	54	73	
e	24	22	
k	32	44	
Totals	232	279	45.4%

with the Late Alexandrians. A significant gap now separates the Alexandrian group from the Byzantine, with which Didymus averages a 60.1% agreement when TR is included (a drop of 5.8% from the Late Alexandrians) and 60.0% when it is not (a drop of 5.9%). Didymus agrees with the Caesarean witnesses at about the same rate--59.0%, a drop of 6.9% from the Late Alexandrians. The close proximity of the Byzantine and Caesarean groups should not be at all surprising, both in view of the alignments of their individual representatives and in view of the inability of prior research to establish a Caesarean tradition in Matthew. The most significant aspect of this collocation of witnesses is the strikingly low support for Didymus by the Western group. Removed by 13.6% from their nearest neighbors, the Western witnesses agree with Didymus in an aggregate of only 45.4% of all variation.

In short, these figures show that in Matthew Didymus is a decidedly Alexandrian witness, standing somewhat closer to the later strand of that tradition. Furthermore, Didymus's text shows little or no evidence of Western contamination.

Residual Methodological Concerns

Before extending this analysis to the other three Gospels, some final methodological issues must be addressed. First, one must question even more rigorously the significance of the relatively even progression of relationships to Didymus among the textual witnesses. Why is it that, with the exception of the Western group, no major breaks occur between representatives of different text-types in Table I? Notably, the Alexandrian support for Didymus ranges from 66.3% (MS 33) to 64.4% (MS B), a difference of 1.9%, while B differs from the Byzantine witness Π by only 1.8%. In this regard, it should be recalled that Colwell and Tune concluded not only that group members will normally agree in ±70% of all variation but that they also will be separated from other group witnesses by about about 10%.[15] Why does this analysis of Didymus not demonstrate such clear-cut affiliations?

These are difficult questions to address, questions which can perhaps receive no final answers. Nevertheless, two common sense considerations serve to mitigate their force: (1) the Patristic data are more difficult to uncover than are those of the Greek MSS, and (2) despite this difficulty, clear alignments of witnesses have emerged in the analysis.

First, the groupings of witnesses should be expected to be less well defined in relationship to a Patristic source than to the continuous Greek text of a NT MS. As previously shown, the Fathers quoted the NT randomly and, often, inaccurately. This makes the recovery of their text always difficult, and sometimes impossible. Methodological advances in textual analysis simply cannot circumvent this problem: occasionally a textual reconstruction will be in error. The critic must therefore proceed with methodological rigor, and apply a degree of caution when using questionable evidence. Both of these factors—occasional errors of reconstruction and systematic caution—will have an unavoidable effect on the statistical analysis: they will tend to "even out" differences among the textual witnesses. Thus the absence of large breaks between individual witnesses of different text-types is not surprising. Were Didymus's continuous Gospel text fully recovered, the textual alignments so far discerned would doubtless become more well defined.

At the same time, it is precisely this consideration which makes the alignments uncovered by the analysis all the more remarkable. Table II (pp. 194-95) shows the unmistakably Alexandrian, anti-Western quality of Didymus's Gospel text.

---
[15] See p. 189 above.

In view of the character of the available data, one must be struck both by the relatively high agreement of Didymus with the Alexandrian witnesses and the disparity between this group and the others. Didymus must have had a very good Alexandrian tradition at his disposal. This not only makes his unequivocal support for a given variant significant for ascertaining the original reading, it also makes the collocation of variants potentially significant for a clearer understanding of the Alexandrian textual tradition as a whole.

This matter of "relatively high agreement" with Alexandrian witnesses leads to a second set of methodological questions. How can one gauge the relative significance of these statistical breakdowns? How, for example, can the significance of a 65.9% agreement of Didymus with another witness be put into perspective? Obviously the proportional significance is suggested by a contrasting 45.4% agreement: Didymus is far more Alexandrian than Western. But these statistics do not show how *good* an Alexandrian witness he is. They do not show, that is, how closely he relates to the other Alexandrian witnesses in comparison with the proximity of these witnesses to one another.

In theory the comparative significance of Didymus's alignments could be ascertained by considering them in relationship to the mutual alignments of all other witnesses. To this end, Table III shows the agreements of all witnesses with one another in the portions of Matthew preserved in Didymus (p. 198).

The real significance of this table can be seen by rank-ordering the affinities of each witness. This procedure will show where Didymus stands in relation to witnesses whose relationships to him have already been established. The questions addressed by such rank-orderings are whether Didymus has a relatively high proportion of agreements with witnesses that appear to be his closest allies, and, conversely, a relatively low proportion of agreements with witnesses that appear to be furthest removed from his text. Leaving aside MS A, the three witnesses with the highest agreements with Didymus are UBS^3, 33, and L. How well Didymus supports the readings found in

Table III

Proportional Relationships of All Witnesses To One Another in Matthew
(163 units of variation)
(Numbers Represent Percentages)

	Did.	TR	UBS³	ℵ	A	B	C	D	E	L	W	Δ	Θ	Π	Q	f¹	f¹³	33	892	1241	a	b	e	k
Did.	--																							
TR	60.7	--																						
UBS³	68.1	72.4	--																					
ℵ	65.4	62.3	84.0	--																				
A	80.0	70.0	70.0	75.0	--																			
B	64.4	68.1	91.4	79.0	55.0	--																		
C	65.0	78.0	82.9	75.6	91.7	75.6	--																	
D	47.0	56.9	61.4	53.8	50.0	55.4	54.3	--																
E	61.3	89.0	74.2	64.2	80.0	68.7	78.0	53.1	--															
L	66.2	69.9	73.1	65.6	72.2	70.5	72.5	48.8	72.4	--														
W	54.7	83.7	75.6	64.4	65.0	71.2	76.9	54.6	85.0	66.7	--													
Δ	59.5	86.5	71.8	64.8	65.0	65.0	78.9	50.8	76.5	69.2	81.3	--												
Θ	55.3	69.1	72.3	60.8	60.0	66.7	63.8	55.0	69.8	66.4	69.3	69.2	--											
Π	62.6	92.6	74.2	61.7	70.0	67.5	80.5	56.2	89.0	69.9	83.7	89.0	70.4	--										
Q	61.7	92.6	72.2	62.1	70.0	66.7	79.5	51.9	88.3	69.7	83.0	84.6	66.5	90.7	--									
f¹	60.1	74.8	79.4	67.3	45.0	69.9	71.5	53.5	68.7	64.1	70.0	69.9	69.7	73.6	72.8	--								
f¹³	61.3	69.3	70.6	59.9	80.0	63.8	70.7	56.2	74.8	71.2	69.4	70.6	75.5	73.6	70.4	63.2	--							
33	66.3	77.3	77.3	68.5	75.0	74.8	81.3	50.0	73.0	72.4	73.7	73.6	65.4	74.8	77.2	73.0	65.0	--						
892	65.8	73.3	80.1	73.1	75.0	75.8	77.2	54.3	73.3	72.2	70.3	73.3	65.0	73.9	73.7	71.4	64.2	80.7	--					
1241	53.7	79.9	69.4	59.4	60.0	65.7	75.8	48.5	80.6	69.3	77.5	80.6	61.5	81.3	80.5	69.4	69.4	70.1	71.2	--				
a	46.2	45.4	46.9	45.0	52.9	41.5	43.2	64.0	46.2	33.9	38.4	43.H	41.7	47.7	43.8	40.0	44.6	42.0	43.8	40.0	--			
b	42.5	44.8	45.4	43.1	47.1	43.5	40.4	64.6	44.4	39.0	36.4	42.7	45.2	45.2	42.7	36.3	45.2	41.1	43.4	38.1	83.7	--		
e	52.2	42.0	51.0	42.9	50.0	51.0	41.7	63.8	41.7	40.0	34.7	49.0	46.9	46.9	40.8	42.9	46.9	42.9	42.6	41.7	76.5	71.7	--	
k	42.1	61.8	51.3	50.7	--	48.7	44.8	69.6	60.5	43.2	50.7	55.3	52.5	60.8	61.8	50.0	47.4	50.0	47.4	41.1	67.1	63.6	53.8	--

Quantitative Analysis /199

these witnesses can be seen in the following rank-orderings.

UBS^3		33		L^3	
1. B	(91.4%)	1. C	(81.3%)	1. UBS^3	(73.1%)
2. ℵ	(84.0%)	2. 892	(80.7%)	2. C	(72.5%)
3. C	(82.9%)	3. UBS^3	(77.3%)	3. 33	(72.4%)
4. 892	(80.1%)	4. TR	(77.3%)	4. E	(72.4%)
5. fam 1	(79.4%)	5. Ω	(77.2%)	5. 892	(72.2%)
6. 33	(77.3%)	6. A	(75.0%)	6. A	(72.2%)
7. W	(75.6%)	7. Π	(74.8%)	7. fam 13	(71.2%)
8. Π	(74.2%)	8. B	(74.8%)	8. B	(70.5%)
9. E	(74.2%)	9. W	(73.7%)	9. Π	(69.9%)
10. L	(73.1%)	10. Δ	(73.6%)	10. TR	(69.9%)
11. TR	(72.3%)	11. fam 1	(73.0%)	11. Ω	(69.7%)
12. Θ	(72.3%)	12. E	(73.0%)	12. 1241	(69.3%)
13. Ω	(72.2%)	13. L	(72.4%)	13. Δ	(69.2%)
14. Δ	(71.8%)	14. 1241	(70.1%)	14. W	(66.7%)
15. fam 13	(70.6%)	15. ℵ	(68.5%)	15. Θ	(66.4%)
16. A	(70.0%)	16. DIDYMUS	(66.3%)	16. DIDYMUS	(66.2%)
17. 1241	(69.4%)	17. Θ	(65.4%)	17. ℵ	(65.6%)
18. DIDYMUS	(68.1%)	18. fam 13	(65.0%)	18. fam 1	(64.1%)
19. D	(61.4%)	19. k	(50.0%)	19. D	(48.8%)
20. k	(51.3%)	20. D	(50.0%)	20. k	(43.2%)
21. e	(51.0%)	21. e	(42.9%)	21. e	(40.0%)
22. a	(46.9%)	22. a	(42.0%)	22. b	(39.0%)
23. b	(45.5%)	23. b	(41.1%)	23. a	(33.9%)

Obviously Didymus does not stand in as close a relationship to these texts as they stand in relationship to him. Similar results are obtained when Didymus's relationships to the witnesses furthest removed from his text are gauged.

200/ Didymus and the Gospels

a		**b**		**k**	
1. b	(83.7%)	1. a	(83.7%)	1. D	(69.6%)
2. e	(76.5%)	2. e	(71.7%)	2. a	(67.1%)
3. k	(67.1%)	3. D	(64.6%)	3. b	(63.6%)
4. D	(64.0%)	4. k	(63.6%)	4. Ω	(61.8%)
5. A	(52.9%)	5. A	(47.1%)	5. TR	(61.8%)
6. Π	(47.7%)	6. UBS^3	(45.5%)	6. Π	(60.8%)
7. UBS^3	(46.9%)	7. fam 13	(45.2%)	7. E	(60.5%)
8. DIDYMUS	(46.2%)	8. Π	(45.2%)	8. Δ	(55.3%)
9. E	(46.2%)	9. θ	(45.0%)	9. e	(53.8%)
10. TR	(45.4%)	10. TR	(44.8%)	10. θ	(52.5%)
11. $\aleph$	(45.0%)	11. E	(44.4%)	11. UBS^3	(51.3%)
12. fam 13	(44.6%)	12. B	(43.5%)	12. W	(50.7%)
13. 892	(43.8%)	13. 892	(43.4%)	13. $\aleph$	(50.7%)
14. Ω	(43.8%)	14. $\aleph$	(43.1%)	14. 33	(50.0%)
15. Δ	(43.8%)	15. Ω	(42.7%)	15. fam 1	(50.0%)
16. C	(43.2%)	16. Δ	(42.7%)	16. B	(48.7%)
17. 33	(42.0%)	17. DIDYMUS	(42.5%)	17. 892	(47.4%)
18. θ	(41.7%)	18. 33	(41.1%)	18. fam 13	(47.4%)
19. B	(41.5%)	19. C	(40.4%)	19. C	(44.8%)
20. 1241	(40.0%)	20. L	(39.0%)	20. L	(43.2%)
21. fam 1	(40.0%)	21. 1241	(38.1%)	21. DIDYMUS	(42.1%)
22. W	(38.4%)	22. W	(36.4%)	22. 1241	(41.1%)
23. L	(33.9%)	23. fam 13	(36.3%)	23. A	(0.0%)

These are puzzling alignments indeed. For MS k Didymus is ranked where one would expect, near the bottom of the list. But he is proportionally as close to MS b as he is to UBS^3 and he stands in closer proximity to MS a than to any other witness. How can these facts be explained?

Before addressing this question directly, it is important to note one other puzzling feature of these lists: many other witnesses in them do not stand where one would expect. Only the Western witnesses show consistent alignments, standing together at the top of the rank-orderings for group members and at the bottom of those for Alexandrian witnesses (with the exception of MS e in relationship to MS k, where both texts are highly fragmentary). Other witnesses tend to fall randomly, showing no inner group adhesion. Taking one example, the Late Alexandrian MS L has as its closest allies, as one would expect, other Alexandrian witnesses: UBS^3 (73.1%), C (72.5%), and 33 (72.4%). But the Byzantine MS E stands in proportionally the same relationship to L as does 33, in stark contrast to the other Byzantine documents (e.g. TR, 69.9%; W, 66.4%). And the otherwise closely related Sinaiticus stands relatively far removed (65.6%). Such unexpected alignments can be found in the rank-orderings of virtually every witness.

What conclusion can be drawn from these findings? Simply this: these textual alignments occur in portions of text which have been collected at random. There is no escaping this circumstance for the simple reason that the evidence derives entirely from the sporadic quotations of a church Father. As a consequence, the alignments which demonstrably occur in these portions of text are not necessarily those that obtain in a full analysis of all witnesses in their total texts. In these arbitrarily preserved passages MS L happens to be closer to E than to ℵ. This does not mean that these relationships are maintained in every portion of their texts of Matthew. Of course there is *some* measure of predictability in the alignments: most Alexandrian witnesses align themselves, even here, with other Alexandrians. But not consistently so.

These considerations require a significant methodological conclusion. For Patristic evidence of this sort, graphics such as Table III are of little or no value. To be sure, if one were comparing the continuous text of one MS against the continuous texts of others, such a graphic would prove useful. One could then ascertain, say, the relative affiliations of ℵ B in relationship to D k, and draw conclusions concerning group membership. This, in fact, has been the approach normally taken in analyses of this kind, starting with the work of Colwell.[16] But as this study shows, the approach does not

---

[16] See the works cited in n.7, p. 188, above.

work well when seeking to portray the affinities of a highly fragmentary and randomly selected collection of data, as is usually the case in Patristic analyses.

How then can the relative significance of the quantified relationships be established? Only by setting the findings in relationship to quantified affiliations already determined for the representative witnesses in prior studies of their continuous texts. Thus the Colwell-Tune rule of thumb that a group witness will agree in approximately 70% of all variation with other group members, with a ±10% disparity between groups, can be used as a starting point. As already suggested, these numbers should be lowered somewhat in view of the special character of Patristic quotations and allusions that occur frequently but sporadically, lowered perhaps to a ±65% agreement of a witness with group members with a 6-8% disparity between groups.

Didymus's Affinities in Mark

Didymus rarely quotes the Gospel of Mark: parts of only ten verses of the Gospel can be isolated in the Toura commentaries. Even more significantly, only ten units of genetically significant variation can be found among these references. Of course, Didymus may well have quoted Mark more frequently than this. But it is practically impossible to isolate Marcan quotations for three reasons: (1) most of Mark's Gospel is not "distinctive," since it was "reproduced" by Matthew and Luke; (2) Didymus rarely cites a uniquely Marcan form of the text; and (3) never does Didymus identify Mark as the author of a quotation. As a result, there are hardly enough data to produce a quantitative analysis. And even when the analysis is undertaken, the results certainly cannot be considered reliable by themselves. This is particularly unfortunate because previous research has isolated the Caesarean text only in Mark.

These caveats notwithstanding, the evidence from Mark can be combined with that from the other Gospels to provide an aggregate picture of Didymus's Gospel text. As Table IV demonstrates (p. 203), Mark's minor role in this total picture is basically consistent with the major roles played by the other Gospels.

Table IV

Witnesses Ranked According to Proportional Agreement With Didymus in Genetically Significant Variation in Mark
(10 units of variation)

1.	Ψ	10/10	(100%)
2.	B	9/10	(90.0%)
3.	892	9/10	(90.0%)
4.	L	9/10	(90.0%)
5.	C	6/7	(85.7%)
6.	UBS^3	8/10	(80.0%)
7.	Δ	8/10	(80.0%)
8.	ℵ	7/10	(70.0%)
9.	Θ	7/10	(70.0%)
10.	Π	6/10	(60.0%)
11.	fam 13	6/10	(60.0%)
12.	579	6/10	(60.0%)
13.	TR	5/10	(50.0%)
14.	A	5/10	(50.0%)
15.	E	5/10	(50.0%)
16.	Ω	5/10	(50.0%)
17.	33	5/10	(50.0%)
18.	1241	5/10	(50.0%)
19.	b	5/10	(50.0%)
20.	D	4/10	(40.0%)
21.	W	4/10	(40.0%)
22.	fam 1	4/10	(40.0%)
23.	a	3/9	(33.3%)
24.	k	1/3	(33.3%)
25.	e	0/1	(0.0%)

Didymus aligns most frequently with Alexandrian witnesses, least frequently with Western. The peculiar alignments of some MSS (e.g. MS 33) derive only from the extreme sparsity of the data. In view of this problem, there is no reason to analyze Didymus's text of Mark any further at this stage.

Didymus's Affinities in Luke

The data for Didymus's text of Luke are considerably more promising. As can be seen in the critical apparatus, Didymus quotes and alludes to Luke extensively. A collation of the representative witnesses in these references reveals 125 units of variation. Significantly, the quantitative analysis set forth in Table V demonstrates textual alignments comparable to those already found in Matthew.

Table V

Witnesses Ranked According to Proportional Agreements With Didymus in Genetically Significant Variation in Luke
(125 units of variation)

1.	UBS^3	91/125	(72.8%)
2.	ℵ	88/123	(71.5%)
3.	B	89/125	(71.2%)
4.	L	88/125	(70.4%)
5.	fam 1	87/124	(70.2%)
6.	579	85/122	(69.7%)
7.	P^{75}	56/81	(69.1%)
8.	892	85/125	(68.0%)
9.	33	83/124	(66.9%)
10.	Ψ	80/125	(64.0%)
11.	fam 13	80/125	(64.0%)
12.	Θ	79/124	(63.7%)
13.	Π	78/125	(62.4%)
14.	A	77/124	(62.1%)
15.	C	27/45	(60.0%)
16.	1241	75/125	(60.0%)
17.	Δ	74/124	(59.7%)
18.	W	72/124	(58.1%)
19.	TR	71/125	(56.8%)
20.	Ω	69/122	(56.6%)
21.	b	36/86	(41.9%)
22.	a	39/94	(41.5%)
23.	D	46/120	(38.3%)
24.	e	30/92	(32.6%)

As in Matthew, Didymus's text of Luke stands closest to the Alexandrian witnesses and furthest from the Western. Between these blocks of witnesses stand the Byzantine and Caesarean MSS in random order. There is, once again, considerable disparity among the Western witnesses themselves.

Only three unexpected alignments occur here: fam 1, which falls in the midst of the Alexandrian group, undoubtedly because of the curious infusion of Alexandrian readings throughout its text;[11] C, which is highly fragmentary in Luke, preserving only 45/125 units of variation; and, once again, 1241, whose textual character is becoming increasingly suspect.[12]

When the MS support for Didymus's text in Luke is broken down by text-types, the relationships charted in Table VI result. (In view of its peculiar alignments, 1241 is once again not counted among the Alexandrian witnesses).

Table VI

Proportional Agreements With Didymus Arranged
By Textual Group in Luke

	Agreements	Disagreements	% Agreement
EARLY ALEXANDRIAN:			
UBS^3	91	34	
P^{75}	56	25	
ℵ	88	35	
B	89	36	
Totals	324	130	71.4%
Totals w/o UBS^3	233	96	70.8%

---

[11] See Metzger, *Text*, p. 215.
[12] See pp. 193, 212.

Table VI (cont.)

	Agreements	Disagreements	% Agreement
LATE ALEXANDRIAN:			
C	27	18	
L	88	37	
W (1:1-8:12)	18	15	
Ψ	80	45	
33	83	41	
579	85	37	
892	85	40	
Totals	466	233	66.7%
(Average Alexandrian)	790	363	68.5%
(Average Alexandrian w/o UBS^3)	699	329	68.0%
CAESAREAN:			
θ	79	45	
fam 1	87	37	
fam 13	80	45	
Totals	246	127	66.0%
BYZANTINE:			
TR	71	54	
A	77	47	
W (8:13-24:53)	54	37	
Δ	74	50	
Π	78	47	
Ω	69	53	
Totals	423	288	59.5%
Totals w/o TR	352	234	60.1%
WESTERN:			
D	46	74	
a	39	55	
b	36	50	
e	30	62	
Totals	151	241	38.5%

Here the relationships of the groups to Didymus are even more clear-cut than in Matthew. Didymus agrees with the Alexandrian witnesses in ±68% of all variants, with a gap of ±8% between this group and the Byzantine. Of the Alexandrian subgroups, Didymus stands closer to the earlier, with a respectable 71.4% agreement. As already intimated, the Caesarean agreement (66.0%) is higher than would be expected because of the extensive agreement of fam 1 with Didymus. Excluding fam 1 from the tabulation would drop the Caesarean total more than two percentage points (to 63.9%). The Western witnesses, on the other hand, agree with Didymus in an astonishingly low 38.5% of all variation. Thus, once again, Didymus is seen to preserve a predominantly Alexandrian text far removed from Western influence.

Didymus's Affinities in John

Didymus quotes John more extensively than any other Gospel. Collations of his quotations and allusions against the representative witnesses reveal 128 units of variation. The proportional relationships thereby uncovered are set forth in Table VII (p. 208).

One is immediately struck by the failure of the quantitative analysis to isolate group support for Didymus's text in John. For the most part, the clear patterns of textual alignment found in the Synoptics simply do not occur here. The only exception to this observation is, notably, the Western group. These witnesses again form a clear block at the end of the list, supporting Didymus in 50% or less of all variation. Particularly noteworthy is the diversity of the Alexandrian attestation. Several Late Alexandrian witnesses head the list (33, C, L), although their distance from leading Caesarean and Byzantine witnesses (fam 13, fam 1, Ω) is negligible. Furthermore, other Alexandrian witnesses are found scattered throughout the list (note P^{75} with 59.6% agreement and 892 with 57.0%). Nor can any uniformity be found among the Byzantine witnesses. Codex Ω ranks seventh on the list, removed only 0.3% from Didymus's closest Alexandrian allies, while codex Δ ranks nineteenth. Even more striking is the consistently even distribution of witnesses. The only significant break between individual witnesses occurs between 892 and b, that is, at the beginning of the Western group. When the Western witnesses are excluded, Didymus's closest ally is separated from the most distant by only 11%.

Table VII
Witnesses Ranked According to Proportional Agreement With Didymus In Genetically Significant Variation in John
(128 units of variation)

1.	33	87/128	(68.0%)
2.	C	36/54	(66.7%)
3.	L	83/128	(64.8%)
4.	fam 13	83/128	(64.8%)
5.	UBS^3	82/128	(64.1%)
6.	fam 1	82/128	(64.1%)
7.	Ω	81/127	(63.8%)
8.	P^{66}	77/121	(63.6%)
9.	B	81/128	(63.3%)
10.	579	81/128	(63.3%)
11.	A	64/102	(62.7%)
12.	Ψ	80/128	(62.5%)
13.	W	66/106	(62.3%)
14.	1241	77/124	(62.1%)
15.	TR	79/128	(61.7%)
16.	P^{75}	59/99	(59.6%)
17.	Θ	76/128	(59.4%)
18.	Π	76/128	(59.4%)
19.	Δ	75/127	(59.1%)
20.	ℵ	73/128	(57.0%)
21.	892	49/86	(57.0%)
22.	b	51/102	(50.0%)
23.	a	50/103	(48.5%)
24.	D	53/117	(45.3%)
25.	e	45/103	(43.7%)

The close proximity of all the witnesses to Didymus in John can be seen even more clearly when the alignments are arranged according to text-types, as is done in Table VIII.

Table VIII
Proportional Agreements With Didymus Arranged By Textual Group in John

	Agreements	Disagreements	% Agreement
EARLY ALEXANDRIAN:			
UBS^3	82	46	
P^{66}	77	44	
P^{75}	59	40	
ℵ (8:39-21:25)	43	31	
B	81	47	
Totals	342	208	62.2%
Totals w/o UBS^3	260	162	61.6%
LATE ALEXANDRIAN:			
C	36	18	
L	83	45	
W	66	40	
Ψ	80	48	
33	87	41	
579	81	47	
892	49	37	
1241	77	47	
Totals	559	323	63.4%
(Average Alexandrian)	901	531	62.9%
(Average Alexandrian w/o UBS^3)	819	485	62.8%

Table VIII (cont.)

	Agreements	Disagreements	% Agreement
CAESAREAN:			
θ	76	52	
fam 1	82	46	
fam 13	83	45	
Totals	241	143	62.8%
BYZANTINE:			
TR	79	49	
A	64	38	
Δ	75	52	
Π	76	52	
Ω	81	46	
Totals	375	237	61.3%
Totals w/o TR	296	188	61.2%
WESTERN:			
ℵ (1:1-8:38)	30	24	
D	53	64	
a	50	53	
b	51	51	
e	45	58	
Totals	229	250	47.8%

Once again, the Western witnesses stand a considerable distance from the other groups. Nonetheless, they support Didymus somewhat more frequently than in Matthew and Luke. Even more significantly, the Alexandrian, Byzantine, and Caesarean witnesses, taken as groups, vary from one another by only 1.6%. One is tempted to draw the conclusion that Didymus represents a thoroughly "mixed" form of text in John, a text that is not distinctively like any one of the groups but that represents a combination of text forms throughout the Gospel. This would account for both the uneven Alexandrian support and the consistently even distribution of witnesses.

Such a conclusion, however, would be premature at this stage. First it must be determined whether these affiliations apply to the whole of Didymus's text of John, or whether, instead, different textual alignments occur in different portions of text. A perusal of the critical apparatus of John suggests that Didymus's text is predominantly Alexandrian through John 6:46. But beginning with John 6:47 one notices a less consistent attestation of Alexandrian readings.

These impressions demand statistical verification. Table IX shows the alignments of the representative witnesses before John 6:47.

Table IX

Witnesses Ranked According to Proportional Agreement With Didymus In Genetically Significant Variation in John 1:1-6:46 (40 units of variation)

1.	C_3	14/17	(82.4%)
2.	UBS^3	31/40	(77.5%)
3.	B	30/40	(75.0%)
4.	33	30/40	(75.0%)
5.	P^{66}	28/38	(73.7%)
6.	Ψ	29/40	(72.5%)
7.	P^{75}	26/37	(70.3%)
8.	L	28/40	(70.0%)
9.	579	27/40	(67.5%)
10.	fam 13	27/40	(67.5%)
11.	fam 1	26/40	(65.0%)
12.	θ	26/40	(65.0%)
13.	A	25/40	(62.5%)
14.	Ω	24/39	(61.5%)
15.	TR	24/40	(60.0%)
16.	Δ	24/40	(60.0%)
17.	892	24/40	(60.0%)
18.	Π	23/40	(57.5%)
19.	$\aleph$	23/40	(57.5%)
20.	W	12/21	(57.1%)
21.	1241	21/37	(56.8%)
22.	b	16/30	(53.3%)
23.	e	14/32	(43.8%)
24.	D	12/30	(40.0%)
25.	a	12/31	(38.7%)

As the table demonstrates, Didymus's alignments for John 1:1-6:46 are strikingly similar to those already uncovered in the Synoptic Gospels. His closest allies are Alexandrian witnesses, most of which agree with him in more than 70% of all variation. This group is closely followed by Caesarean witnesses, with 67.5%-65.0% agreement, and Byzantine, with 62.5%-57.5%. The Western representatives fall to the bottom of the list and evidence widespread divergence among themselves (53.3%-38.7% agreement). Notable exceptions to these clear alignments are several Late Alexandrian witnesses which provide an unexpectedly low support for Didymus's text: 1241, whose textual character has already come under suspicion; W, whose text is known to preserve a curious amount of mixture; and 892.

Table X shows the alignments for John 1:1-6:46 by textual group.

Table X

Proportional Relationships With Didymus Arranged According to Textual Group in John 1:1-6:46

	Agreements	Disagreements	% Agreement
EARLY ALEXANDRIAN:			
UBS^3	31	9	
P^{66}	28	10	
P^{75}	26	11	
B	30	10	
Totals	115	40	74.2%
Totals w/o UBS^3	84	31	73.0%

Table X (cont.)

	Agreements	Disagreements	% Agreement
LATE ALEXANDRIAN:			
C	14	3	
L	28	12	
W	12	9	
Ψ	29	11	
33	30	10	
579	27	13	
892	24	16	
1241	21	16	
Totals	185	90	67.3%
Totals w/o W and 1241	152	65	70.0%
(Average Alexandrian, w/o W, 1241)	267	105	71.8%
(Average Alexandrian, w/o W, 1241, UBS^3)	236	96	71.1%
CAESAREAN:			
θ	26	14	
fam 1	26	14	
fam 13	27	13	
Totals	79	41	65.8%
BYZANTINE:			
TR	24	16	
A	25	15	
Δ	24	16	
Π	23	17	
Ω	24	15	
Totals	120	79	60.3%
Totals w/o TR	96	63	60.4%

Table X (cont.)

	Agreements	Disagreements	% Agreement
WESTERN:			
ℵ	23	17	
D	12	18	
a	12	19	
b	16	14	
e	14	18	
Totals	77	86	47.2%

Didymus's alignments in John 1:1-6:46 are even more clear-cut than in Matthew and Luke. Here Didymus agrees most extensively with Alexandrian witnesses (± 70%), his agreements with the earlier strand of this tradition being significantly greater than those for the later. The Caesarean group is unified in its support, allying with Didymus somewhat less that the average Alexandrian witness (by 4.7%), but somewhat more than the average Byzantine (by 5.4%). Once again, the Western witnesses are far removed from the next closest group, supporting Didymus in only 47.2% of all variation (a drop of 13.2% from the Byzantine group). These data for John 1:1-6:46 bear out what has already been shown for the other Gospels-- Didymus's text is predominantly Alexandrian with few Western affinities.

That Didymus's textual consanguinity shifts dramatically in the remaining portion of the Fourth Gospel is shown clearly by Table XI (p. 215). Here one finds even less clear group affiliation than in the quantified relationships charted for the whole Gospel (see Table VII p. 208). Alexandrian, Caesarean, and Byzantine witnesses are interspersed throughout the table in a baffling sequence. Note, for example, the positions of the Alexandrian MSS 33 (second, with 64.8% agreement), L (ninth, with 62.5%), P_{66} (thirteenth, with 59.0%), B (sixteenth, with 58.0%), and P_{75} (twenty-first, with 53.2%)! Furthermore, the gaps between witnesses are slight throughout the sequence with no outstanding breaking points, even between

Table XI

Witnesses Ranked According to Proportional Agreement with
Didymus In Genetically Significant Variation in John 6:47-21:25
(88 units of variation)

1.	Ω	57/88	(64.8%)
2.	33	57/88	(64.8%)
3.	1241	56/87	(64.4%)
4.	fam 1	56/88	(63.6%)
5.	fam 13	56/88	(63.6%)
6.	W	54/85	(63.5%)
7.	A	39/62	(62.9%)
8.	TR	55/88	(62.5%)
9.	L	55/88	(62.5%)
10.	579	54/88	(61.4%)
11.	Π	53/88	(60.2%)
12.	C	22/37	(59.5%)
13.	P^{66}	49/83	(59.0%)
14.	Δ	51/87	(58.6%)
15.	UBS^3	51/88	(58.0%)
16.	B	51/88	(58.0%)
17.	Ψ	51/88	(58.0%)
18.	Θ	50/88	(56.8%)
19.	ℵ	50/88	(56.8%)
20.	892	25/46	(54.3%)
21.	P^{75}	33/62	(53.2%)
22.	a	38/72	(52.8%)
23.	b	35/72	(48.6%)
24.	D	41/87	(47.1%)
25.	e	31/71	(43.7%)

the Western witnesses and the rest. These observations add up to an inevitable conclusion: from John 6:47 to the end of the Gospel, Didymus's text cannot be counted as predominantly Alexandrian, or, for that matter, as predominantly related to any of the standard text-types. It is a highly eclectic text in which variants from each of the several traditions (least, of course, from the Western) are represented in random fashion.

This conclusion can be borne out by considering the group support for Didymus's text in John 6:47-21:25.[13]

Table XII

Proportional Relationships To Didymus Arranged According To Textual Group in John 6:47-21:25

	Agreements	Disagreements	% Agreement
EARLY ALEXANDRIAN:			
UBS^3	51	37	
P^{66}	49	34	
P^{75}	33	29	
ℵ (8:39-21:25)	43	31	
B	51	33	
Totals	227	164	58.1%
Totals w/o UBS^3	176	127	58.1%
LATE ALEXANDRIAN:			
C	22	15	
L	55	33	
W	54	31	
Ψ	51	37	
33	57	31	
579	54	34	
892	25	21	
1241	56	31	
Totals	374	233	61.6%
(Average Alexandrian)	601	397	60.2%
(Average Alexandrian w/o UBS^3)	550	360	60.4%

---

[13]Although John 20:19 is the last verse of the Gospel that Didymus quotes, it will be assumed that his textual affinities remain constant to the end of the Gospel.

	Agreements	Disagreements	% Agreement
CAESAREAN:			
Θ	50	38	
fam 1	56	32	
fam 13	56	32	
Totals	162	102	61.4%
BYZANTINE:			
TR	55	33	
A	39	23	
Δ	51	36	
Π	53	35	
Ω	57	31	
Totals	255	158	61.7%
Totals w/o TR	200	125	61.5%
WESTERN:			
ℵ (6:47-8:38)	7	7	
D	41	46	
a	38	34	
b	35	37	
e	31	40	
Totals	152	164	48.1%

This tabulation validates the observations made previously on the basis of the support of individual witnesses. The Western group is furthest removed from Didymus's text, standing 10.0% behind the next nearest group (the Early Alexandrian!). The other text-types stand extremely close together, with no more than 1.1% variance among them when the TR and UBS^3 are not counted. What this must indicate is the highly eclectic character of Didymus's text in the latter part of the Fourth Gospel. Here Didymus does not support any one of the groups particularly well—his text has not become predominantly Western or Byzantine, for example. Instead the distinctively Alexandrian character of his text has simply given way to elements of the other traditions. Now Didymus is

218/ Didymus and the Gospels

seen to represent a thoroughly "mixed" text. This conclusion will be borne out by a consideration of Didymus's support of group readings in Chapter V.

Before turning to such a consideration, however, it may be useful to set forth Didymus's textual relations for his entire Gospel text. This involves a simple tabulation of the figures already set forth for each of the Gospels individually (Table XIII).

Table XIII
Proportional Relationships to Didymus Arranged According To Textual Grouping for All Four Gospels

	Matthew	Mark	Luke	John	Totals	
EARLY ALEXANDRIAN						
UBS^3	111/163	8/10	91/125	82/128	292/426	68.5%
P^{66}				77/121	77/121	63.6%
P^{75}			56/81	59/99	115/180	63.9%
ℵ	106/162	7/10	88/123	43/74	244/369	66.1%
B	105/163	9/10	89/125	81/128	284/426	66.7%
Total Early Alexandrian:					1012/1522	66.5%
LATE ALEXANDRIAN						
C	80/123	6/7	27/45	36/54	149/229	65.1%
L	104/157	9/10	88/125	83/128	284/420	67.6%
W			18/33	66/106	84/139	60.4%
Δ		8/10			8/10	80.0%
Ψ		10/10	80/125	80/128	170/263	64.6%
33	108/163	5/10	83/124	87/128	283/425	66.6%
579		6/10	85/122	81/128	172/260	66.2%
892	106/161	9/10	85/125	49/86	249/382	65.2%
1241	(72/134)	5/10	(75/125)	77/124	229/393	58.3%
Total Late Alexandrian (including 1241)					1628/2521	64.6%
Average Alexandrian					2627/4023	65.3%

Quantitative Analysis /219

Table XIII (cont.)

CAESAREAN						
θ	88/159	7/10	79/124	76/128	250/421	59.4%
fam 1	98/163	4/10	87/124	82/128	271/425	63.8%
fam 13	100/163	6/10	80/125	83/128	269/426	63.1%
Total Caesarean:					790/1272	62.1%
BYZANTINE						
TR	99/163	5/10	71/125	79/128	254/426	59.6%
A	(16/20)	5/10	77/124	64/102	162/256	63.3%
E	100/163	5/10			105/173	60.7%
W	88/161		54/91		142/252	56.3%
Δ	97/163		74/124	75/127	246/414	59.4%
Π	102/163	6/10	78/125	76/128	262/426	61.5%
Ω	100/162	5/10	69/122	81/127	255/421	60.6%
Total Byzantine:					1426/2368	60.2%
WESTERN						
ℵ				30/54	30/54	55.6%
D	62/132	4/10	46/120	53/117	165/379	43.5%
W		2/3			2/3	66.7%
a	60/130	3/9	39/94	50/103	152/336	45.2%
b	54/127	5/10	36/86	51/102	146/325	44.9%
e	24/46	0/1	30/92	45/103	99/242	40.9%
k	32/76	1/3			33/79	41.8%
Total Western:					627/1418	44.2%

These figures show the clear Alexandrian affinities of Didymus's text, but they cannot be accepted without reservation in view of the observations made previously in this chapter. Three adjustments must be made before the quantitative analysis reflects Didymus's textual relationships as accurately as possible: (1) Didymus's text of the latter portion of John, beginning with John 6:47, must be separated off from the rest of his Gospel text; (2) MSS 1241 and W, in view of their curiously variegated texts, should be removed from the analysis; and (3) UBS^3 and TR, which are not, strictly speaking, representatives of any text-type, should be left out of consideration. When these changes are made the results appear conclusive (Table XIV).

Table XIV
Proportional Agreement With Didymus Arranged According To Text Group in Matthew, Mark, Luke, and John 1:1-6:46

EARLY ALEXANDRIAN: P^{66} (Jn.), P^{75} (Lk., Jn.), ℵ (Mt., Mk, Lk), B

Matthew	211/325	64.9%
Mark	16/20	80.0%
Luke	233/329	70.8%
Jn. 1:1-6:46	84/115	73.0%
Totals	544/789	68.9%

LATE ALEXANDRIAN: C, L, Δ (Mk.), Ψ (Mk., Lk, Jn.), 33, 579 (Mk., Lk., Jn.), 892

Matthew	398/604	65.9%
Mark	53/67	79.1%
Luke	448/666	67.3%
Jn. 1:1-6:46	152/217	70.0%
Totals	1051/1554	67.6%
Average Alexandrian	1595/2343	68.1%

CAESAREAN: Θ; fam 1; fam 13

Matthew	286/485	59.0%
Mark	17/30	56.7%
Luke	246/373	66.0%
Jn. 1:1-6:46	79/120	65.8%
Totals	628/1008	62.3%

BYZANTINE: A; E (Mt., Mk.); Δ (Mt., Lk., Jn.); Π; Ω

Matthew	415/671	61.8%
Mark	21/40	52.5%
Luke	298/495	60.2%
Jn. 1:1-6:46	96/159	60.4%
Totals	830/1365	60.8%

Table XIV (cont.)

WESTERN: ℵ (Jn.); D; W (Mk.); a; b; e; k (Mt., Mk.)

Matthew	232/511	45.4%
Mark	13/33	39.4%
Luke	151/392	38.5%
Jn. 1:1-6:46	77/163	47.2%
Totals	473/1099	43.0%

These quantified relationships for Didymus's Gospel text up to John 6:46 can profitably be compared with those already set forth for Jn. 6:47-21:25 (Table XV: UBS^3, TR, W, and 1241 are not considered.)

Table XV

Comparison of Support for Didymus Among Textual Groups
In the Latter Part of John

	Totals for Mt., Mk., Lk., and Jn. 1:1-6:46	Jn. 6:47-21:25
Early Alexandrian:	68.9%	58.1%
Late Alexandrian	67.6%	60.7%
(Average Alexandrian)	68.1%	59.6%
Caesarean	62.3%	61.4%
Byzantine	60.8%	61.5%
Western	43.0%	48.1%

This comparison demonstrates on a broader scale what had already been shown from John's Gospel itself: a shift in consanguinity occurs in Didymus's text of Jn. 6:47-21:25. The eclectic character of this portion of text is seen particularly in the remarkable absence of clear-cut group support for or against Didymus: the Late Alexandrian, Caesarean, and Byzantine groups all fall within one percentage point of each other. Only the Western witnesses stand at some distance from Didymus's text, although even this group stands closer to Didymus here than in any other portion of the Gospels.

222/ Didymus and the Gospels

Some preliminary conclusions concerning Didymus's text of the Gospels can be drawn from this quantitative analysis. It was argued above that to be classified as a group member, a Patristic witness must maintain no less than a 65% relationship with members of a group, with at least 6-8% distance between groups.[14] This is precisely what is found in the case of Didymus. For most of his Gospel quotations and allusions, Didymus stands as a clear witness to the Alexandrian text. He bears a particularly close relationship to the early strand of this tradition, though the distance between the Early and Late Alexandrian witnesses is not striking (1.3%!).

Didymus's text bears no particular relationship to either the Byzantine or the so-called Caesarean text. This observation is significant primarily for its negative implications: (1) Didymus cannot be used to shed light on the history of the Caesarean text, which some have thought originated in his own home town some 150 years earlier;[15] and (2) his text cannot be used to isolate a proto-Byzantine text in fourth-century Alexandria.[16]

Of further significance is Didymus's great distance from the Western witnesses. Although the Western text did exert some influence over the Alexandrian tradition in Didymus's day,[17] this influence apparently had no effect on Didymus himself.

These preliminary conclusions can be expanded and supported by the corroborating evidence afforded by an examination of Didymus's attestation of group readings. Such an examination will be made in the following chapter.

---

[14] See pp. 195-202 above.
[15] See n. 40, p. 20 above.
[16] See n. 39, p. 20 above.
[17] See n. 36, p. 20 above.

Chapter V

The Gospel Text of Didymus: Group Profiles

Up to this point, Didymus's textual affinities have been determined strictly by comparing his text with individual representatives of the known text-types. With this emphasis on individual MSS, no attention has been paid to Didymus's support for <u>readings</u> that distinguish the various textual groups. Yet this kind of support is equally significant, since Didymus can scarcely be classified as a good Alexandrian witness unless he preserves primarily Alexandrian group readings. Thus it is necessary to supplement the preceding quantitative analysis with a comprehensive examination of Didymus's relationship to readings characteristic of different textual groups.

Over the past thirty years, several proposals have been made for the analysis of group readings. None of these proposals has received widespread critical acceptance.[1] Most

---

[1] Taking his lead from E. A. Hutton's <u>Atlas of Textual Criticism</u> (Cambridge: University Press, 1911), E. C. Colwell was the first to make a truly systematic proposal. To determine the possibility of group affiliation prior to the quantitative analysis, Colwell suggested tabulating a witness's support of "multiple readings." "Multiple readings" were narrowly defined as readings "in which the minimum support for each of at least three variant forms of the text is either one of the major strands of the tradition, or the support of a previously established group..., or the support of some one of the ancient versions..., or the support of some single manuscript of admittedly distinctive character" ("Method in Locating," 27-28). To demonstrate the relationship thus indicated, Colwell proposed considering the document's attestation of the unique readings of the group.

Colwell had hoped that the initial analysis of multiple readings would save time in making a preliminary judgment of a document's textual affinities. But such an assessment would save time only if lists of multiple readings were readily available, which they are not. And while a consideration of singular readings will indicate primary group members, such readings are practically useless for establishing secondary membership, since they are typically the first to be assimilated by mixture with readings of other groups. Furthermore, neither of these initial steps can indicate what must be established by a thorough quantitative analysis in any case--viz. how closely a document relates to all others in total variation. For these reasons many subsequent researchers bypassed Colwell's first two steps. Other researchers, how-have failed to match the level of sophistication achieved by the quantitative analysis of individual MSS;[2] others have represented ad hoc creations not applicable to a wide range of textual witnesses.[3] Not even the Claremont Profile Method--

---

ever, refrained from making an analysis of group readings until basic textual affiliation had been established by the clearest means possible, the quantitative analysis. As will be seen shortly, this latter approach is to be preferred. An assessment of group readings will not save time, as Colwell anticipated, but it can serve to clarify and refine the findings of a purely quantitative analysis. For a fuller treatment of this issue, see my article "The Use of Group Profiles for the Classfication of NT Documentary Evidence," JBL, forthcoming.

[2] This is true, e.g., of the profile method used by Carroll Osburn in his otherwise valuable study, "The Text of the Pauline Epistles in Hippolytus of Rome," The Second Century 2 (1982) 97-124. For this analysis Osburn used E. A. Hutton's earlier method of "Triple Readings," tabulating Hippolytus's support of readings attested uniquely by members of one of the three major text-types. The problems of such an approach are now well known: it bases its judgments only on "distinctive" readings (which are never defined) and does not consider the readings "distinctive" of any subgroups. This kind of analysis can give a very basic picture of a document's textual affinities, but nothing more. For Osburn's study the method was sufficient to demonstrate his major contention, that Hippolytus cannot be used to establish the existence of a Byzantine tradition in the second century.
  Much worse is Alexander Globe's study "The Gospel Text of Serapion of Thmuis," NovTest 26 (1984) 97-127. Globe's group profile method assumes the critic's ability to ascertain the character and provenance of textual corruption prior to the analysis! That is to say, Western variants are called Western, or Caesarean variants Caesarean, not because they are supported primarily by Western or Caesarean documents, but because in Globe's opinion, the readings represent corruptions which originated in the West or in Caesarea. Not infrequently Globe makes such judgments quite independently of the extent and character of the MS support for the readings, on the slim basis of their earliest extant representatives. In actuality, of course, the earliest occurrence of a variant tells us nothing of its place of origin.

[3] This applies to Gordon Fee's groundbreaking study of the text of John in Origen and Cyril (see n. 7, p. 6 above). In this analysis Fee established group profiles empirically rather than theoretically, that is, by determining group alignments in the portions of John preserved in Origen's and Cyril's quotations and allusions. For this reason, the seventeen textual groupings that Fee isolated cannot be applied in the analysis of other witnesses for different portions of text.

the most influential proposal to date--can be regarded as adequate for a thorough and in-depth analysis.[4] I have argued elsewhere that this method is well suited for making a quick determination of a document's essential consanguinity.[5] But since it evaluates only one pattern of group reading, it fails to consider enough data to allow an accurate assessment of a document's textual affinities. In simple terms, the Claremont Profile Method classifies a MS on the basis of its attestation of readings found extensively among witnesses of one group, independent of a thorough quantitative analysis and irrespective of "distinctive" readings, that is, readings preserved exclusively by members of one textual group or another.[6] A full and accurate determination of group affiliation, however, requires (1) a full-scale quantitative analysis which demonstrates the document's proportional relationship to other witnesses in total variation, such as is found in the

---

[4] For initial statements concerning the rationale and application of the Claremont Profile Method, see Eldon Jay Epp, "The Claremont Profile-Method for Grouping New Testament Minuscule Manuscripts," in *Studies in the History and Text of the New Testament*, ed. Boyd L. Daniels and Jack M. Suggs (SD, 29. Salt Lake City: University of Utah Press, 1967) 27-37; Ernest C. Colwell, Paul R. McReynolds, Irving A. Sparks, and Frederik Wisse, "The International Greek New Testament Project: A Status Report," *JBL* 87 (1968) 187-97. The method was devised by McReynolds and Wisse while doctoral candidates at Claremont Graduate School. For full statements and consistent applications of the method see their dissertations: Paul R. McReynolds, "The Claremont Profile Method and the Grouping of Byzantine New Testament Manuscripts" (Ph.D. dissertation, Claremont Graduate School, 1968); Frederik Wisse, "The Claremont Profile Method for the Classification of the Byzantine New Testament Manuscripts: A Study in Method" (Ph.D. dissertation, Claremont Graduate School, 1968). Wisse later revised his dissertation and updated the discussion in his monograph *The Profile Method for Classifying and Evaluating Manuscript Evidence* (SD, 44. Grand Rapids: Eerdmans, 1982).

[5] "The Use of Group Profiles."

[6] Ibid. Wisse's decision not to apply a full quantitative analysis and his refusal to consider readings unique to the various groups led him to make erroneous classifications of documents in Luke. The most outstanding instance was his assignation of MSS Bezae and Vaticanus to the same group! This misclassification is easily detected by a quantitative analysis.

preceding chapter, and (2) a <u>comprehensive</u> evaluation of group readings: both those preserved extensively among members of a group and those unique to each of the groups.

Three preliminary profiles have been devised to provide such a comprehensive evaluation for the Gospel quotations and allusions of Didymus.[7] (1) An inter-group profile is concerned with readings characteristically preserved by witnesses of only one of the known textual groups (a category not considered by the Claremont Profile Method). Two sets of readings are profiled: those supported <u>mainly</u> by members of only one group (as defined strictly below) and those supported <u>only</u> by members of one group. The latter set of readings has itself been divided into two sub-categories: readings supported by most group members (and no other witnesses) and those supported only by a few group members (and no others). (2) An intra-group profile is concerned with readings found extensively among members of a group, regardless of how well they are also attested by members of other groups. Once again two sets of readings are profiled: those supported by <u>all</u> the representative witnesses of a group and those supported by at least <u>two-thirds</u> of these representatives. (3) A combination profile is concerned with the extent and strength of a reading's attestation both within a given group and among the various groups. The readings profiled under this category are those supported by all or most representatives of a group (as determined by the intra-group profile) but by few or no other witnesses (as determined by the inter-group profile).

It would be helpful at this stage to define as narrowly as possible the terms used to describe each of these group relationships.

Inter-Group Relationships

<u>Distinctive Readings</u>: Generally, readings distinct to a group, i.e. those shared by most group members and found in no other witnesses. For this particular analysis of Didymus,

---

[7] In the article just cited, I give a more extended rationale for these profiles, and illustrate their superiority with the data collected for the present study.

distinctive group readings have been defined as follows:
> Distinctively Alexandrian: Readings found in at least two Early Alexandrian witnesses, half of the Late Alexandrian, and no others.
> Distinctively Western: Readings found in at least one Greek witness and two Old Latin MSS (when their witness can be adduced) and no others. When the Old Latin cannot be used, readings found in two Greek witnesses.
> Distinctively Caesarean: Readings found in all the Caesarean witnesses and no others.
> Distinctively Byzantine: Readings found in all but one of the Byzantine witnesses and no others.

Exclusive Readings: Readings found exclusively among witnesses of one group, i.e. those shared by at least two group members and no others (excluding distinctive readings).

Primary Readings: Readings that are shared by at least two group members and that have greater group than non-group support. "Greater group support" is defined (a) in the case of "uniform" primary readings (see the intra-group profile below) as readings supported neither uniformly by another group, nor predominantly by more than one other group, nor by more than two other groups when one of them supports it predominantly; (b) in the case of "predominant" primary readings (see below) as readings supported neither uniformly nor predominantly by another group; and (c) in all other cases, as readings supported by more group than non-group witnesses.

Intra-Group Relationships

Uniform Readings: Readings shared by all group witnesses with text.

Predominant Readings: Readings shared by at least two-thirds of all group witnesses with text.[8]

---

[8] Naturally, to be consistent with the methodological principles sketched previously, all of the preceding categories of group witnesses can be applied only to units of genetically significant variation in which two or more of the representative witnesses agree against the rest. Furthermore, in view of the preceding quantitative analysis, it was decided not to take into account the witness of either W or 1241 when

It is now possible to describe the three preliminary profiles in terms of these narrowly defined group relationships. The first two profiles are "simple"--one ascertaining the extent to which Didymus attests the distinctive, exclusive, and primary readings of each group, the other determining his support of uniform and predominant readings. The third profile is "complex"--showing Didymus's attestation of readings which are simultaneously uniform or predominant and distinctive, exclusive, or primary.

Profile One: Inter-Group Readings

The following table shows the frequency with which Didymus supports the distinctive, exclusive, and primary readings of the four major control groups. The fractions represent the number of Didymus's agreements over the total number of readings. It was decided to separate the readings of John 6:47-21:25 from the rest of the Gospel text as a means of determining on independent grounds whether a shift of consanguinity occurs in that portion of text.

Table XVI
Didymus's Attestation of Inter-Group Readings

	Distinctive	Exclusive	Primary	Totals
Matthew				
Alexandrian:	1/2	4/8	9/19	14/29
Byzantine:	0/0	0/1	5/23	5/24
Caesarean:	0/0	0/7	6/18	6/25
Western:	0/13	3/19	11/27	14/59
Mark				
Alexandrian:	1/1	0/1	3/3	4/5
Byzantine:	0/0	0/0	0/2	0/2
Caesarean:	0/0	0/0	0/0	0/0
Western:	0/2	0/2	1/2	1/6

---

establishing uniform or distinctive readings.

Table XVI (cont.)

	Distinctive	Exclusive	Primary	Totals
Luke				
Alexandrian:	1/1	2/8	14/23	17/32
Byzantine:	0/0	0/0	2/13	2/13
Caesarean:	0/0	0/0	6/9	6/9
Western:	0/15	0/18	7/17	7/50
John 1:1-6:46				
Alexandrian:	0/0	0/5	4/4	4/9
Byzantine:	0/0	0/0	0/2	0/2
Caesarean:	0/0	0/0	0/2	0/2
Western:	0/4	0/5	2/9	2/18
Totals: Matthew-John 6:46				
Alexandrian:	3/4	6/22	30/49	39/75
	(75.0%)	(27.3%)	(61.2%)	(52.0%)
Byzantine:	0/0	0/1	7/40	7/41
	(--)	(0.0%)	(17.5%)	(17.1%)
Caesarean:	0/0	0/7	12/29	12/36
	(--)	(0.0%)	(41.4%)	(33.3%)
Western:	0/34	3/44	21/55	24/133
	(0.0%)	(6.8%)	(38.2%)	(18.0%)
John 6:47-21:25				
Alexandrian:	1/1	2/11	2/6	5/18
	(100%)	(18.2%)	(33.3%)	(27.8%)
Byzantine:	0/0	0/0	0/4	0/4
	(--)	(--)	(0.0%)	(0.0%)
Caesarean:	0/0	1/1	0/3	1/4
	(--)	(100%)	(0.0%)	(25.0%)
Western:	1/4	4/21	6/14	11/39
	(25.0%)	(19.0%)	(42.9%)	(28.2%)

Before evaluating these data, it may prove helpful to consider the significance of the inter-group profile in general terms. For a witness to be classified as a group member, it obviously must support a high proportion of distinctive group readings. The category "distinctive" itself, of course, can be useful only when representative witnesses have been chosen--scarcely ever do all witnesses of a text-type agree on a given variant reading. For this reason, a newly analyzed witness cannot be expected to agree in every case with readings found exclusively among the majority of already selected group representatives. But what can be expected is that Alexandrian witnesses outside the control group of MSS will *frequently* preserve such distinctive readings, and that rarely will they preserve readings distinctive to other groups.

Furthermore, one would expect any group witness to contain a relatively high proportion of exclusive and primary group readings. Here a special degree of caution must be applied. Because these latter kinds of inter-group readings involve group splits, with the majority of group members sometimes opposing the exclusive or primary text, one should not be overly sanguine about establishing the same proportion of agreement in such readings as obtains in a quantitative analysis of the individual witnesses. That is to say, a 65-70% agreement with exclusive or primary readings is far more than can be anticipated, since this would inevitably involve a frequent opposition to the group's majority text. What *can* be expected is a strikingly higher attestation of the exclusive and primary readings of one group than of those of the others.

On the basis of these theoretical observations, it should be clear that prior to John 6:47, Didymus's profile conforms to what one would expect of a good Alexandrian witness. He preserves a high proportion of distinctively Alexandrian readings--varying in only one of four instances.[9] No distinc-

---

[9] Didymus's text in the one variant reading is somewhat uncertain, involving the presence of the article in Matt. 25:41. Both immediately before and after the reading in question Didymus preserves singular variants (omit ἀπ' ἐμοῦ; κεκατηραμένοι for κατηραμένοι). Of the remaining three instances, the plural form τὰς παραβολάς of Mark 4:10 appears fairly certain, although it occurs in an allusion, while the distinctive readings of Matt. 18:6 and Luke 24:49 are beyond question.

tive readings are found among the Caesarean and Byzantine control groups. But there is an impressive number of distinctive Western readings (thirty-four)[10] of which Didymus preserves <u>none</u>. This statistic confirms what has already been shown by the quantitative analysis: Didymus was basically unaffected by the Western tradition.

Furthermore, Didymus preserves a markedly higher proportion of Alexandrian exclusive and primary readings than of any other group. Didymus does not preserve the sole Byzantine exclusive reading,[11] nor any of the seven Caesarean exclusive readings,[12] and only three of the forty-four Western.[13] By contrast, he agrees with Alexandrian exclusive readings in more than one out of every four instances.[14] In addition, Didymus's 61.2% agreement with Alexandrian primary readings[15]

---

[10]Matt. 4:4; 5:42; 10:28; 10:29; 11:21; 11:28; 15:8; 16:18; 18:22; 22:13; 24:30; 25:33; 28:19; Mark 7:6; 9:49; Luke 2:37; 8:15; 9:62; 10:20; 11:13; 11:50; 12:19; 12:20 (2x); 14:29; 16:23; 18:14; 19:12; 19:43; 20:25; John 1:6; 4:14; 4:28; 5:19.

[11]Matt. 26:53.

[12]Matt. 7:23; 7:26; 13:43; 14:21; 15:14 (2x); 25:16.

[13]All three are from Matthew; all three consist of agreements with Old Latin MSS against all other witnesses (12:37; 21:31 [2x]). Western exclusive readings not supported by Didymus: Matt. 5:19; 5:42; 6:14; 7:23; 10:29; 10:34; 11:20; 12:37; 13:11 (2x); 13:17; 13:45; 13:47; 18:6; 26:53; 28:19; Mark 3:17; 7:6; Luke 2:36; 5:10; 6:45; 7:41; 12:18; 12:19; 13:27; 14:29 (2x); 16:8; 16:25; 18:7; 18:8; 19:21; 19:42 (2x); 21:20; 24:32; John 1:18 (2x); 1:29; 3:16; 5:46.

[14]As anticipated, this proportion of agreement is much lower that Didymus's overall agreement with the Alexandrian witnesses only because the exclusive readings in nearly every case represent an Alexandrian minority opposing all other witnesses. Didymus preserves the Alexandrian exclusive readings of Matt. 5:4; 12:24; 20:32; 21:19; Luke 6:45; 11:15; while varying at Matt. 7:6; 7:14; 11:21; 24:40; Mark 9:49; Luke 1:17; 14:29; 15:22; 16:8; 17:10; 20:35; John 3:16 (2x); 5:18; 5:29; 5:45.

[15]Didymus agrees with Alexandrian primary readings in the following texts: Matt. 5:41; 7:9 (2x); 10:28 (2x); 12:35; 21:2; 23:30; 24:3; Mark 7:6; 11:2 (2x); Luke 2:35; 2:36; 2:37; 4:17; 6:38; 7:28 (2x); 10:19; 10:20; 11:15; 12:8; 18:14 19:42; 20:25; John 4:20; 4:36; 5:38; 5:47. Disagreements: Matt. 6:24; 10:28; 11:21; 15:6; 16:19; 19:28; 22:45; 26:31; 26:53 (2x); Luke 6:45; 6:46; 13:27; 14:26; 14:28; 18:7; 19:43; 20:25; 21:20.

232/ Didymus and the Gospels

contrasts sharply with his support for all the other groups: Caesarean, 41.4% agreement;[16] Western, 38.2%;[17] and Byzantine, 17.5%.[18]

When Didymus's support of the three different kinds of inter-group readings is tabulated together (the Totals column), one can see with particular clarity his comparative proximity to the Alexandrian text. He agrees with over half of the Alexandrian group readings, but with only a third of the Caesarean, and with less than a fifth of the Byzantine and Western. Thus it should be clear that Didymus is not only a good Alexandrian witness (as shown especially by his attestation of distinctive readings) but that his deviations from the Alexandrian tradition are not toward a Western or Byzantine text.

One other feature of this profile worth observing is the change in Didymus's alignments beginning with John 6:47. The paucity of the data makes it difficult to compare only the two parts of John, although the strikingly closer relationship to the Western readings in the second part of the Gospel should not be overlooked (11/39 [28.2%] as contrasted with 2/18 [11.1%]). But a comparison of Didymus's total Gospel text before John 6:47 with that which follows validates the conclusion drawn earlier: the character of Didymus's text shifts dramatically for the final two-thirds of John's Gospel. Par-

---

[16] Agreements with Caesarean primary readings: Matt. 1:6; 3:12; 11:20; 22:13; 24:36; 26:53; Luke 1:34; 6:38; 9:23; 14:28; 21:20; 22:32. Disagreements: Matt. 7:23; 7:26; 10:28 (4x); 11:18; 15:14; 23:30 (2x); 25:6; 26:53; Luke 2:37; 20:35; 23:21; John 4:20; 5:47.

[17] Agreements with Western primary readings: Matt. 3:12; 5:9; 6:20; 7:9 (2x); 7:24; 7:26; 22:13; 23:2; 24:36; 26:53; Mark 7:6; Luke 4:18; 10:20; 16:15; 16:23; 17:10 (2x); 24:49; John 1:3; 6:46. Disagreements: Matt. 1:16; 4:19; 5:20; 5:48; 6:1; 6:14; 11:20; 12:24; 13:43; 14:21; 15:6; 23:37; 25:41; 26:53; 27:40 (2x); Mark 4:10; Luke 1:68; 3:8; 9:23; 14:26; 17:10; 19:12; 19:21; 19:42; 20:36; 23:21; John 5:8; 5:29; 5:47; 6:38 (4x).

[18] Agreements with Byzantine primary readings: Matt. 4:4; 15:6; 15:14; 23:30; 26:31; 28:19; Luke 4:29; 19:43. Disagreements: Matt. 1:6; 5:25; 5:48; 7:9 (2x); 7:21; 7:24; 15:8; 21:2; 22:13; 23:25; 23:37; 24:3; 24:36 (3x); 26:52; 24:53; Mark 4:10; 11:2; Luke 1:69; 2:36; 4:17; 4:18; 6:38; 10:13; 16:25; 18:14; 19:42; 20:25; 22:32; John 6:29; 6:46.

ticularly worth noting are: (1) the drop in Didymus's support for Alexandrian readings from 52.0% to 27.8%;[19] and (2) the greater attestation of Western readings (up from 18.0% to 28.2%). Only in this portion of text does Didymus preserve a distinctive Western reading,[20] and he contains nearly three times the proportion of exclusive Western readings as in the rest of his Gospel text (19.0% as contrasted with 6.8%).[21] Obviously these data are too sparse to allow final judgments of Didymus's textual affinities. There are scarcely any Byzantine group readings here, for example. All the same, it cannot be overlooked that Didymus has changed from being a very good supporter of the Alexandrian tradition to being a rather mediocre one. And at least in part this shift has involved a greater influx of Western readings.

Two major drawbacks to this first profile have already been intimated. First, it is based on few data that tend to be unevenly distributed among the textual groups. When no distinctive Byzantine or Caesarean readings are found among a Father's Biblical quotations and allusions, the profile cannot very well illuminate his affinities with the Byzantine or Caesarean texts. With other Patristic sources, of course, the data will be more numerous. Second, a witness's failure to support a group's exclusive or primary readings may result from its preservation of the variant found in the majority of the group's witnesses. This in fact often proves to be the case for Didymus. These two drawbacks suggest the need to corroborate the findings of the inter-group profile with a profile which considers purely intra-group relationships.

---

[19] He agrees with the only distinctively Alexandrian readings in this part of John (10:28), but agrees with only two of the exclusive readings (8:39; 9:39) while varying from nine others (7:37; 7:39 [2x]; 9:39; 10:9; 10:29; 10:33; 12:2; 14:10). He also preserves two primary readings (13:13; 14:10) while failing to support four others (6:47; 8:48; 10:15; 14:10).

[20] John 6:70. He varies from three others (6:62; 8:45; 10:35).

[21] Agreements with Western exclusive readings: John 9:28; 10:36; 14:27; 18:5. Disagreements: 8:12; 8:34; 8:40; 8:48; 9:2; 10:10; 10:11 (2x); 10:15; 10:29; 13:27; 14:10; 14:23 (2x); 15:5; 16:33; 17:3.

234/ Didymus and the Gospels

Profile Two: Intra-Group Readings
   The second profile charts the attestation of uniform and predominant readings without regard to the distribution of readings among various groups. To be included in the profile, a reading must vary from at least one other reading that is attested by at least two representatives of any group. This delimitation serves to exclude from consideration instances of accidental agreement among otherwise unrelated MSS.

Table XVII
Didymus's Attestation of Intra-Group Readings

	Uniform	Predominant	Total
Matthew:			
Alexandrian:	49/57 (86.0%)	29/45 (64.4%)	78/102 (76.5%)
Byzantine:	60/87 (69.0%)	9/16 (56.3%)	69/103 (67.0%)
Caesarean:	45/59 (76.3%)	26/56 (46.4%)	71/115 (61.7%)
Western:	25/52 (48.1%)	12/29 (41.4%)	37/81 (45.7%)
Mark:			
Alexandrian:	4/4 (100%)	3/5 (60.0%)	7/9 (77.8%)
Byzantine:	4/8 (50.0%)	0/0 (--)	4/8 (50.0%)
Caesarean:	4/5 (80.0%)	0/4 (0.0%)	4/9 (44.4%)
Western:	1/4 (25.0%)	2/4 (50.0%)	3/8 (37.5%)
Luke:			
Alexandrian:	33/37 (89.2%)	28/35 (80.0%)	61/72 (84.7%)
Byzantine:	39/61 (63.9%)	10/18 (55.6%)	49/79 (62.0%)
Caesarean:	47/55 (85.5%)	17/33 (51.5%)	64/88 (72.7%)
Western:	8/30 (26.6%)	7/18 (38.9%)	15/48 (31.3%)
John 1:1-6:46:			
Alexandrian:	11/11 (100%)	13/14 (92.9%)	24/25 (96.0%)
Byzantine:	17/23 (73.9%)	0/3 (0.0%)	17/26 (65.4%)
Caesarean:	19/23 (82.6%)	3/6 (50.0%)	22/29 (75.9%)
Western:	5/10 (50.0%)	1/6 (16.7%)	6/16 (37.5%)

Table XVII (cont.)

	Uniform	Predominant	Total
Totals: Matthew-John 6:46			
Alexandrian:	97/109 (89.0%)	73/99 (73.7%)	170/208 (81.7%)
Byzantine:	120/179 (67.0%)	19/37 (51.4%)	139/216 (64.4%)
Caesarean:	115/142 (81.0%)	46/99 (46.5%)	161/241 (66.8%)
Western:	39/96 (40.6%)	22/57 (38.6%)	61/153 (39.9%)
John 6:47-21:25			
Alexandrian:	20/27 (74.1%)	19/24 (79.2%)	39/51 (76.5%)
Byzantine:	42/59 (71.2%)	2/2 (100%)	44/61 (72.1%)
Caesarean:	38/51 (74.5%)	6/13 (46.2%)	44/64 (68.8%)
Western:	8/17 (47.1%)	11/17 (64.7%)	19/34 (55.9%)

Once again some preliminary remarks about this profile may be helpful. A witness obviously cannot be classified as a *bona fide* member of a group unless it contains a high proportion of the readings shared by all or most group members. One would expect a higher attestation of uniform readings than predominant, since failure to support a predominant reading of a group occurs whenever a witness attests a primary or exclusive reading of the group's minority. Furthermore, since the predominant reading of one group will often be that of another, this profile will not reveal the kind of radical disparities among groups as those seen in the first profile, where two of the three categories of group readings were mutually exclusive. What it does demonstrate is a witness's significantly higher support for readings of one group than for those of the others, in approximately the same proportion as was attained in the quantitative analysis of individual witnesses.

In view of these considerations, it can be seen that the intra-group profile demonstrates beyond reasonable doubt that Didymus's closest affinities lie with the Alexandrian text, and that the consanguinity of his text shifts after John 6:46. Most significant is the tabulation of *uniform* readings. Didymus supports all of the Alexandrian uniform readings in Mark and John 1:1-6:46, all but eight of fifty-seven in Matthew,[22] and all but four of thirty-seven in Luke.[23] This 89.0% agreement contrasts sharply with his support of the other groups, particularly the Byzantine (67.0% agreement) and Western (40.6% agreement).

That a good group witness could vary from representative witnesses in about 10% of all uniform readings should not be surprising. The representative witnesses themselves serve to define "uniformity": these automatically agree in 100% of such readings. Any extraneous witness will naturally preserve some variation. This can be demonstrated by considering Didymus's eight variations from the uniform Alexandrian text of Matthew. It is interesting to note that if codex L were removed from the group of Alexandrian witnesses and collated against the other five representatives in Matthew, it too would preserve eight places of variation (57/65, 87.7% agreement).[24] Thus Didymus's overall agreement of 89% in Alexandrian uniform readings prior to John 6:47 is not only significantly higher than his support of other groups, it is also significantly high in and of itself.

Staying for the moment with uniform readings, one is struck by the shifts that occur beginning with John 6:47. In effect, Didymus's support of the Caesarean and especially the Alexandrian groups drops significantly,[25] while his attestation of Byzantine and Western readings increases. As a result, the differences among the non-Western groups are now negligible (±3%), while the Western witnesses make a somewhat

---

[22] The eight exceptions are Matt. 4:4; 12:37; 21:31 (2x); 22:13; 22:45; 23:2; 26:31. Three of these (12:37; 21:31 [2x]) are agreements with Old Latin MSS against all others.

[23] The exceptions: Luke 10:20; 16:23; 17:10; 21:20.

[24] 6:24; 7:9; 7:14; 7:21; 7:23; 7:24; 11:18; 15:14.

[25] It is particularly worth noting that Didymus never varies from the Alexandrian uniform readings in John 1:1-6:46, but does so seven times in the rest of the Gospel (6:70; 9:28; 10:29; 10:36; 13:27; 14:27; 18:5). Three of these (9:28; 10:36; 14:27) represent agreements with Old Latin MSS against all others. Overall, Didymus's support of Alexandrian uniform readings drops more than 15% in this portion of his Gospel text; his support of Caesarean uniform readings drops over 6%.

better showing (up nearly 7% to a 47.1% agreement). The conclusion cannot be escaped that Didymus's textual affinities are much less pronounced for the latter part of John's Gospel, evidencing a greater influx of Western and Byzantine readings.

A similar profile emerges in the tabulation of <u>predominant</u> readings. Before John 6:47, Didymus is again shown to be a strong witness to the Alexandrian text, which he supports in 73.7% of all instances. The next closest group, the Byzantine, is removed by a full 22% (with 51.4% agreement), the Caesarean by 26% (46.5% agreement), and the Western by 35% (38.6% agreement). As already noted, Didymus supports fewer Alexandrian predominant readings than uniform because he often attests the variant of the group's minority in primary and exclusive readings.

When Didymus's support for predominant group readings is combined with that for the uniform, the profile of intra-group relationships becomes clear. Up to John 6:47, Didymus is a strong supporter of the Alexandrian text (81.7% agreement), a rather mediocre witness to the Caesarean and Byzantine groups (66.8% and 64.4% agreement respectively), and a poor representative of the Western group (39.9% agreement). Beginning with John 6:47 the alignments shift: the wide disparities among the Alexandrian, Byzantine, and Caesarean groups narrow sharply (here they are separated by 8% rather than 17%), while the Western group now stands much closer to Didymus (up 16% from 39.9% to 55.9%).

The major drawback of this second profile is that the proportion of Didymus's agreements with the Alexandrian, Byzantine, and Caesarean groups is inevitably raised by the common occurrence of exclusive and distinctive Western readings--that is, by instances of two or three Western witnesses agreeing against all others. The distinctive and exclusive readings of the other groups, though less frequent, have a similar effect on the profile. Readings of this kind reveal less about a witness's overall affinities with the different text-types than about its failure to support a particularly aberrant form of one of the textual groups. But this negative kind of relationship was already tabulated under the cate-

238/ Didymus and the Gospels

gories of the first profile. Obviously what is needed is a profile which can combine the concerns of the first profile with those of the second, so as to ascertain a witness's agreements with the uniform and predominant readings of a group that happen also to be distinctive, exclusive, or primary.

Profile Three: Combination Inter- and Intra-Group Readings

The relationship of an individual witness to a group can best be gauged by tabulating its support for readings found uniformly or predominantly among group members, but among no or few other witnesses. Naturally there will be fewer data in a profile of this sort. Nonetheless, enough exist in Didymus's case to provide a clear portrait of his group affinities.

Table XVIII
Didymus's Support of Uniform and Predominant Readings That Are Also Distinctive, Exclusive, or Primary

	Uniform	Predominant	Total
Matthew:			
Alexandrian:	5/7	4/7	9/14
Byzantine:	2/12	0/3	2/15
Caesarean:	4/5	2/19	6/24
Western:	8/29	6/18	14/47
Mark:			
Alexandrian:	1/1	2/2	3/3
Byzantine:	0/1	0/0	0/1
Caesarean:	0/0	0/0	0/0
Western:	0/3	1/2	1/5
Luke:			
Alexandrian:	3/4	7/10	10/14
Byzantine:	2/11	0/1	2/12
Caesarean:	3/5	3/4	6/9
Western:	3/18	3/12	6/30

Table XVIII (cont.)

	Uniform	Predominant	Total
John 1:1-6:46:			
Alexandrian:	1/1	2/2	3/3
Byzantine:	0/2	0/1	0/3
Caesarean:	0/1	0/0	0/1
Western:	2/7	0/4	2/11
Totals: Matthew-John 6:46			
Alexandrian:	10/13 (76.9%)	15/21 (71.4%)	25/34 (73.5%)
Byzantine:	4/26 (15.4%)	0/5 (0.0%)	4/31 (12.9%)
Caesarean:	7/11 (63.6%)	5/23 (21.7%)	12/34 (35.3%)
Western:	13/57 (22.8%)	10/36 (27.8%)	23/93 (24.7%)
John 6:47-21:25			
Alexandrian:	0/0	1/1	1/1 (100%)
Byzantine:	0/4	0/0	0/4 (0.0%)
Caesarean:	0/0	1/4	1/4 (25.0%)
Western:	1/5	6/10	7/15 (46.7%)

Once again, the profile up to John 6:47 shows that Didymus's strongest affinities lie with the Alexandrian group. He supports a full 76.9% of the Alexandrian uniform readings,[26] as opposed to 63.6% of the Caesarean readings,[27] 22.8% of the Western,[28] and a scant 15.4% of the Byzantine.[29]

---

[26] His agreements: Matt 5:28; 10:28; 18:6; 21:2; 24:3; Mark 11:2; Luke 2:36; 4:17; 11:15; John 5:38. Disagreements: Matt. 22:45; 26:31; Luke 17:10.

[27] This relatively high level of agreement is best attributed to the pronounced Alexandrian element in the Caesarean witnesses, in contrast with those of the Western and Byzantine groups. See below, pp. 261-62. Didymus's agreements: Matt 1:6; 3:12; 11:20; 22:13; Luke 1:34; 9:23; 21:20. Disagreements: Matt 15:14; Luke 2:37; 23:21; John 5:47.

[28] Western agreements: Matt. 3:12; 6:20; 7:9; 7:24; 7:26; 22:13: 23:2; 24:36; Luke 4:18; 17:10; 24:49; John 1:3; 6:46. Western disagreements: 1:16; 4:4; 4:19; 5:19; 5:42; 10:29; 11:20; 11:21; 11:28; 13:43; 14:21; 15:6; 15:8; 16:18; 18:22; 22:13; 24:30; 25:33; 25:41; 26:53; 27:40; Mark 4:10; 7:6; 9:49; Luke 2:37; 8:15; 9:23; 9:62; 10:20; 11:13; 12:19; 12:20;

Even more telling is the tabulation of predominant readings. Here Didymus attests 71.4% of the Alexandrian readings,[30] but only 21.7% of the Caesarean,[31] and 27.8% of the Western.[32] He supports none of the predominant Byzantine readings.[33] The combination of these figures in the totals column makes Didymus's affinities crystal clear. While supporting 73.5% of all Alexandrian readings of this profile, he attests only 35.3% of the Caesarean readings, 24.7% of the Western, and 12.9% of the Byzantine. The sparsity of relevant group readings in the latter portion of John's Gospel precludes a complete comparison with the rest of Didymus's Gospel text, although it is worth noting that Didymus's attestation of Western readings nearly doubles from 24.7% to 46.7%.[34]

One way to put this profile into perspective is by contrasting Didymus with all other witnesses with respect to

---

14:29; 16:23; 18:14; 19:12; 19:43; 20:25; 20:36; John 1:6; 4:14; 5:19; 6:38 (2x).

[29] Byzantine agreements: Matt. 15:6; 15:14; Luke 4:29; 19:43. Disagreements: Matt. 1:6; 7:9; 7:24; 15:8; 21:2; 22:13; 23:37; 24:36 (2x); 26:53; Mark 11:2; Luke 1:69; 4:17; 4:18; 6:38; 10:13; 16:25; 18:14; 19:42; 20:25; John 5:38; 6:46.

[30] Alexandrian agreements: Matt. 7:9; 10:28; 12:35; 23:30; Mark 4:10; 11:2; Luke 2:37; 6:38; 7:28; 10:19; 10:20; 20:25; 24:49; John 4:20; 4:36. Disagreements: Matt. 10:28; 11:21; 25:41; Luke 14:28; 18:7; 19:43.

[31] Caesarean agreements: Matt. 24:36; 26:53; Luke 6:38; 14:28; 22:32. Disagreements: Matt. 7:23 (2x); 7:26 (2x); 10:28 (3x); 11:18; 13:43; 14:21; 15:14 (2x); 23:30 (2x); 25:6; 25:16; 26:53; Luke 20:35.

[32] Western agreements: Matt. 5:9; 6:34; 7:9; 21:31 (2x); 26:53; Mark 7:6; Luke 16:15; 16:23; 17:10. Disagreements: Matt. 5:48; 6:1; 6:14 (2x); 7:14; 7:23; 10:28; 10:34; 13:11; 23:37; 26:53; 28:19; Mark 7:6; Luke 11:50; 12:19; 12:20; 14:26; 16:25; 17:10; 19:42; 21:20; 23:21; John 1:18; 5:8; 5:47; 6:38.

[33] Byzantine disagreements: Matt. 5:25; 7:21; 24:3; Luke 22:32; John 6:29.

[34] Alexandrian agreements in this portion of John: 10:28 (predominant). Caesarean agreements: 10:29 (predominant). Western agreements: uniform--17:12; predominant--6:70; 9:39; 10:16; 10:36; 13:27; 13:27. Byzantine disagreements: 8:39; 10:27; 14:23; 17:12 (all uniform). Caesarean disagreements: 8:48; 10:16; 10:32 (all predominant). Western disagreements: uniform--8:40; 8:45; 10:35; 17:21; predominant--6:62; 7:37; 10:10; 10:29.

their support of the Alexandrian group readings. Obviously witnesses closest to the Alexandrian text will contain such readings with the greatest frequency.

There would be no reason to include Alexandrian witnesses in a rank-ordering of MSS according to support of <u>uniform</u> Alexandrian readings. By definition, the Alexandrians all share these readings.[35] When the other witnesses are ranked by this standard, however, a significant result is obtained. Table XIX confirms Didymus's strong Alexandrian affinities: he stands well above all other witnesses on the list.

<u>Table XIX</u>
Witnesses Ranked According to Support of Uniform
Distinctive, Exclusive, or Primary Alexandrian Readings
In Matthew, Mark, Luke, and John 1:1-6:46

1.	Didymus	10/13 (76.9%)
2.	fam 13	9/13 (69.2%)
3.	1241	7/12 (58.3%)
4.	W	7/13 (53.8%)
5.	Θ	6/13 (46.2%)
6.	a	4/9 (44.4%)
7.	b	4/9 (44.4%)
8.	fam 1	5/13 (38.5%)
9.	e	2/6 (33.3%)
10.	Ω	4/13 (30.8%)
11.	A	2/7 (28.6%)
12.	E	2/8 (25.0%)
13.	D	3/13 (23.1%)
14.	Δ	3/13 (23.1%)
15.	Π	3/13 (23.1%)
16.	k	0/0 (--)

An even more significant result is obtained by ranking the witnesses according to agreements in <u>predominant</u> distinctive, exclusive, or primary readings of the Alexandrian group.

---

[35] With the exception of 1241, which, as noted, was left out of consideration for this classification.

242/ Didymus and the Gospels

Since the Alexandrian witnesses split in these readings, they can be included in the tabulation as well. But it should be recognized that group members outside of the control group will normally contain fewer of these readings than those inside, since they were not used to establish the boundaries of the category. This consideration makes the position of Didymus in the rank-ordering of Table XX the more remarkable.

Table XX
Witnesses Ranked According to Support of Predominant
Distinctive, Exclusive, or Primary Readings
In Matthew, Mark, Luke, John 1:1-6:46

1.	P^{75}	9/9 (100%)
2.	P^{66}	2/2 (100%)
3.	ℵ	18/21 (85.7%)
4.	B	18/21 (85.7%)
5.	L	18/21 (85.7%)
6.	C	13/16 (81.3%)
7.	Didymus	15/21 (71.4%)
8.	579	9/13 (69.2%)
9.	1241	11/17 (64.7%)
10.	892	13/21 (61.9%)
11.	Ψ	8/13 (61.5%)
12.	33	12/20 (60.0%)
13.	e	5/11 (45.5%)
14.	fam 1	9/21 (42.9%)
15.	W	6/19 (31.6%)
16.	Δ	6/21 (28.6%)
17.	D	5/20 (25.0%)
18.	b	2/12 (16.7%)
19.	A	2/15 (13.3%)
20.	E	1/9 (11.1%)
21.	Θ	2/21 (9.5%)
22.	Π	2/21 (9.5%)
23.	Ω	2/21 (9.5%)
24.	fam 13	2/21 (9.5%)
25.	a	1/14 (7.1%)
26.	k	0/3 (0.0%)

As this rank-ordering demonstrates, the third profile not only indicates that Didymus preserves the Alexandrian text—it shows that he does so even better than some members of the Alexandrian control group. Didymus is obviously not a primary representative of the text-type (cf. his standing in relationship to the Early Alexandrian witnesses P^{66} P^{75} ℵ and B). But just as obviously he must be considered a strong secondary witness to it, at least as strong as, or perhaps somewhat stronger than, the minuscule MSS of the "Late" Alexandrian subgroup (MSS 33, 579, 892, 1241).

This conclusion can be further sharpened by yet another configuration of MSS in their combined witness, as set forth in a fourth profile. Unlike the three preliminary profiles, the fourth cannot be used for every textual witness, but only for those whose basic Alexandrian affinities have already been established.

Profile Four: Didymus's Relationship to Alexandrian Witnesses

The so-called "later" Alexandrian witnesses are generally grouped together because they contain a greater "impurity" of text than the "earlier" Alexandrians. One way to gauge the level of impurity in these witnesses is by collating them against the relatively purer representatives of the Alexandrian group. To some extent, of course, this has already been done in the quantitative analysis. But that analysis did not allow for comparisons of individual MSS with group or subgroup readings, and so did not permit judgments to be made concerning the relative purity of individual group members. These judgments can be made, however, by isolating the purest Alexandrian witnesses from the rest and using them as a standard of comparison.

Thus the fourth profile attempts to determine Didymus's relative standing among the Alexandrian witnesses with respect to the text shared by the group's purest members. For each Gospel, all witnesses were collated against the uniform and predominant Early Alexandrian readings (i.e. readings supported by all or by at least two-thirds of the Early Alexandrian MSS with text). The resultant rank-orderings indicate

244/ Didymus and the Gospels

how well each MS preserves the Alexandrian text in its least adulterated form. Since ℵ and B are the only Early Alexandrian representatives in Matthew and Mark, only a list of uniform readings will be given for these Gospels (Tables XXI and XXII). In Luke the witness of P^{75} and in John that of both P^{66} and P^{75} are also available. Hence for these two Gospels separate lists can be provided for uniform and predominant Early Alexandrian readings (Tables XXIII and XXIV).

Table XXI
Witnesses Ranked According to Proportional Agreement With the Uniform Early Alexandrian Text in Matthew (116 units of variation)

1.	C	70/85	(82.4%)
2.	892	95/116	(81.9%)
3.	33	90/116	(77.6%)
4.	Didymus	87/116	(75.0%)
5.	L	83/114	(72.8%)
6.	fam 1	84/116	(72.4%)
7.	W	82/116	(70.7%)
8.	Ω	80/115	(69.6%)
9.	E	79/115	(68.7%)
10.	Δ	79/116	(68.1%)
11.	Π	78/116	(67.2%)
12.	1241	63/94	(67.0%)
13.	A	9/12	(66.7%)
14.	Θ	74/113	(65.5%)
15.	fam 13	73/116	(62.9%)
16.	D	51/94	(54.3%)
17.	k	26/53	(49.1%)
18.	e	18/38	(47.4%)
19.	a	44/93	(47.3%)
20.	b	37/89	(41.6%)

Table XXII

Witnesses Ranked According to Proportional Agreement With the Uniform Early Alexandrian Text in Mark (8 units of variation)

1.	C	6/6	(100%)
2.	Ψ	3/3	(100%)
3.	Didymus	7/8	(87.5%)
4.	L	7/8	(87.5%)
5.	Δ	7/8	(87/5%)
6.	892	7/8	(87.5%)
7.	33	4/5	(80.0%)
8.	579	6/8	(75.0%)
9.	A	6/8	(75.0%)
10.	Π	6/8	(75.0%)
11.	fam 13	6/8	(75.0%)
12.	1241	6/8	(75.0%)
13.	E	5/8	(62.5%)
14.	Θ	5/8	(62.5%)
15.	Ω	5/8	(62.5%)
16.	fam 1	4/8	(50.0%)
17.	b	4/8	(50.0%)
18.	W	3/8	(37.5%)
19.	a	3/8	(37.5%)
20.	k	1/3	(33.3%)
21.	D	2/8	(25.0%)
22.	e	0/1	(0.0%)

Table XXIII
Witnesses Ranked According to Proportional Agreement With the Early Alexandrian Text in Luke

Uniform Readings (94 units of variation)				Uniform and Predominant Readings (106 units of variation)			
1.	L	86/94	(91.5%)	1.	L	93/106	(87.7%)
2.	579	83/92	(88.3%)	2.	579	87/103	(84.5%)
3.	Didymus	79/94	(84.0%)	3.	Didymus	86/106	(81.1%)
4.	33	78/93	(83.9%)	4.	Ψ	82/106	(77.4%)
5.	Ψ	76/94	(80.9%)	5.	33	81/105	(77.1%)
6.	C	28/36	(77.8%)	6.	892	80/106	(75.5%)
7.	892	72/94	(76.6%)	7.	C	31/42	(73.8%)
8.	Π	70/94	(74.5%)	8.	1241	76/106	(71.2%)
9.	A	68/94	(73.1%)	9.	fam 13	75/106	(70.8%)
10.	1241	68/94	(72.3%)	10.	Π	74/106	(69.8%)
11.	Θ	68/94	(72.3%)	11.	Θ	73/106	(68.9%)
12.	fam 13	67/94	(71.3%)	12.	A	71/105	(67.6%)
13.	Δ	66/94	(70.2%)	13.	Δ	70/106	(66.0%)
14.	fam 1	64/94	(68.1%)	14.	W	69/106	(65.1%)
15.	Ω	63/94	(67.0%)	15.	fam 1	69/106	(65.1%)
16.	W	62/94	(66.0%)	16.	Ω	67/106	(63.2%)
17.	a	39/75	(52.0%)	17.	a	42/80	(52.5%)
18.	b	32/67	(47.8%)	18.	b	34/73	(46.6%)
19.	D	43/93	(46.2%)	19.	D	48/105	(45.7%)
20.	e	29/76	(38.2%)	20.	e	31/81	(38.3%)

Table XXIV
Witnesses Ranked According to Proportional Agreement With the Early Alexandrian Text in John 1:1-6:46

Uniform Readings (18 units of variation)			Uniform and Predominant Readings (31 units of variation)		
1. C	9/9	(100%)	1. C	15/15	(100%)
2. 33	17/18	(94.4%)	2. 33	28/31	(90.3%)
3. L	17/18	(94.4%)	3. Didymus	27/31	(87.1%)
4. Ψ	15/18	(83.3%)	4. L	26/31	(83.9%)
5. Didymus	14/18	(77.8%)	5. Ψ	24/31	(77.4%)
6. 579	14/18	(77.8%)	6. 579	23/31	(74.2%)
7. Θ	14/18	(77.8%)	7. A	23/31	(74.2%)
8. 892	13/18	(72.2%)	8. fam 1	23/31	(74.2%)
9. fam 1	13/18	(72.2%)	9. Θ	23/31	(74.2%)
10. A	13/18	(72.2%)	10. 1241	22/30	(73.3%)
11. 1241	12/17	(70.6%)	11. 892	22/31	(71.0%)
12. Δ	12/18	(66.7%)	12. fam 13	22/31	(71.0%)
13. Ω	12/18	(66.7%)	13. Δ	21/31	(67.7%)
14. fam 13	12/18	(66.7%)	14. Π	21/31	(67.7%)
15.	11/18	(61.1%)	15. Ω	20/30	(66.7%)
16. W	6/10	(60.0%)	16. W	9/15	(60.0%)
17. D	8/14	(57.1%)	17. a	11/24	(45.8%)
18. a	9/18	(50.0%)	18. b	11/24	(45.8%)
19. b	8/18	(44.4%)	19. e	11/24	(45.8%)
20. e	7/18	(38.9%)	20. D	9/23	(39.1%)

As can seen from these tables, Didymus stands in approximately the same relationship to the Early Alexandrian witnesses in all of the Gospels up to John 6:47. When the agreements presented in these tables are combined, an aggregate picture emerges of Didymus's relative support of the Early Alexandrian text. This will first be done with respect to uniform readings (Table XXV, p. 248).

This table provides a clear demonstration of Didymus's Alexandrian affinities--he stands among the group of Late

Table XXV
Witnesses Ranked According to Proportional Agreement with Uniform Early Alexandrian Readings in Matthew, Mark, Luke, and John 1:1-6:46
(236 units of variation)

1.	C	119/136	(87.5%)
2.	579	103/118	(87.3%)
3.	L	193/234	(82.5%)
4.	Ψ	94/115	(81.7%)
5.	33	189/232	(81.5%)
6.	Didymus	187/236	(79.2%)
7.	892	187/236	(79.2%)
8.	A	96/131	(73.3%)
9.	1241	149/213	(70.0%)
10.	fam 1	165/236	(69.9%)
11.	Π	165/236	(69.9%)
12.	Δ	164/236	(69.5%)
13.	Θ	161/233	(69.1%)
14.	E	84/123	(68.3%)
15.	Ω	160/235	(68.1%)
16.	W	153/228	(67.1%)
17.	fam 13	158/236	(66.9%)
18.	D	104/209	(49.8%)
19.	k	27/56	(48.2%)
20.	b	81/182	(44.5%)
21.	a	95/214	(44.4%)
22.	e	54/193	(40.6%)

Alexandrian witnesses. Especially to be noted here is the 6% drop between 892 and A, showing the basic cohesion of the Alexandrian group.

Nevertheless, this profile should be further refined by taking into account the twenty-five instances of <u>predominant</u> Early Alexandrian readings in Luke and John. The decision to use such readings is based on the assumption that the variation of one witness of the subgroup derives either from the vagary of the witness itself or from corruption of one strand

of the group by a different element of the textual tradition.
When these predominant readings are accepted as also representing the Alexandrian tradition in its purest form, the
relationship of each witness to this tradition is shown as
clearly as possible (Table XXVI).

Table XXVI
Witnesses Ranked According to Proportional Agreement With
Uniform and Predominant Early Alexandrian Readings
In Matthew, Mark, Luke, and John 1:1-6:46

1.	579	126/142	(88.7%)
2.	C	128/148	(86.5%)
3.	L	209/259	(80.7%)
4.	Didymus	207/261	(79.3%)
5.	33	203/257	(79.0%)
6.	892	205/261	(78.2%)
7.	Ψ	109/140	(77.9%)
8.	1241	167/238	(70.2%)
9.	A	109/156	(69.9%)
10.	fam 1	180/261	(69.0%)
11.	Π	179/261	(68.6%)
12.	E	84/123	(68.3%)
13.	Θ	177/261	(67.8%)
14.	Δ	175/258	(67.8%)
15.	fam 13	176/261	(67.4%)
16.	W	163/245	(66.5%)
17.	Ω	172/259	(66.4%)
18.	k	27/56	(48.2%)
19.	D	110/230	(47.8%)
20.	a	100/225	(44.4%)
21.	b	86/194	(44.3%)
22.	e	60/144	(41.7%)

The general contours of this final profile are not surprising. The Late Alexandrian witnesses stand closest to the
Early Alexandrians, the Western witnesses are furthest removed, while the Byzantine and Caesarean witnesses gravitate

to the middle. The Late Alexandrians agree with the purest form of Alexandrian text in 78-88% of all instances. As would be expected from the earlier quantitative analysis, MS 1241 falls far behind the other Alexandrian witnesses (removed 7.7% from Ψ, its closest Alexandrian neighbor). Judged by this standard, the text of 1241 appears to be much closer to the Byzantine and Caesarean groups (standing only 0.3% ahead of A). The witnesses of this middle group are remarkably consistent with one another in their attestation of Early Alexandrian readings, with less than 4% difference separating the highest ranked witness from the lowest. Between the Byzantine and Western witnesses is a gap of 12%, the Western witnesses alone sharing less than half the readings found in the Early Alexandrian text.

As already suggested, the superiority of this final profile resides in its ability to isolate Alexandrian group readings by eliminating the vagaries of individual Early Alexandrian witnesses. This makes Didymus's position in Table XXVI particularly striking. Here he is shown to be a strong Alexandrian witness--as strong an Alexandrian witness as some of the leading representatives of the Late Alexandrian subgroup (L, Ψ, 33, and 892). This finding leads one to conclude that Didymus should be ranked among the Late Alexandrian witnesses.

Both W. Linss and C. Martini previously maintained that Didymus represents the early Alexandrian tradition. But one would expect that if Didymus were an Early Alexandrian witness, he would have stood above all other Alexandrian MSS in this final profile. Such obviously is not the case. One other way to use this fourth profile to test Didymus's location within the Alexandrian tradition is to chart his agreements when the Early and Late Alexandrian witnesses clearly split. No such splits occur in Didymus's text of Mark, but a total of thirty occur in Matthew, Luke, and John 1:1-6:46.[36]

---

[36]Matt. 1:6; 5:4; 6:1; 6:20; 7:9; 7:14; 7:26; 11:20; 12:24; 16:19; 22:44; 24:36; 24:40; 26:53 (2x); Luke 6:45; 6:46; 9:62; 11:15; 13:27; 14:26; 14:34; 16:25; 21:20; 23:21; 24:49; John 1:18; 3:16; 5:47; 6:38.

Notably, Didymus's support for the predominant reading of each group in these splits is nearly even: he agrees with the Early Alexandrians in sixteen and the Late Alexandrians in fourteen. So slight a difference is clearly not enough to justify ranking Didymus among the Early Alexandrians. This conclusion can be substantiated by examining the attestation of the Late Alexandrian witnesses in those splits where their readings are not uniform (i.e. where one-third or less support the Early Alexandrian reading). Notably, of the nine occurrences of such readings in Luke and John 1:1-6:46, MS 579 agrees with the Early Alexandrian reading in five![37] There remains no argument contrary to the conclusion already drawn: in his Gospel text up to John 6:47 Didymus is a good representative of the Late Alexandrian subgroup.

The fourth profile can also serve to document the shift in the consanguinity of Didymus's text beginning with John 6:47. Table XXVII (p. 252) presents a rank-ordering of witnesses according to their support of uniform and predominant Early Alexandrian readings in this portion of text.

On the whole, this profile resembles the one made previously for the rest of Didymus's Gospel text (p. 249). The Late Alexandrian witnesses, with the exception of MS 579, top the list, supporting the Early Alexandrians in at least 76% of all readings. The Western witnesses fall significantly below all others, attesting the Early Alexandrian readings in slightly more than half of all instances. The Byzantine and Caesarean witnesses group together in the middle of the table, somewhat lower than the Alexandrians and significantly higher than the Westerns.

Given this essential continuity with the earlier profile, one is particularly struck by the position now occupied by Didymus. Rather than standing in the midst of the Late Alexandrian witnesses, Didymus has fallen near the bottom of the middle section occupied by Byzantine and Caesarean witnesses.

---

[37] It should be recalled that 579 was not used as a representative witness in Matthew. It agrees with the Early Alexandrians in Luke 6:45; 11:15; 14:26; 16:25; and 21:20, but not in Luke 13:27; 24:49; John 1:18; and 6:38.

Table XXVII
Witnesses Ranked According to Proportional Agreement With Uniform and Predominant Early Alexandrian Readings in John 6:47-21:25
(68 units of variation)

1.	C	36/37	(97.3%)
2.	L	60/68	(88.2%)
3.	W	55/66	(83.3%)
4.	33	54/68	(79.4%)
5.	Ψ	53/68	(77.9%)
6.	892	26/34	(76.5%)
7.	Ω	52/68	(76.5%)
8.	Π	51/68	(75.0%)
9.	Θ	50/68	(73.6%)
10.	Δ	47/68	(69.1%)
11.	579	47/68	(69.1%)
12.	A	35/51	(68.6%)
13.	fam 13	46/68	(67.6%)
14.	Didymus	44/68	(64.7%)
15.	fam 1	44/68	(64.7%)
16.	1241	43/68	(63.2%)
17.	b	33/60	(55.0%)
18.	a	31/60	(51.7%)
19.	D	35/68	(51.5%)
20.	e	31/61	(50.8%)

Instead of an impressive 79.3% agreement with the Early Alexandrians, Didymus now maintains a mediocre 64.7% agreement.

One other consideration demonstrates the shift in Didymus's textual affinities for this portion of the Gospels. A comparison of Didymus with the Early and Late Alexandrian witnesses when their texts split produces a different result from that obtained earlier for the rest of his Gospel text (pp. 250-51). Instead of containing a slightly greater attestation of the purer Alexandrian readings, as represented in the Early Alexandrian text, Didymus now evidences a convincing proclivity to the Late Alexandrian type of text, supporting these less pure representatives of the tradition in eight of ten instances.[38] This does not suggest that Didymus is a good witness of the Late Alexandrian subgroup in the latter part of the Fourth Gospel (cf. the preceding profile!). In these Alexandrian splits Didymus necessarily preserves one reading or the other. His attestation of the later strain of the Alexandrian tradition, therefore, simply demonstrates that in John 6:46-21:25 the consanguinity of his text changed through an increased occurrence of textual contamination.

---

[38]Early Alexandrian agreements: 14:10; 17:12; Late Alexandrian: 7:39 (2x); 10:15; 10:29; 12:2; 14:10; 17:3; 17:21.

Chapter VI

Conclusions

The most enduring contribution of the present study will undoubtedly be its accumulation of significant data: here all the NT quotations and allusions of a fourth-century Alexandrian witness have been presented and collated. Not until all the data from all other important sources are similarly accumulated will we be able to sketch as accurately as possible the history of the NT text. And only then will we draw nearer to the ultimate goal of textual criticism: the accurate reconstruction of the NT autographs.

At the same time this study has made other, more general contributions to the ongoing task of textual reconstruction. The purposes of this final chapter are (1) to rehearse the methodological refinements proposed in the course of this study for the analysis and classification of NT witnesses, and (2) to draw out the implications of the analysis of Didymus for the early history of the NT text, particularly as it was transmitted in Alexandria.

Methods of Textual Analysis and Classification

A number of significant methodological advances have been made by other textual analyses in recent years. These advances have made an important impact on the present study in four major areas: (1) The Use of a Quantitative Analysis. Textual affinities cannot be ascertained by counting a witness's agreements with MSS representing known textual groups only when they vary from an extrinsic and artificial standard such as the TR. Instead, textual consanguinity must be determined by tabulating alignments in __all__ units of genetically significant variation.[1] (2) The Alignments of Alexandrian Witnesses. Alexandrian MSS can be expected to agree with one another in approximately 70% of all variation, while standing at a distance of about 10% from MSS representing other

---

[1] See pp. 187-90 above.

groups.[2] (3) The Phenomenon of Block Mixture. Since scribes sometimes made use of more than one exemplar, a textual witness may evidence radical and sudden shifts of consanguinity. A textual analysis must therefore be conducted so as to detect unexpected realignments.[3] (4) Profiles of Group Readings. A quantitative analysis that considers a witness's proximity to individual representatives of known textual groups cannot be used exclusively to determine textual alignments. Instead a supplementary analysis of <u>readings</u> characteristic of each group must be used to confirm and refine the findings of the quantitative analysis.[4]

Not only did the present study rely on earlier methodological advances, it also sought to make refinements of its own in the methods of analysis now in common use. With respect to the use of a quantitative analysis, this study proposed that a document's relation to the representative witnesses of known textual groups can be crystalized somewhat by looking at a composite of the data group by group, rather than restricting the comparison only to the proportional relationships of the individual MSS themselves. That is to say, a quantitative analysis should be used to ascertain the <u>average</u> relationship of a previously unclassified witness to the members of each group <u>qua</u> group representatives.[5] This step serves to reduce somewhat the problems attendant to the idiosyncracies of this or that individual MS.[6]

A second refinement has to do with the extent of agreement that a quantitative analysis can be expected to yield for

---

[2] See pp. 189-90 above. As discussed below, these figures should be lowered somewhat for the non-continuous texts of Patristic sources. See also pp. 195-202.

[3] Thus Didymus's text shifts dramatically beginning with John 6:47 and continuing to the end of the Gospel. See the discussion of pp. 207-18.

[4] See pp. 223-25 above.

[5] See the tables on pp. 194-95; 205-06; 209-10; 212-14; 216-17.

[6] It will be realized that the group profiles effect a similar end through an entirely different means.

a Patristic author. It was argued that Patristic sources preserving frequent but sporadic quotations of the NT may not evidence group affiliation as clearly as other sources, such as Greek MSS which contain a continuous text. The reasons for this comparative lack of clarity were not hard to locate. Only those passages a church Father chose to quote, and only those quoted passages that happen to survive, are available for analysis. This random character of the data combines with other problems unique to the Patristic sources--the loose citation habits of the Fathers and the occasional corruption of their citations in the course of transmission--to make the analysis of a Patristic witness particularly difficult. No methodological advances can surmount these problems: occasionally a proposed textual reconstruction will be incorrect. The critic must therefore proceed with methodological rigor and apply a degree of caution when using questionable evidence. Both of these factors--occasional errors of reconstruction and systematic caution--will have an unavoidable effect on the quantitative analysis: they will tend to "even out" the differences among textual witnesses.[7]

Thus it was shown that Didymus's text is strongly Alexandrian, more strongly Alexandrian in fact, than even some of the the witnesses of the Alexandrian control group.[8] Yet the proportional relationships of Didymus's text charted by the quantitative analysis are not as clear cut as is normally expected of Alexandrian witnesses. For these reasons it was proposed that the normal rule of thumb that Alexandrian witnesses agree in ± 70% of all variation and be removed from leading representatives of other groups by a distance of 10%[9] be somewhat modified for sources such as Didymus. The character of the data urges the lowering of these figures to levels of agreement as low as 65%, with gaps between groups of around

---
[7] See the discussion on pp. 195-96 above.
[8] See esp. the third and fourth profiles on pp. 238-53 above.
[9] See the discussion of pp. 189-90 above.

6-8%.[10]

The major methodological proposals developed in this study concern the use of the Comprehensive Group Profile Method for clarifying and refining the findings of a quantitative analysis. Since a quantitative analysis considers the relationships of an extraneous witness only to individual representatives of known textual groups, or to their composite testimonies as group witnesses, it must be supplemented with a corrolary analysis which considers the readings that characterize the various groups, irrespective of whether these readings are attested by this or that individual witness. Previous profile methods have lacked adequate sophistication, applicability, or thoroughness to allow for a complete analysis.[11] Hence three profiles were developed for the study of Didymus's text, profiles which can be used for any witness whose text has been fully collated and, preferably, already subjected to a quantitative analysis.

First, an inter-group profile was used to ascertain the extent of Didymus's attestation of readings found mainly by representatives of only one of the control groups ("primary" group readings) or only by representatives of one group ("distinctive" readings when the majority of group witnesses attest the reading; "exclusive" readings when a minority of at least two do).[12] Next an intra-group profile was used to determine Didymus's support of readings found among all the witnesses of any group ("uniform" readings) or among most of these witnesses ("predominant" readings).[13] Finally, a combination profile was devised to conflate the concerns of the other two by tabulating Didymus's attestation of readings supported by most or all members of one group, but by few or no other witnesses (i.e. uniform or predominant readings that are also

---

[10] See the discussion of pp. 195-202 above.
[11] See the discussion on pp. 223-25 above.
[12] See pp. 228-33.
[13] See pp. 234-38.

distinctive, exclusive, or primary).[14]

These profiles demonstrated convincingly that Didymus is a strong representative of the Late Alexandrian text. A fourth profile was developed to confirm these findings by considering a different configuration of readings.[15] Unlike the other profiles, the fourth can be used only for witnesses already determined to be Alexandrian. Here the Early Alexandrian MSS are used as a collation base, on the assumption that their uniform (or predominant) text best represents the Alexandrian tradition in its purest form. When other witnesses are collated against this hypothetical standard, their levels of Alexandrian "purity" can be readily gauged. The application of this final profile to Didymus demonstrated beyond reasonable doubt that he preserves a good strand of the "Late" Alexandrian tradition.

The Character and History of the Alexandrian Text

Since the data from the present study derive entirely from the Alexandrian tradition of the mid- to late- fourth century, they cannot be used to make sweeping generalizations concerning the entire history of the NT text. At the same time, however, once these data have been analyzed and Didymus has been firmly situated in the "Late" Alexandrian tradition, it is appropriate to ask what light his text can shed on the thorny problems already raised concerning the history of the Alexandrian text.[16]

The Western Text in Alexandria

It has long been debated whether the Western text[17] began

---
[14] See pp. 238-43.
[15] See pp. 243-53.
[16] See pp. 19-21 above.

[17] Here we do not need to concern ourselves with the question of the integrity of the Western text. Most textual scholars now acknowledge that Western witnesses do not cohere as closely as do those of other groups, but instead preserve a "wild" form of text that was extremely early and widespread. See, for example, Kurt Aland, "The Significance of the Papyri for Progress in New Testament Research," *The Bible in Modern*

to exert its influence late in Alexandria,[18] or instead was influential early, only to be gradually eliminated in later times.[19] This larger problem cannot be resolved by looking at only one point along the continuum of the Alexandrian tradition. Nevertheless, it is significant that Didymus preserves a tradition which is virtually free from Western influence. Judging from the evidence afforded both by the quantitative analysis of individual witnesses and by the profiles of group readings, the Western tradition was making practically no inroads into the mainstream of the Alexandrian text in Didymus's day.

This conclusion is not materially affected by the shift in consanguinity detected in Didymus's text for the latter part of John's Gospel. It is true that Didymus's support of individual Western witnesses and his attestation of Western group readings both improve at this point. But when viewed from the larger perspective, his Western affiliations are strikingly weak even here: he still stands closer to the Alexandrian text in every respect. Hence the textual shift does not suggest that Didymus used Western manuscripts for this portion of John. It does suggest that the distinctively Alexandrian element of his text was modified by an increased proclivity toward an eclectic text. In this part of the Fourth Gospel, Didymus preserves readings of various traditions--least of all the Western--in no recognizable pattern of attestation.[20]

The Byzantine Text in Alexandria

As was shown by the labors of von Soden, K. Lake, and E. Colwell,[21] the Byzantine text is no monolith, but rather

---

Scholarship, ed. J. Philip Hyatt (Nashville: Abingdon, 1965) 336; Ernest C. Colwell, Studies in Methodology, 53; Gordon D. Fee "Codex Sinaiticus," 44.

[18] So Streeter, The Four Gospels, 60, 118.

[19] So P. L. Hedley, "The Egyptian Text of the Gospels and Acts," CQR 118 (1934) 223.

[20] On the presence of the Western text in Alexandria, see n. 36, p. 20 above.

[21] See Hermann von Soden, Die Schriften des Neuen Testa-

comprises a complicated network of various streams of tradition. Leading representatives of the more important Byzantine subgroups were selected for the present analysis of Didymus: A, E, Π, Ω.[22] Didymus stands in virtually identical relationships to each of these witnesses, and hence to the subgroups they represent. In no case does he evidence a significant affiliation with any of the branches of the Byzantine text, whether by his support of group witnesses or by his attestation of group readings. In most instances Didymus supports Byzantine group readings only when these are shared by other groups. It should not be overlooked, in this connection, that he attests a lower proportion of uniform or predominant Byzantine readings that are also distinctive, exclusive, or primary than he does for any other group--the Western included.[23]

These findings indicate that no "proto-Byzantine" text existed in Alexandria in Didymus's day or, at least if it did, it made no impact on the mainstream of the textual tradition there.[24] Thus the support of Didymus for Byzantine witnesses, which is significantly greater than that for the Western, does not suggest that he drew some of his readings from an already existent Byzantine tradition.[25] It suggests

---

ments (Berlin: Alexander Drucker, 1902-11); Kirsopp Lake, "The Ecclesiastical Text," Excursus I of K. Lake, Robert P. Blake, and Silva New, "The Caesarean Text of Mark, HTR 21 (1928) 338-57; E. C. Colwell, "The Complex Character of the Late Byzantine Text of the Gospels," JBL 54 (1935) 211-21. See also Wisse, Profile Method, 1-18.

[22] On these MSS and the subgroups they represent, see Russell Champlin, Family E and its Allies in Matthew (SD, 28; Salt Lake City: University of Utah Press, 1967) 1-11, and Silva Lake, Family Π and the Codex Alexandrinus: The Text According to Mark (SD, 5; London: Christophers, 1937) 65-71.

[23] See pp. 238-39 above.

[24] Notably, once again, the shift evidenced in Didymus's text at John 6:47 does not signify a particularly closer relationship to the Byzantine text.

[25] H. Sturz (The Byzantine Text-Type) repeatedly asserts that "the Byzantine readings" derive from at least the second century, from a stream of transmission independent of the

rather that the Byzantine editors derived their text, in part, from elements found in the Alexandrian tradition. This conclusion, of course, has also been drawn by G. Zuntz and others on entirely different grounds.[26]

The Caesarean Text in Alexandria

As was observed earlier, the Caesarean Text has been isolated only in Mark's Gospel, for which the data from Didymus are scantiest. Nonetheless, it is significant that neither here nor in any other portion of the Gospels does Didymus give any indication of the existence of a Caesarean text in fourth-century Alexandria.

How is it, then, that the quantitative analysis and group profiles show Didymus standing closer to the Caesarean group than to the Byzantine and Western, groups which are known to exist as distinct entities? The question is not so perplexing when it is recalled that the so-called Caesarean witnesses represent "mixed" texts in which the Alexandrian element is especially prominent. In this regard it cannot be overlooked that in the textual realignments of the latter part of John, Didymus's diminished attestation of the Alexandrian text is matched by a corresponding drop in his support for the Caesarean, while his support for the other groups increases. His agreements with the Caesarean witnesses, therefore, seem to

---

Western and Alexandrian traditions. In his view, the readings of this third type of text crept into Western and Alexandrian witnesses through various kinds of mixture. But if this were true, why did this kind of text have such an infinitesimal effect on Didymus? Unfortunately Sturz has made an unwarranted leap: having discovered that some Byzantine readings could be found in the early papyri, he assumed the early origin of <u>all</u> Byzantine readings. But the presence of some Byzantine readings in second-century MSS simply does not prove that the text-type itself--i.e. all of its readings in their characteristic combinations--existed at that time. Furthermore, Sturz's evidence itself is highly questionable: actually very few of the 150 Byzantine readings he finds in the second- and third-century papyri are "distinctively" Byzantine in any sense of the term. As one example drawn from a myriad of others, Sturz classifies a reading such as ψυχῇ ὑμῶν of Luke 12:22 as "distinctively" Byzantine, though, on his own showing, it is supported by Old Latin, Syriac, and Coptic versions, as well as by Clement of Alexandria and Athanasius!

[26] G. Zuntz, <u>Text of the Epistles</u>.

262/ Didymus and the Gospels

derive from mutual affinities with the Alexandrian text, not from any particular relationship he bore to a distinctively Caesarean tradition.

The Early and Late Alexandrian Texts

Martini's preliminary investigation of the Gospel text of Didymus led him to conclude that Didymus represents the Early Alexandrian text, a type of text Martini labeled "prerecensional."[27] Since Didymus resembles this older form of text as late as the fourth century, Martini questioned whether the designation of other witnesses as "Late Alexandrian" is at all appropriate.[28] He drew attention to the fact that some of the readings of this "late" text are quite early, citing the reading of P^{75} in John 8:39 as an example. From this Martini concluded that the so-called Late Alexandrian text must in fact have been quite early.[29] He suggested that it derived from a slight correction of an extremely ancient, unedited line of text preserved also in Alexandria.[30] In Martini's view, both the unedited Alexandrian text (represented best by P^{75} B) and the edited version existed side by side for several centuries.

A close examination of Martini's argument shows that Didymus actually has very little to do with it. Even if Didymus were an Early Alexandrian witness, he could be used only to show the continued persistence of this type of text in the fourth century. But this would be no new discovery. Martini himself demonstrated this very phenomenon by his examination of another fourth-century Alexandrian witness, Codex Vaticanus![31] To demonstrate that the designation "Late Alexandrian" is inadequate, therefore, Martini was forced to by-pass the evidence from Didymus and look to the older papyri

---

[27] Martini, "Late Alexandrian Text," 295.
[28] Ibid., 295.
[29] Ibid., 295-96.
[30] Ibid., 295-96.
[31] Il problema della recensionalita del codice B alla luce del papiro Bodmer XIV (Rome, 1966).

for earlier elements of this tradition.

The present study shows at least one of the inadequacies of Martini's analysis. Didymus actually does bear a close relationship to the so-called Late Alexandrian witnesses. Although the quantitative analysis shows that his overall agreements are greater with the Early Alexandrian witnesses,[32] the difference between the two Alexandrian groups is negligible (1.3%), and in Matthew and Mark Didymus actually stands closer to the Late Alexandrians. Furthermore, the fourth profile makes it certain that Didymus cannot be classified as a member of the Early Alexandrian group: other Late Alexandrian witnesses resemble the Early Alexandrian text more closely than Didymus does![33] Thus Didymus must be considered a Late Alexandrian witness.

But this classification raises the question also posed by Martini: what does it mean to call a witness Late Alexandrian? In view of the conclusions already reached in this study, the question can be somewhat modified: how is it that a witness which stands closest to Early Alexandrian witnesses must be considered Late Alexandrian? The solution to this enigma will illuminate the real character of the history of the Alexandrian text.

When critics speak of two distinct types of text in Alexandria, as does Martini, they tend to confuse the historical relationship of these texts. It has been convincingly demonstrated that the P^{75} B type of text does not represent a recension of any kind--i.e. it cannot be considered an edition or revision of earlier texts.[34] What then of the Alexandrian MSS that differ from this unrevised, unedited type of text? Do they derive from an Alexandrian recension? Obviously to some extent these MSS differ from the pure line of text best preserved in P^{75} B. It is not so obvious that these other

---

[32] See pp. 220-21 above.

[33] See pp. 243-51 above.

[34] See Gordon D. Fee, "P75, P66, and Origen"; Calvin Porter, "Papyrus Bodmer XV (P75) and the Text of Codex Vaticanus," JBL 81 (1962) 363-76; and Martini, Il problema.

264/ Didymus and the Gospels

witnesses preserve a distinct type of text, i.e. that their agreements represent a form of text which has been derived from an early Alexandrian recension of the purer line of text. This, of course, was Hort's conception taken over without apology by Martini--Alexandria preserved an unedited (=Neutral) and an edited (=Alexandrian) type of text.[35] But the foible of Hort's theory has long been recognized: he could cite no Greek MS which represents this latter kind of text in an unmixed form. Martini himself has in a sense highlighted the problem by pointing to an early occurrence of a "late" reading in P^{75}. Although Martini does not draw this conclusion, he very well could have: the so-called Late Alexandrian witnesses do not represent a distinct type of text deriving from a recension at all; rather, they indicate a movement away from the purest line of Alexandrian text by various witnesses at various times.

This is not, of course, a new conception.[36] But it does receive corroboration from the present analysis of Didymus. The quantitative analysis which shows Didymus's close relationship to Early Alexandrian witnesses, coupled with the fourth profile which shows him to be Late Alexandrian, suggests that the notion of two distinct types of Alexandrian text is inaccurate. There was one type of text in Alexandria, with Alexandrian witnesses preserving it in varying levels of purity.

---

[35]Martini's questioning of the existence of a "Late" Alexandrian text--i.e., of a distinctive form of text deriving from a third- or fourth-century recension--has, in effect, simply pushed the date of the "recension" back into the second century. Thus the conclusions of the present study differ from Martini's in one important respect: here it is being contended that early corruptions of the purest Alexandrian tradition do not necessarily derive from a recension, i.e., from an intentional and deliberate production of an edition or revision. They could just as well have resulted from arbitrary improvements of the Biblical text at different times by different scribes who were trained in the same classical tradition for which Alexandria was so famous. As shown below, this way of construing the development of the "Late" Alexandrian text seems to explain more adequately the textual character of Didymus's Gospel quotations and allusions.

[36]See, e.g., Streeter, The Four Gospels, 59-61.

Conclusions /265

If this conclusion is correct, a whole new set of designations for the Alexandrian subgroups is necessary. The labels "Early" and "Late Alexandrian," used merely as a matter of convenience in the present study, do serve to highlight one aspect of the relationship of these subgroups: the purest representatives tend to be early, the less pure late. But when a fourth-century witness such as Didymus is labeled Late Alexandrian, while a contemporary witness such as codex ℵ is called Early Alexandrian, some confusion may result. Of course these designations simply indicate that one of the witnesses preserves the earlier form of text. But given the circumstance that "early" and "late" readings coexist in the earliest sources,[37] one wonders about the adequacy of the labels.

Martini puzzled over this problem as well, but expressed a reticence about returning to the Hortian classification of a "Neutral" text.[38] This designation is still commonly used, but it too is misleading. To be sure, this type of text is preserved in a second-century witness (P^{75}) which itself does not appear to represent a textual revision or edition. Obviously, then, it represents "a very ancient line of a very ancient text." But that does not make it "Neutral," i.e. "original." And once the designation is extended so as to include "primary" and "secondary" Neutrals, as is done by Fee and others,[39] the term has lost much of its meaning. The idea of a "secondary Neutral" witness is bizarre in the extreme!

From the foregoing discussion it should be seen that the Alexandrian subgroups are best labeled according to their relative preservation of the purest form of the text in Alexandria. The most satisfactory designations of these subgroups, therefore, are "Primary Alexandrian" and "Secondary Alexandrian." The label "Primary Alexandrian" presupposes nothing about the overall superiority or the unrevised charac-

---
[37] See Martini, "The Late Alexandrian Text," 295.
[38] See, for example, the studies of Fee ("The Text of John in Origen and Cyril") and Globe ("Serapion of Thmuis").
[39] "The Text of John in Origen and Cyril," 387.

ter of this text, nor does it suggest that the text is found among all early Alexandrian witnesses but among none of the later. "Secondary Alexandrian" signifies a relative contamination of the distinct Alexandrian text, without presupposing either the relative inferiority of this kind of text or its late date of origin. Furthermore, by suggesting a relatively impure preservation of a distinctive form of text, the latter designation avoids the misconception that the MSS of this group themselves derive from a recension of some sort. When the text in Alexandria is understood in this way, it becomes clear how a witness such as Didymus can agree most extensively with "Primary Alexandrian" witnesses while being classified as "Secondary Alexandrian": his text is on the same level of impurity as other secondary witnesses, but does not always share with them the same contaminations.

It will be evident from what has already been said that the character of Didymus's text counters the older view of Bousset, von Soden, and others that the Alexandrian text represents an official recension made in the third or fourth century.[40] Were there such an ecclesiastically sanctioned text, one would certainly expect to find a much greater homogeneity in the Alexandrian tradition. One would especially suppose that the text of a prominent church leader--the head of the Alexandrian catechetical school!--would differ little from that preserved in the magnificent Alexandrian codices produced during his lifetime. Particularly unfounded is the conjecture of S. Jellicoe, that Didymus himself was a popularizer of the Hesychian recension, that it was actually he who persuaded Jerome of its exceptional quality when the latter visited him for two weeks in A.D. 386.[41]

The text of the NT was fluid in fourth-century Alexandria, though not nearly as fluid as in other centers of ancient Christendom. A good deal of evidence exists to indicate

---

[40] See note 35, p. 19 above.
[41] *JBL* 82 (1963) 409ff.

that particular efforts were taken to preserve textual purity there.[42] And at least one line of Alexandrian text was very ancient, unrevised, and unedited. The Gospel quotations and allusions of Didymus help to demonstrate the degree of control that this pure line of transmission exercised over the entire Alexandrian tradition: textual variation tended to be away from this norm. But the trend toward variation was so widespread that by the time of Didymus most Alexandrian witnesses had lost the exceptional purity of the P^{75} B line of text.

---

[42] See especially Zuntz, <u>Text of the Epistles</u>, 271-76.

Appendix One
Didymus in the Apparatus of NA^{26}

The following is a complete list of readings for which Didymus's support can now be cited or corrected in the apparatus of NA^{26}. The list includes only those readings for which supporting documents are already cited. Parentheses indicate that Didymus's reading differs slightly from the one given in the apparatus. Readings for which Didymus's support should be <u>corrected</u> in the apparatus are marked with an asterisk.

Matt 1:6   omit ο βασιλευς

Matt 1:16   (τον ανδρα Μαριας, εξ ης εγεννηθη Ιησους ο λεγομενος χριστος)

Matt 5:4   add νυν

Matt 5:25   μετ' αυτου εν τη οδω

Matt 5:41   (εαν εγγαρευση)

Matt 6:1   ελεημοσυνη

Matt 6:14   ουρανιος τα παραπτωματα υμων

Matt 6:21   σου$^{(2)}$

Matt 7:6   καταπατησουσιν Did^{pt}/καταπατησωσιν Did^{pt}

Matt 7:9   omit εστιν

Matt 7:9   omit εαν

Matt 7:10   (η και ιχθυν αιτησει)

Matt 7:13   omit η πυλη Did^{pt}

Matt 7:14   τι

Matt 7:21   add τοις

Matt 7:24   ομοιωθησεται

Matt 7:26   την οικιαν αυτου

Matt 8:12   εξελευσονται Did^{pt}/(εκβληθησονται) Did^{pt}

Matt 10:28 φοβεισθε$^{(1)}$

Didymus in the NA²⁶ /269

Matt 10:28   φοβηθητε (2)
Matt 10:33   καγω αυτον
Matt 11:20   add ο Ιησους
Matt 12:24   βεεζεβουλ
Matt 12:35   add τα
Matt 15:6   την εντολην
Matt 15:8   ο λαος ουτος
*Matt 15:14 εις βοθρον πεσουνται
Matt 16:19   κλεις
Matt 18:6   περι
Matt 18:7   omit εκεινω
Matt 18:10   omit εν ουρανοις
Matt 19:28   υμεις
Matt 21:2   κατεναντι
Matt 21:19   add ου
Matt 22:13   (δησαντες αυτου ποδας και χειρας εκβαλετε)
Matt 22:44   omit ο
Matt 22:45   (add εν πνευματι)
Matt 23:2   καθεδρας Μωσεως
Matt 23:30   κοινωνοι αυτων
Matt 23:37   ορνις επισυναγει
Matt 23:37   omit αυτης
Matt 24:3   add της
Matt 24:36   add ουδε ο υιος
Matt 24:40   δυο εσονται
Matt 25:41   add οι
Matt 25:41   το ητοιμασμενον

270/ Didymus and the Gospels

Matt 26:31   διασκορπισθησεται
Matt 26:52   απολουνται
Matt 26:53   omit αρτι
Matt 26:53   πλειους
Matt 26:53   omit η
Matt 26:53   λεγ(ε)ωνων αγγελων
Matt 27:40   omit και
Matt 28:19   omit ουν

Mark 4:10   (τας παραβολας)
Mark 7:6   ο λαος αυτος
Mark 11:2   (ουδεις ουπω ανθρωπων)
Mark 11:2   εκαθισεν

Luke 1:17   (προελευσεται)
Luke 1:69   omit τω
Luke 2:35   δε
Luke 2:37   εως
Luke 4:17   βιβλιον του προφητου Ησαιου
Luke 6:21   (γελασουσιν)
Luke 6:38   (ω γαρ μετρω)
Luke 6:45   omit αυτου
Luke 7:28   Ιωαννου ουδεις εστιν
Luke 9:23   add καθ' ημεραν
Luke 9:62   (επιβαλων την χειρα επ' αροτρον και βλεπων εις τα οπισω)
Luke 10:13 εγενηθησαν
Luke 10:19 δεδωκα
*Luke 10:19 ου μη Did^{pt}/omit Did^{pt}

Luke 10:20   δαιμονια
Luke 10:20   εγγεγραπται
Luke 11:15   βεεζεβουλ
Luke 12:8   ομολογησει Did^{pt}/ομολογηση Did^{pt}
Luke 12:20   απαιτουσιν Did^{pt}
Luke 13:27   ουκ οιδα υμας ποθεν εστε
Luke 14:26   εαυτου Did^{pt}/αυτου Did^{pt}
Luke 14:26   δε
Luke 14:26   εαυτου ψυχην
Luke 14:26   ειναι μου μαθητης Did^{pt}/μου ειναι μαθητης Did^{pt}
Luke 14:34   omit και
Luke 14:34   αλας
Luke 15:22   add   την
Luke 16:23   (αναπαυομενον)
Luke 18:14   παρ' εκεινον
Luke 19:42   omit σου
Luke 19:43   (περιβαλουσιν)
Luke 21:20   omit την
Luke 23:21   σταυρου σταυρου
Luke 24:49   omit Ιερουσαλημ
Luke 24:49   εξ υψους δυναμιν

John 1:3   ουδεν
John 3:18   add   δε
John 4:36   omit και
John 5:29   οι δε
John 5:47   πιστευετε
John 6:46   του πατρος

272/ Didymus and the Gospels

John 6:57	add μου
John 6:62	ιδητε
John 6:70	εις εξ υμων
John 7:39	ελεγεν
John 7:39	ου
John 7:39	πιστευοντες
John 8:12	εμοι
*John 8:39	εστε Did^{pt}/ητε Did^{pt}
*John 8:39	ποιειτε
John 9:6	(επεχρισεν)
John 10:16	συναγαγειν
John 10:16	ακουσουσιν
John 10:16	(γενησονται)
John 10:18	ηρεν Did^{pt}/αιρει Did^{pt}
John 10:27	ακουουσιν
John 10:29	add μου$^{(2)}$
John 10:30	add μου Did^{pt}
John 10:32	καλα εργα εδειξα υμιν
John 10:32	add μου
John 11:26	omit εις εμε
John 12:2	omit εκ
John 13:37	(την ψυχην μου υπερ σου) Did^{pt}/(υπερ σου την ψυχην μου) Did^{pt}
John 14:10	(add ο)
John 14:10	αυτου
John 14:23	ποιησομεθα
John 17:3	γινωσκουσιν
John 17:12	omit εν τω κοσμω

Didymus in the NA²⁶ /273

John 17:21   omit εν
John 18:5   Ναζαρηνον

Appendix Two
Didymus in the Apparatus of UBS^3

The following is a complete list of readings for which Didymus's support can now be cited or corrected in the apparatus of UBS^3. The format is the same as Appendix One.

Matt 1:16   (τον ανδρα Μαριας, εξ ης εγεννηθη Ιησους ο λεγομενος Χριστος)

Matt 3:12   (εις την αποθηκην)

Matt 7:13   η πυλη Did^{pt}/omit Did^{pt}

Matt 7:14   τι

Matt 7:14   η πυλη

Matt 7:24   ομοιωθησεται

Matt 8:12   (εκβληθησονται) Did^{pt}/εξελευσονται Did^{pt}

Matt 15:6   την εντολην

Matt 18:7   ουαι τω ανθρωπω

*Matt 24:36 ουδε ο υιος

Matt 27:40 omit και

Mark 7:6   τιμα

Mark 9:49   (πας γαρ πυρι αλισθησεται)

Luke 1:17   (προελευσεται)

Luke 1:35   γεννωμενον εν σοι

Luke 1:68   κυριος

Luke 2:11   Χριστος κυριος

Luke 6:38   ω μετρω

Luke 7:28   γυναικων

Luke 9:62   επιβαλων την χειρα επ' αροτρον και βλεπων εις το οπισω (στραφεις for βλεπων)

275/ Didymus and the Gospels

Luke 11:13   πνευμα αγιον
Luke 12:20   απαιτουσιν την ψυχην σου απο σου Did^pt/(την
             ψυχην σου αιτουσιν απο σου Did^pt/ την ψυχην
             σου απαιτουσιν απο σου Did^pt
Luke 13:27   ουκ οιδα υμας ποθεν εστε
Luke 19:42   ειρηνην

John 8:34   της αμαρτιας
*John 8:39   ποιειτε
John 9:6   επεχρισεν
John 10:11   τιθησιν
John 10:15   τιθημι
John 10:16   (γενησονται)
*John 10:18 αιρει Did^pt/ηρεν Did^pt
John 10:29   πατρος μου
John 10:32   πατρος μου
John 17:21   εν ωσιν

Selected Bibliography

I. Biblical Texts and Editions

Aland, Kurt. Synopsis Quattuor Evangeliorum, 8th ed. Stuttgart: Deutsche Bibelanstalt, 1973.

Aland, Kurt; Black, Matthew; Martini, Carlo M.; Metzger, Bruce M.; and Wikgren, Allen. The Greek New Testament, 3rd ed. New York: United Bible Societies, 1975.

Barnabitae, Cardi Vercellone Sodalis, and Basiliani, Iosephi Cozza Manachi, eds. Bibliorum Sacrorum Graecus Codex Vaticanus. 1868. Reproduced, Detroit: Brown and Thomas, 1982.

Beerman, Gustav, and Gregory, Caspar René, eds. Die Koridethi Evangelien. Leipzig: J.C. Hinrichs, 1913.

Champlin, Russell. Family E and its Allies in Matthew (SD, XXVIII) Salt Lake City: University of Utah Press, 1966.

Ferrar, William Hugh. A Collation of Four Important Manuscripts of the Gospels. Edited by T. K. Abbott. London: Macmillan & Co., 1877.

Geerlings, Jacob. Family Π in John (SD, XXIII). Salt Lake City: University of Utah Press, 1963.

⎯⎯⎯⎯. Family Π in Luke (SD, XXII). Salt Lake City: University of Utah Press, 1962.

⎯⎯⎯⎯. Family Π in Matthew (SD, XXIV). Salt Lake City: University of Utah Press, 1964.

⎯⎯⎯⎯. Family 13--The Ferrar Group: The Text According to John (SD, XXI). Salt Lake City: University of Utah Press, 1962.

⎯⎯⎯⎯. Family 13--The Ferrar Group: The Text According to Luke (SD, XX). Salt Lake City: University of Utah Press, 1961.

⎯⎯⎯⎯. Family 13--The Ferrar Group: The Text According to Matthew (SD, XIX). Salt Lake City: University of Utah Press, 1961.

Hansell, Edward H., ed. Novum Testamentum Graece: Antiquissimorum Codicum Textus in Ordine Parallelo Dispositi Accedit Collatio Codices Sinaitici. 3 vols. Oxford: Clarendon Press, 1864.

Harris, J. Rendel. "An Important Manuscript of the New
    Testament," JBL 9 (1890) 31-59.
Hort, Fenton John Anthony, and Westcott, Brooke Foss, eds. The
    New Testament in the Original Greek, I, Cambridge: Mac-
    millan, 1881.
Jülicher, Adolf. Itala: Das Neue Testament in altlatein-
    ischer Überlieferung. Berlin: Walter de Gruyter & Co., IV,
    1963; I-III, eds. Kurt Aland and Walter Matzkow, 1970.
Lake, Helen, and Lake, Kirsopp, eds. Codex Sinaiticus
    Petropolitanus: The New Testament. Oxford: Clarendon
    Press, 1911; reproduced Detroit: Brown & Thomas, 1982.
Lake, Kirsopp. Codex 1 of the Gospels and Its Allies. (TS,
    3). Cambridge: University Press, 1902.
Lake, Kirsopp, and Lake, Silva. Family 13 (The Ferrar Group):
    The Text According to Mark (SD, XI). London: Christo-
    phers, 1941.
Lake, Kirsopp, and New, Silva. Six Collations of New Testament
    Manuscripts (HTS, XVII). Cambridge Mass.: Harvard
    University Press, 1932.
Lake, Silva. Family Π and the Codex Alexandrinus: The Text
    According to Mark (SD, V). London: Christophers, 1937.
Legg, S. C. E., ed. Novum Testamentum Graece: Evangelium
    Secundum Marcum. Oxford: University Press, 1935.
    _____, ed. Novum Testamentum Graece: Evangelium Secundum
    Matthaeum. Oxford: University Press, 1940.
Martin, Victor, ed. Papyrus Bodmer II: Évangile de Jean 1-
    14. Geneva: Bibliotheca Bodmeriana, 1956.
    _____, ed. Papyrus Bodmer II, Supplément: Évangile de
    Jean chap. 14-21. Geneva: Bibliotheca Bodmeriana,
    1958.
Nestle-Aland Novum Testamentum Graece. 26th ed. Text edited
    by Kurt Aland, Matthew Black, Carlo M. Martini, Bruce M.
    Metzger, and Allen Wikgren. Apparatus edited by Kurt
    Aland and Barbara Aland with the Institute for the Study
    of the Text of the New Testament (Westphalia). Stutt-
    gart: Deutsche Bibelgesellschaft, 1979.

Rettig, H. C. M., ed. <u>Codex Sangallensis</u>. Zurich: Frederich Shulthess, 1836.

Schmidtke, Alfred, ed. <u>Die Evangelien: Eines alten Unzialcodex</u>. Leipzig: J. C. Hinrichs, 1903.

Scrivener, Frederick H. A., ed. <u>Novum Testamentum: Textus Stephanici A. D. 1550</u>. Cambridge: Deighton Bell, 1877.

von Soden, Hermann Freiherr. <u>Die Schriften des Neuen Testaments in ihren ältesten erreichbaren Textgestalt</u>. II, <u>Text mit Apparat</u>. Gottingen, 1913.

Tischendorf, Constantinus, ed. <u>Monumenta Sacra Inedita</u>. Leipzig, 1846.

_____, ed. <u>Novum Testamentum Graece. Ex Sinaitico Codice</u>. Leipzig: F. A. Brockhaus, 1865.

II. Editions of Didymus's Commentaries found at Toura

Didymus. <u>Kommentar zum Ecclesiastes</u>. I.1 (<u>Papyrologische Texte und Abhandlungen</u>, 25). Gerhard Binder and Leo Liesenborghs, eds. Bonn: Rudolf Habelt Verlag GMBH, 1979.

_____. <u>Kommentar zum Ecclesiastes</u>. II (<u>Papyrologische Texte und Abhandlungen</u>, 22). Michael Gronewald, ed. Bonn: Rudolf Habelt Verlag GMBH: 1977.

_____. <u>Kommentar zum Ecclesiastes</u>. III (<u>Papyrologische Texte und Abhandlungen</u>, 13). Johannes Kramer, ed. Bonn: Rudolf Habelt Verlag GMBH, 1970.

_____. <u>Kommentar zum Ecclesiastes</u>. IV (<u>Papyrologische Texte und Abhandlungen</u>, 16). Johannes Kramer and Bärbel Krebber, eds. Bonn: Rudolf Habelt Verlag GMBH, 1972.

_____. <u>Kommentar zum Ecclesiastes</u>. V (<u>Papyrologische Texte und Abhandlungen</u>, 24). Michael Gronewald, ed. Bonn: Rudolf Habelt Verlag GMBH, 1979.

_____. <u>Kommentar zum Ecclesiastes</u>. VI (<u>Papyrologische Texte und Abhandlungen</u>, 9). Gerhard Binder and Leo Liesenborghs, eds. Bonn: Rudolf Habelt Verlag GMBH, 1969.

_____. *Kommentar zu Hiob*. I (*Papyrologische Texte und Abhandlungen*, 1). Albert Henrichs, ed. Bonn: Rudolf Habelt Verlag GMBH, 1968.

_____. *Kommentar zu Hiob*. II (*Papyrologische Texte und Abhandlungen*, 2). Albert Henrichs, ed. Bonn: Rudolf Habelt Verlag GMBH, 1968.

_____. *Kommentar zu Hiob*. III (*Papyrologische Texte und Abhandlungen*, 3). Ursula Hagedorn, Dieter Hagedorn, and Ludwig Koenen, eds. Bonn: Rudolf Habelt Verlag GMBH, 1968.

_____. *Psalmenkommentar*. I (*Papyrologische Texte und Abhandlungen*, 7). Louis Doutreleau, Adolphe Gesché, and Michael Gronewald, eds. Bonn: Rudolf Habelt Verlag GMBH, 1969.

_____. *Psalmenkommentar*. II (*Papyrologische Texte und Abhandlungen*, 4). Michael Gronewald, ed. Bonn: Rudolf Habelt Verlag GMBH, 1968.

_____. *Psalmenkommentar*. III (*Papyrologische Texte und Abhandlungen*, 8). Michael Gronewald, ed. Bonn: Rudolf Habelt Verlag GMBH, 1969.

_____. *Psalmenkommentar*. IV (*Papyrologische Texte und Abhandlungen*, 6). Michael Gronewald, ed. Bonn: Rudolf Habelt Verlag GMBH, 1969.

_____. *Psalmenkommentar*. V (*Papyrologische Texte und Abhandlungen*, 12). Michael Gronewald, ed. Bonn: Rudolf Habelt Verlag GMBH, 1970.

_____. *Der Psalmenkommentar von Tura, Quaternio IX*. Aloys Kehl, ed. Cologne: Westdeutscher Verlag, 1964.

_____. *Sur la Genèse. Texte inédit d'apres un papyrus de Toura: Introduction, texte critique, traduction et notes*. 2 vols. (SC, 233, 244) Paris: Les Éditions du Cerf, 1976, 1978.

_____. *Sur Zacharie. Texte inédit d'apres un papyrus de Toura: Introduction, texte critique, traduction et notes*. 3 vols. (SC, 83-85). Louis Doutreleau, ed. Paris: Les Éditions du Cerf, 1962.

III. Books and Articles

Aland, Kurt. "The Significance of the Papyri for Progress in New Testament Research," in *The Bible in Modern Scholarship*, ed. J. Philip Hyatt. Nashville: Abingdon Press, 1965.

_____. *Studien zur Überlieferung des Neuen Testaments und seines Textes*. Berlin: Walter de Gruyter, 1967.

Altaner, Berthold. "Ein grosser, aufsehen erregender patrologischer Papyrusfund," *ThQ* 127 (1947) 332-33.

_____. "Wer ist der Verfasser des Tractatus in Isaiam VI, 1-7?" *ThRev* 42 (1943) 147-51.

Altaner, Berthold, and Stuiber, Alfred. *Patrologie: Leben, Schriften, und Lehre der Kirchenväter*, 8th ed. Freiburg: Herder, 1978.

Andresen, Carl. "Didymos 3," in *Lexicon der Alten Welt*. Zurich: Artemis Verlag, 732-33.

Bardenhewer, Otto. *Geschichte der altkirchlichen Literatur*, vol. III. Darmstadt: Wissenschaftliche Buchgesellschaft, 1962.

Bardy, Gustav. "Pour l'histoire de l'école d'Alexandrine," *Vivre et Penser* 2 (1942) 80-109.

_____. *Didyme l'Aveugle*. Paris: Beauchesne, 1910.

Barnard, P. M. *The Biblical Text of Clement of Alexandria*. (TU, V) Cambridge: University Press, 1899.

Bebb, J. M. "The Evidence of the Early Versions and Patristic Quotations on the Text of the Books of the New Testament," in *Studia Biblica et Ecclesiastica*. Oxford: Clarendon Press, 1890, 195-240.

Beranger, Louis. "Sur deux énigmes de 'De Trinitate' de Didyme l'Aveugle," *RechSR* 51 (1963) 155-67.

Bienert Wolfgang A. *"Allegoria" und "Anagoge" bei Didymos dem Blinden von Alexandria*. Berlin: Walter de Gruyter, 1972.

Bizer, Chr. "Studien zu den pseudoathanasian Dialogen. Der Orthodoxos und Aëtios." Ph.D. Dissertation, Bonn, 1966.

Boismard, M.-E "A Propos de Jean V, 39," *RB* 55 (1948) 5-34.

_____. "Critique textuelle et citations patristiques," RB 57 (1950) 388-408.

_____. "Dans le sein de Père (Joh 1,18)," RB 59 (1952) 23-39.

_____. "Lectio brevior, potior," RB 58 (1951) 161-68.

_____. "Le papyrus Bodmer II," RB 64 (1957) 363-98.

_____. "Problèmes de critique textuelle concernent le quatrième évangile," RB 60 (1953) 347-71.

Bousset, Wilhelm. "Die Recension des Hesychius," in Textkritische Studien zum Neuen Testament. Leipzig: J. C. Hinrichs, 1894, 74-110.

Brooks, James Arthur. "The Text of the Pauline Epistles in the Stromata of Clement of Alexandria." Ph.D. Dissertation, Princeton Theological Seminary, 1966.

Ceillier, Remy. Historie générale des Auteurs Sacrés et Ecclésiastiques, V. 2nd ed. Paris: Louis Vives, 1860.

Chavoutier, L. "Querelle origèniste et controverses trinitaires à propos du Tractus contra Origenem de visione Isaiae," VC 14 (1960) 9-14.

Colwell, Ernest C. "The Complex Character of the Late Byzantine Text of the Gospels," JBL 54 (1935) 211-21.

_____. Studies in Methodology in Textual Criticism of the New Testament. Grand Rapids: Eerdmans, 1969.

Colwell, Ernest C.; McReynolds, Paul R.; Sparks, Irving A.; and Wisse, Frederick. "The International Greek New Testament Project: A Status Report," JBL 87 (1968) 187-97.

Cullmann, Oscar. "Die neuesten Papyrusfunde von Origenestexten und gnostischen Schriften," ThZ 5 (1949) 153-57.

Dietsche, W. Didymus von Alexandrien als Verfasser der Schrift uber die Seraphvision. Freiburg: Blumer, 1941.

Doutreleau, Louis. "Étude d'une tradition manuscrite: Le 'De Spiritu Sancto' de Didyme" in Kyriakon: Festschrift Johannes Quasten, eds. Patrick Granfield and Josef A. Jungmann. Vol. I. Münster: Verlag Aschendorff, 1970.

_____. "Le 'De Spiritu Sancto' de Didyme et ses éditeurs," RechSR 51 (1963) 383-406.

_____. "Le 'De Trinitate' est-il l'oeuvre de Didyme l'Aveugle?" RechSR 45 (1957) 514-57.

_____. "Que savons-nous aujourd'hui des Papyrus de Toura?" RechSR 43 (1955) 161-93.

Doutreleau, Louis, and Koenen, Ludwig. "Nouvelle inventaire des papyrus de Toura," RechSR 55 (1967) 547-64.

Duplacy, Jean, and Suggs, M. Jack. "Les citations grecques et la critique du texte de Nouveau Testament: le passé, le present et l'avenir," in Le Bible et les pères. Edited by André Benoit and Pierre Prigent. Paris: Presses Universitaires de France, 1971, 187-213.

Eldridge, Laurence. The Gospel Text of Epiphanius of Salamis. (SD, XLI). Salt Lake City: University of Utah Press, 1969.

Epp, Eldon J. "The Claremont Profile Method for Grouping New Testament Minuscule Manuscripts," in Studies in the History and Text of the New Testament in honor of Kenneth Willis Clark. Edited by Boyd L Daniels and M. Jack Suggs (SD, XXIX). Salt Lake City: University of Utah Press, 1967, 27-38.

Fee, Gordon D. "Codex Sinaiticus in the Gospel of John: A Contribution to Methodology in Establishing Textual Relationships," NTS 15 (1968-69) 23-44.

_____. "Origen's Text of the New Testament and the Text of Egypt," NTS 28 (1982) 348-64.

_____. "P^{75}, P^{66}, and Origen: The Myth of Early Textual Recension in Alexandria," in New Dimensions in New Testament. Edited by Richard N. Longenecker and Merrill C. Tenney. Grand Rapids: Zondervan, 1974, 19-45.

_____. "The Text of John and Mark in the Writings of Chrysostom," NTS 26 (1979-80) 525-47.

_____. "The Text of John in Origen and Cyril of Alexandria: A Contribution to Methodology in the Recovery and Analysis of Patristic Citations," Bib 52 (1971) 357-94.

_____. "The Text of John in the Jerusalem Bible: A Critique of the Use of Patristic Citations in New Testament Textual Criticism," JBL 90 (1971) 163-73.

Fischer, Bonifatius. "Das Neue Testament in lateinischer Sprache. Der gegenwärtige stand seiner Erforschung und seine Bedeutung fur die grieschen Textgeschichte," in Die Alten Übersetzungen des Neuen Testaments, Die Kirchenväterzitate und Lektionare. Edited by Kurt Aland. Berlin: Walter de Gruyter, 1972, 1-92.

Funk, F. X. "Die zwei letzen Bücher der Schrift Basilius' des Gr. gegen Eunomius," Kirchengeschichtliche Abhandlungen und Untersuchungen, II. Paderborn: Ferdinand Schöningh, 1899, 291-329.

Gauche, William J. Didymus the Blind: An Educator of the Fourth Century. Washington: Catholic University of America, 1934.

Geerlings, Jacob and New, Silva. "Chrysostom's Text of the Gospel of Mark," HTR 24 (1931) 121-42.

Gesché, Adolph. La Christologie du 'Commentaire sur les Psaumes' découvert à Toura. Gembloux: J. Duculot, 1962.

de Ghellinck, J. "Récentes découvertes de littérature chrétienne antique," NRTh 71 (1949) 83-86.

Globe, Alexander. "Serapion of Thmuis as Witness to the Gospel Text Used by Origen in Caesarea," NovT 26 (1984) 97-127.

Goodspeed, Edgar J. The Newberry Gospels. Chicago: University Press, 1902.

Grant, Robert M. "The Citation of Patristic Evidence in an Apparatus Criticus," in New Testament Manuscript Studies. Edited by Merrill Parvis and Allen P. Wikgren. Chicago: University Press, 1950, 117-24.

Greenlee, J. Harold. The Gospel Text of Cyril of Jerusalem (SD, XVII). Copenhagen: Ejnar Munksgaard, 1955.

Griesbach, Johann Jakob. Symbolae Criticae. 2 vols. Halle, 1785.

Guérand, O. "Note préliminaire sur les papyrus d'Origèn découverts à Toura," RHR 131 (1946) 85-108.

Günthor, P. Anselm. Die 7 pseudoathanischen Dialoge: ein Werk Didymus' des Blinden von Alexandrien. Rome: Herder, 1941.

Hedley, P. L. "The Egyptian Text of the Gospels and Acts," CQR 118 (1934) 23-39; 188-230.

Heron, Alistair. "The Two Pseudo-Athanasian Dialogues Against the Anomeans," JTS, n.s. 24 (1973) 101-22.

Hills, E. F. "A New Approach to the Old Egyptian Text," JBL 4 (1950) 345-62.

Hönscheid, Jürgen. Didymus der Blinde: De trinitate, Buch I. Meisenheim am Glan: Verlag Anton Hain, 1975.

Holl Kurt. "Über die Gregor von Nyssa zugeschreiben Schrift 'Adversus Arium et Sabellium,'" ZKG 25 (1904) 390-98.

Hort, Fenton John Anthony, and Westcott, Brooke Foss. The New Testament in the Original Greek, II, Introduction and Appendix. Cambridge: Macmillan, 1881.

Hurtado, Larry. Text-Critical Methodology and the Pre-Caesarean Text. Grand Rapids: Eerdmans, 1981.

Hutton, Edward Ardron. An Atlas of Textual Criticism. Cambridge: University Press, 1911.

Jellicoe, Sidney, "The Hesychian Recension Reconsidered," JBL 82 (1963) 409-18.

Kenyon, Frederic G. Handbook to the Textual Criticism of the New Testament, 2nd ed. London: Macmillan & Co., 1912.

_____. "Hesychius and the Text of the New Testament," in Memorial Lagrange. Edited by Hugues Vincent. Paris: J. Gabalda, 1940, 245-50.

Klijn, A. J. "Papyrus Bodmer II (John i-xiv) and the Text of Egypt," NTS 3 (1956-57) 327-34.

Klostermann, Erich. Didymus von Alexandria In Epistolas Canonicas Enarratio. Leipzig: J. C. Hinrichs, 1905.

_____. "Der Papyrusfund von Tura," ThLZ 73 (1948) 47-50.

Koenen, Ludwig. "Ein theologischer Papyrus des Kölner Sammlung: Kommentar Didymos' des Blinden zu Zach 9,11 u. 16," Archiv fur Papyrusforschung 17 (1960) 61-105.

_____. "Zu den Papyri aus dem Arsenioskloster bei Tura," ZPE 2 (1968) 44-53.

Kramer, Bärbel. "Didymus von Alexandrien," in Theologische Realenzyklopädie, VIII. Berlin: Walter de Gruyter, 1981, 741-46.

Lachmann, Karl. "Rechenshaft über seine Ausgabe des Neuen Testaments," ThStK 3 (1830) 817-45.

Lake, Kirsopp. "The Ecclesiastical Text." Excursus 1 of Robert P. Blake, Kirsopp Lake, and Silva New, "The Caesarean Text of Mark," HTR 21 (1928) 338-57.

_____. "Texts from Mount Athos," in Studia Biblica et Ecclesiastica, V. Oxford: Clarendon Press, 1903.

Lake, Kirsopp, and Lake, Silva. "The Byzantine Text of the Gospels," in Memorial Lagrange. Edited by Hugues Vincent Paris: J. Gabalda, 1940, 251-58.

Laurence, Richard. Remarks Upon Griesbach's Classification of Manuscripts. Oxford, 1814. Reprinted in Biblical Repertory 2 (1826) 33-95.

Lebon, J. "Le Pseudo-Basile (Adv. Eunom. IV-V) est bien Didyme D'Alexandrie," Le Museon 59 (1937) 61-83.

Leipoldt, Johannes. Didymus der Blinde von Alexandria (TU, XIV). Leipzig: J. C. Hinrichs, 1905.

Linss, Wilhelm Cahill. "The Four Gospel Text of Didymus." Ph.D. Dissertation, Boston University, 1955.

Marcos, Natalio Fernandez. "El Texto Biblico de Didimo en El Commentario Zacarias Del Papiro De Tura," Sef 36 (1976) 267-84.

Martini, Carlo M. "Is There a Late Alexandrian Text of the Gospels?" NTS 24 (1977-78) 285-96.

_____. Il problema della recensionalita del codice B alla luce del papiro Bodmer XIV (AnBib, XXVI) Rome: Pontifical Biblical Institute, 1966.

Mees, M. Die Zitate aus dem Neuen Testament bei Clemens von Alexandrien. Rome, 1970.

Metzger, Bruce M. The Early Versions of the New Testament: Their Origin, Transmission, and Limitations. Oxford: Clarendon Press, 1977.

_____. "Patristic Evidence and the Textual Criticism of the New Testament," NTS 18 (1971-72) 379-400.

_____. *The Text of the New Testament: Its Transmission, Corruption, and Restoration*, 2nd ed. New York: Oxford University Press, 1968.

Migne, J.-P. *Patologiae Cursus Completus Series Graeca Prior*. Vol.XXXIX. Paris, 1863.

Mingarelli, J. A. *Didymi Alexandrini de Trinitate Libri Tres*. Bonn, 1769. Reprinted in Migne PG XXXIX, 139-216.

Mühlenberg, Ekkehard. *Psalmenkommentare aus der Katenenüberlieferung*, 3 vols. Berlin: Walter de Gruyter, 1975-78.

Müller-Wiener W. "Zu den Papyri aus dem Arsenioskloster bei Tura, Teil II," ZPE 2 (1968) 53-63.

Muncey, R. W. *The New Testament Text of Saint Ambrose*. Cambridge: University Press, 1959.

Murphy, Harold S. "Eusebius' New Testament Text in the *Demonstratio Evangelica*," JBL 78 (1954) 162-68.

Oliver, Harold Hunter. "The Text of the Four Gospels, As Quoted in the *Moralia* of Basil the Great." Ph.D. Dissertation, Emory, 1961.

Osburn, Carroll. "The Text of the Pauline Epistles in Hippolytus of Rome," Second Century 2 (1982) 97-124.

Patrick, John. "The Biblical Text in Clement," Appendix F in *Clement of Alexandria*. London: Wm. Blackwood & Sons, 1914.

Porter, Calvin L. "Papyrus Bodmer XV (P75) and the Text of the Codex Vaticanus," JBL 81 (1962) 363-76.

Prigent, Pierre. "Les citations des Pères grecs et la critique textuelle du Nouveau Testament," in *Die alten Übersetzung des Neuen Testaments, die Kirchenväterzitate und Lektionare*. Edited by Kurt Aland. Berlin: Walter de Gruyter, 1972, 436-54.

Puech H.-Ch. "Les nouveaux écrits d'Origène et de Didyme découverts à Toura," RHPhR 31 (1951) 293-329.

Quasten, Johannes. *Patrology*. Vol. III, *The Golden Age of Greek Patristic Literature*. Utrecht: Spectrum, 1966.

de Regnon, T. *Études de théologie positive sur la Sainte Trinité*, III. Paris, 1898.

Richards, W. L. *The Classification of the Greek Manuscripts of the Johannine Epistles*. SBLDS, 35; Missoula: Scholars Press, 1977.

Sanders, Henry A. "The Egyptian Text of the Four Gospels and Acts," *HTR* 26 (1933) 79-98.

_____. "A New Collation of MS 22 of the Gospels," *JBL* 33 (1914) 91-117.

_____. *The Washington Manuscript of the Four Gospels*. New York: Macmillan & Co. 1912.

Sandys, John Edwin. *A History of Classical Scholarship*, 2nd ed. Vol. I. Cambridge: University Press, 1906.

Seiler, Ingrid. *Didymus der Blinde: De trinitate Buch 2, Kapitel 1-7*. Meinsenheim am Glan: Verlag Anton Hain, 1975.

von Soden, Hermann Freiherr. *Die Schriften des Neuen Testaments in ihren ältesten erreichbaren Textgestalt*. I, *Untersuchungen*. 3 vols. Berlin, 1902-10.

Stolz, Eugen. "Didymus, Ambrosius, Hieronymus," *TQ* 87 (1905) 371-401.

Streeter, Burnett Hillman. *The Four Gospels: A Study of Origins*. 5th impression. London: Macmillan & Co., 1936.

Sturz, Harry A. *The Byzantine Text-Type and New Testament Textual Criticism*, 3rd syllabus edition. La Mirada, Cal.: Biola College Bookstore, 1980.

Suggs, M. Jack. "The Use of Patristic Evidence in the Search for a Primitive New Testament Text," *NTS* 4 (1957-58) 131-57.

Swanson, Reuben J. "The Gospel Text of Clement of Alexandria." Ph.D. Dissertation, Yale University, 1956.

Tarelli, C. C. "The Chester Beatty Papyrus and the Western and Byzantine Texts," *JTS* 41 (1940) 253-60.

Tate, Martin. "Zur Theologie des Markell von Ankyra I," *ZKG* 75 (1964) 217-70.

Wisse, Frederick. *The Profile Method for Classifying and Evaluating Manuscript Evidence* (SD, 44). Grand Rapids: Eerdmans, 1982.

Young, Frances. *From Nicaea to Chalcedon: A Guide to the Literature and Its Background*. Philadelphia: Fortress Press, 1983.

Zevvopoulos, Gerassimos. "The Gospels Text of Athanasius." Ph.D. Dissertation, Boston University, 1955.

Zoepfl, Fiedrich. *Didymi Alexandrini in epistolas canonicas brevis enarratio*, in *Neutestamentliche Abhandlungen*, IV, ed. M. Meinertz. Münster: Aschendorffsche Verlagsbuchhandlung, 1914.

Zuntz, Günther. *The Text of the Epistles: A Disquisition Upon the* Corpus Paulinum. London: Oxford University Press, 1953.

www.ingramcontent.com/pod-product-compliance
Lightning Source LLC
Chambersburg PA
CBHW031707230426
43668CB00006B/138